Merry

Hopefully you will have to use this oneday

Love Kiel
xxx

Moving to Australia

a guide for expats, lovers

and the otherwise curious

Andrea Spirov

Copyright © 2010 Andrea Spirov. All rights reserved.
Second edition

Many of the designations used by manufacturers and sellers to distinguish their products are claimed as trademarks. Where those designations appear in this book and the author was aware of a trademark, the designations have been italicised or made bold.

While every precaution has been taken in the preparation of this book, the author and publisher assume no responsibility for errors or omissions, or for damages resulting from the use of the information contained herein. The information was researched and is thought to be correct at the time of writing. The author recommends that you confirm all information before taking any action.

If you have questions or comments on this book, or if you would like to be put on the mailing list for future updates, please email the author at andreaspirov@gmail.com

Table of Contents

Introduction   14

Chapter One: Visas - How to survive your dealings with DIAC (grab a copy of *The Three Pillars of Zen*)   19

  Visitor Visas   22

    Electronic Travel Authority (ETA Visitor Subclass 976) or eVisitor (Subclass 651)   22

    Tourist Visa (Subclass 676)   25

    Working Holiday Visa (Subclass 417)   26

    Work and Holiday Visa (Subclass 462)   27

  Employer Sponsored Work Visas   27

    Business (Long Stay) Visa (Subclass 457)   27

    Employer Nomination Scheme (Subclass 121/856)   29

    Regional Sponsored Migration Scheme (Subclass 119/857)   30

  Skilled Migration Visas   30

    Skilled – Independent (Migrant) Visa (Subclass 175)   31

    Skilled – Sponsored (Migrant) Visa (Subclass 176)   42

    Skilled – Regional Sponsored (Provisional) Visa (Subclass 475)   43

  Family Migration Options (including my experience with the Spouse Visa)   45

    Prospective Marriage Visa (PMV) (Subclass 300)   49

    Onshore Partner temporary visa (subclass 820) and permanent visa (subclass 801) AND Offshore Partner Temporary Visa (Subclass 309) and Permanent Visa (Subclass 100)   51

    Parent and Child visas   56

  Student visas   56

Available visas not discussed in this chapter	58
Applying for a Visa	61
Penal, Character and Health Clearances	65
Whether to use a migration agent	67
Once you have the visa	70
Australian resources	71
US resources	72
UK and Commonwealth Country resources	72
Expat and migrant communities and other international resources	73

Chapter Two: What happens when you assume? That's right...common misperceptions of Australia and living overseas	75

Chapter three: And where will you live? Six states and two territories to choose from	81
New South Wales (NSW)	82
Sydney	83
Country New South Wales	85
Victoria (VIC)	86
Melbourne	86
Country Victoria	88
Queensland (QLD)	89
Brisbane	90
Beyond Brisbane	91
Western Australia (WA)	92
Perth	92
Regional Western Australia	94

South Australia (SA)	95
Adelaide	95
Country South Australia	96
Tasmania (TAS)	97
Hobart	97
Country Tasmania	97
Australian Capital Territory (ACT)	98
Northern Territory (NT)	99
Darwin	99
Regional Northern Territory	99
Additional relocation resources	100

Chapter Four: Exit strategy - How to close up shop at home, relocate to Australia and answer questions like "You're doing what?!"	101
Preparing to leave your current country of residence	102
Your employment and financial situation	102
Current housing	105
People moving with you	108
Pets	110
Checklist of things to do before you leave	112
Packing, selling, moving, storing and shipping	116
Those you leave behind	125
Arriving in Australia and the first 60 days	129
Entering Australia	129
Finding a place to live	130
Moving in and Settling in	135

Checklist for after you arrive: Days 1 to 15 — 137
Checklist for after your arrivev: Days 15 to 30 — 144
Checklist for after you arrive: Days 30 to 60 — 145

Chapter Five: Money in, money out: Working, spending and where to put the rest — 147
  Working in Australia — 147
    Your resume and the job search — 149
    Finding a job — 150
    Job search resources — 152
  Taxes — 153
    Tax resources — 156
  Banking, loans and Investments — 157
    Banks in Australia — 157
    Superannuation (if you're working, you'll have a fund) — 160
  Australian currency and spending it — 162
    Cash — 162
    Credit and Debit (EFTPOS) cards — 163
    Cheques and Money Orders — 164
    Australia Post — 165
    Shopping — 165
    Gambling — 167
    Saving money — 168
    Complaints — 171

Chapter Six: Health - Insurance, Doctors and Medicare — 172
  Medicare — 172

It begins with your either your General Practitioner (GP) or the Emergency Room (ER)   176

    Resources for medical care   180

  Private health insurance   181

    Resources for private health insurance   182

Chapter Seven: Food, products and services - What to expect   184

  Alcohol   184

    Beer   184

    Cocktails and spirits   186

    Wine   187

    Bottle Shops   189

    Legalities   190

  Bakeries   191

  Books   193

  Cars   193

    Buying a car   193

    Car buying and selling resources   195

    Some notes on driving in Australia   195

    Car maintenance resources   196

  Clothing   197

    Fashion resources   199

  Coffee   199

  Dairy   201

    Resources   203

  Electrical items   203

    Resources   205

Fast Food	206
Grocery	207
Supermarkets	207
Specialty food stores	210
Markets	212
Halal	212
Resources	212
Health	213
Ice Cream and Gelato	214
Jewellery	214
Kosher	215
Resources	215
Legal	216
Barristers and solicitors	216
Wills	216
Resources	217
Manchester	218
Bed and sheet sizes in Australia	218
Meat	218
Fish and Seafood	220
Nursery	221
Office	221
Pies, Pizza and Pub Grub	222
Pies	222
Pizza	223
Pub Grub	223
Restaurants	224

Restaurant guides and resources	226
Service	227
Snacks	228
Biscuits	228
Chocolate and confectionary	229
Potato and corn chips and popcorn	230
Other snacks	230
Stamps and shipping	231
Other parcel handling services in Australia	231
Transport	232
Taxis	232
Trains	233
Buses	233
Airport trains and shuttles	234
Used goods	234
Websites for buying second-hand	235
OpShops and Consignment stores	235
Vegetables and Fruits	235
Listed by Australian name (other names)	235
Water	237
Resources	238
Prices for 100 commonly used items in Australian Dollars	239
Items that are hard to find Down Under (with some potential substitutions)	243

Chapter Eight: Getting along - culture differences and how to meet people   246

Be nice about it	248
Transitioning from American English to British English	250
Collective nouns	250
Dates and expressions of time	250
Past-tense	250
Spelling	251
Terminology	252
An introductory guide to Aussie slang	254
Aussie social customs	256
Formalities (or lack of)	257
Personality differences	259
For the love of sport	261
Social Resources	264
Chapter Nine: Studying, buying property and other FAQs	265
What if I want to study?	265
Choosing a program	265
Resources	266
Costs and applying to school	267
Resources	268
Grades in Australia	269
How do I buy property in Australia?	269
Determine how much you can afford to spend on your home	271
Finding a property	275
Settlement	278
Resources	279
How safe is Australia?	279

Resources	281
When can I become a citizen?	282
What about all the dangerous creatures in Australia?	283
Resources for general safety in Australia	287
Chapter Ten: Travel - Here, there and everywhere	**288**
Travel within Australia	289
Cars: Hire or drive your own	289
Flights	291
Train travel	293
Buses	294
Additional domestic travel resources	295
International Travel from Australia	296
Resources	297
Going "home"	297
Appendix	**300**
Australian National Holidays	300
Fixed	300
Variable	300
Australia's National Anthem	301
Advance Australia Fair	301
Resources for parents	301
Online communities	302
School holidays	303
Other helpful resources	303
Further reading	303

Introduction

The bus wound its way down the narrow road of a hill somewhere in Crete as I sat chatting to a friend about politics. Not an ideal topic of conversation for a holiday in the southernmost part of Europe, I admit. But we were exhausted after a delayed flight from New York and there was a war going on, after all. It was barely autumn in 2004 and I'd joined some friends on what was supposed to be a three-country jaunt planned around Oktoberfest in Munich. And it was for them. Fate, however, had other plans for me.

We arrived in one of the tiniest coastal towns I've ever spent time in. It was smack dab in the middle of southern Crete, the giant island in the Mediterranean about halfway between continental Europe and Egypt. Not long after, as we sipped local moonshine in a beautiful olive grove, the hostel owner gave us an introduction to the place. He mentioned something about couples...married couples. Yes, apparently the hostel boasted several couples that met in the idyllic surroundings and later married and had children.

Well, we don't have any children yet but I did meet my husband in this place, about fifteen minutes later when he introduced himself as our fifth roommate in the dorm room we were shown to. I'd never believed in love at first sight but there it was, though I didn't know it in that instant, of course. Over the next few days I got to know this wonderful man and ended up letting my friends go on to Germany while John and I made our way to Santorini, and then promised to visit each other in the next couple of months. There was, you see, one hitch in this otherwise perfect union.

He was Australian.

Six years later, we are happily settled in Melbourne and I am an Australian citizen. The journey to this point has been one of discovery, frustration, fun, excitement and a lot of learning. I didn't read any books or ask for any advice prior to making the decision to come to Australia. In the beginning, I arrived here to be with my boyfriend and see a new place. I decided to migrate after we evaluated all of our options and determined that to be the best course for us. These choices were made with our hearts first. It then became a necessity to fill requirements to make them happen. It would have been handy to have an instruction manual for reference because we had so many questions and so many fears. We also spent countless hours waiting and wondering, living in limbo and trying to stay sane while carrying on with life through it all.

If you're reading this, you've either been offered an employment opportunity in Australia or fallen in love with an Aussie. Or perhaps you're thinking of coming to Oz for a working holiday or to start a new life away from your home country. Maybe you're just curious about this vast, interesting place. Whatever your reasons, I want to reassure you that a move can be made. In this book I will share my experiences with you and also those of other expatriates (expats) I have met during my time here. I will walk you step by step through the relocation process and provide listings of resources that will help you along the way. I've made the journey you're thinking about embarking on. I've asked the questions, made the mistakes, done the research and survived all of it. You can too. I wish a book like this had been available when I first came to Australia in 2005. It would have made things so much easier. I'm very glad I can share what I've discovered with you and give you a head start into the process.

In chapter one, I will discuss the most important item that you will deal with in your move to Australia: your visa. Without it, there is no point to any of the rest. I learned early on that you couldn't just come in and out of Australia on a tourist visa and expect to stay for any significant length of time. You will eventually need to review your options and apply for a visa to remain in the country. This chapter will outline the visas that you can apply for and I will also share my experience applying for the partner/spouse visa. You'll also learn some helpful hints for putting together your application and what to expect throughout the experience.

In chapter two, some of the myths and misconceptions about Australian life and being an expat will be debunked. My only experience with this country before I moved here was knowledge imparted by a couple of Aussie friends I met while working in the United States (US). Luckily I had actually heard of Perth before I met my husband (it is his hometown). Otherwise I might not have had the courage to take a chance and go there. While many people around the world have visited Australia, I've found that Americans generally know very little about the country. Assumptions are often made that just because everyone speaks English, there won't be any sort of culture shock. This is simply not the case. If you come from the United Kingdom (UK) or another country in the Commonwealth (of which Australia is a member), you may find the differences to be less stark. Coming from the US, however, I find Australia to be very different in some incredibly important ways, despite the many similarities. Wherever you come from, the points made in this chapter will preview what you can expect from life in Australia and help you to evaluate whether your transition is likely to be successful.

In the third, fourth and fifth chapters, I will examine the practical matters of migration. Be prepared to essentially shut down your life in your home country before heading Down Under. You'll find tips and explanations for a variety of circumstances along with helpful resources in both Australia and your home country. I will also tell you a little bit about places to live in Australia. I have travelled at least once to all of the states and have lived in both Melbourne and Perth. I will also direct you to some location-specific websites that will help you get settled wherever you decide to land. In chapter five, I will discuss money matters, including working in Australia, what to expect cost-wise and a thorough introduction to banks, retirement accounts and other financial information you'll need to know before arriving in Australia.

Chapters six through ten are dedicated to life and living in Australia. I'll introduce you to the healthcare system, which is very good but quite different from the US (at least for now). We'll look at consumables, including food, products and services that are part of an individual's daily living. Again, Australia has its own brands and these will probably be somewhat different from what you are used to in your home country. Most of the time, you can find what you're looking for; it may just be called something else or look a little different. I've included a list of items and brands that are difficult to find in Australia and what you can use as a substitute if one is available. I'll also tell you a little about the people of Australia and give you some tips on how to get along and what to expect. Finally, I've included a chapter of answers to frequently asked questions about topics from studying in Australia to buying property here.

In the final chapter, I'll explore travel in Australia, from driving to domestic and overseas travel. Australia sits in close proximity to some of the most amazing places in the world that you've probably heard of, but were too far away from to visit. This is just one of the many delightful things you will discover as a resident of Australia.

Probably the only thing that you won't find in this book is extensive information about the Australian school system (kindergarten, primary school and high school). As I do not have children and only have experience with the university system, I do not feel qualified to discuss very much about moving to Australia with children. I will, however, point you in the direction of many very useful resources that I learned about in my time working for two Australian parenting websites. These resources will lead you in any direction on parenting in Australia that you need to go. Like parents anywhere else, most Australians want to ensure that their children receive the best education available and there is a wide variety of free information should you require it.

In this book, I've tried to be frank about my experiences and in some parts I'm critical of Australia, even if not overtly. I've done this because I think it is very important that people considering migration to a new country have no illusions about their decision. It will not be easy. It will not be everything you expected. It may be better than you expected. It may not be. The results of your move will be dictated by your individual circumstances and, most importantly, your attitude. I have no regrets about my decision to move to Australia. Over five years since I first stepped off a plane into the humid summer Sydney air and felt the warmth on my face and heard my first on-soil "G'day," I have had thousands of experiences in this magical country. Some of them were marvellous, some of them were irritating and some of them were downright infuriating. But all of them have been unique and exciting learning experiences that have taught me as much about myself as they have about the country. I love this place and am proud to be a citizen. I hope you will enjoy it as much as I have.

I wish you good luck and good fortune!

Andrea

1.

Chapter One: Visas - How to survive your dealings with DIAC (grab a copy of *The Three Pillars of Zen*)

So you've decided to move to Australia. Or you're thinking about it. Either way, you probably have a reason for doing so and hopefully your reason is covered by one of the many visas available. Like the US (and, let's face it, many countries around the world today), Australia has been shaped and changed by immigrants from all parts of the world. It's history as an English penal colony is long overshadowed by the country's reputation as a land of opportunity. You will often hear it called the "lucky country."

In a population of around 22 million people, over one quarter of Australia's residents were born overseas, migrating from over 200 countries. Thus, over 200 different languages are spoken around the country. English is, however, the official language. With its stable economy and high quality of living, Australia is a very attractive prospect for people desiring a new place to live, employment opportunities or just a change of pace.

I became a permanent resident of Australia (and eventually a citizen) by lodging an application for an onshore Partner visa (subclasses 820/801). While I was waiting for the temporary residency visa to be granted (the first part of a two-stage process), I was able to remain in Australia on a bridging visa, which extended the conditions of the visa I entered the country with. Bridging visas are usually granted automatically when you are moving from one type of visa to another, so if you are already in Australia and looking for a way to stay, you don't necessarily have to leave and come back again. This will depend on the type of visa you are on already and the type of visa you want to apply for.

Please note that I am not a licensed migration agent. The information contained in this chapter has been gathered directly from Australia's Department of Immigration and Citizenship (DIAC) website or from my own experience and is current as of May 2010. I have also included information I have heard from other people who have dealt with DIAC and their own migration issues. The information found in this eBook is intended to provide general knowledge on migration issues and does not constitute legal or official advice of any kind. Everyone's circumstances are different and you are advised to seek the advice of a licensed, professional migration agent if your unique circumstances require additional explanation or attention. Your first point of reference for the latest official information should be the DIAC website: http://www.immi.gov.au

Additionally, I have not covered every type of visa available from the Australian Government. There are simply too many different types of visas and situations to do them all justice. At the end of the chapter I have listed the names and subclasses of the omitted visas where available. This should not be considered an exhaustive list. If you think that you might be eligible for a visa not described or listed here or if you want more detailed information about any of the visas I have discussed, please visit DIAC's website.

Please read through all of the information found on the DIAC website thoroughly for each visa you are considering. There are generally many comprehensive requirements and eligibility criteria that you will need to fulfil and provide evidence for. The following information is only intended as an overview to get you thinking about the types of visas you might be eligible for and point you in the right direction. Once you think you might be eligible for a visa and have chosen the one that is most appropriate for your circumstances, you should then rely directly on the DIAC website or the advice of a registered migration agent should you choose to use one. Information and requirements change all the time. At the end of this chapter I have included the website addresses of several wonderful online discussion forums where you can exchange messages with thousands of migrants who have gone through the same process. Should you choose to apply without the assistance of a migration agent (as many people do successfully all the time), you can join these communities and ask for advice and assistance from some really friendly, knowledgeable people who are happy to lend their support. You might also make some new friends along the way.

An additional piece of information and advice I will also add: leave yourself plenty of time for everything. Visas are not approved overnight. In many cases, you will wait many months through different stages of the visa process. And if you are applying for a visa for long-term migration, there will be stages. It is a process. I survived it and you will too, but you should arm yourself with lots of patience and tolerance for gathering documents and administrative work. There will be times when you want to rip your hair out and curse your decision to move to another country. But recognise that people who wish to migrate to your home country deal with the same bureaucracy, frustrations and lengthy wait times. You will get through it, I promise.

Let's examine the different types of visas you can apply for to enter and remain in Australia. Please note that all estimated wait times are approximate and depend on a complete application being submitted with no delays due to questions or missing items required by DIAC.

Visitor Visas

Electronic Travel Authority (ETA Visitor Subclass 976) or eVisitor (Subclass 651)

As the fastest, cheapest and easiest way to enter Australia is on a tourist visa (if you hold an eligible passport for the ETA or eVisitor programs), I want to get these out of the way first.

Electronic tourist visas are intended for two purposes only: tourism and visiting friends and relatives. With an ETA, you can apply online[1] yourself or through your travel agent or airline and receive a tourist visa in seconds. You will not receive a stamp or label in your passport; however, your details will be electronically recorded on Australian Government systems. When you check-in for your flight to Australia, the airline staff will be able to confirm electronically that you are eligible to board your flight. You will not be allowed onto the plane without an ETA or another type of visa in your passport. The eVisitor program works the same way, except that you apply on a different website[2].

There are two types of ETA: the Visitor ETA, which allows you to travel to Australia as a tourist or to visit friends or relatives who live in Australia. It is valid for multiple visits within a 12-month period, which commences from the date of issue. You are not

---

[1] Australian Electronic Travel Authority website: http://www.eta.immi.gov.au/

[2] eVisitor online applications: http://www.immi.gov.au/e_visa/evisitor.htm

allowed to work while you are in Australia and the maximum length of time you can remain in the country is three months per visit.

The other type of ETA is the Short Validity Business ETA, which allows you to enter Australia to attend business meetings, conventions or conferences. This visa has the same conditions as the Visitor ETA. It is not intended for actors, musicians or commercial filmmakers, who should apply for an Entertainment visa instead.

You cannot work or study on an electronic tourist visa. Except in very limited circumstances on the Short Validity Business electronic visa, working is a breach of your visa and can result in your removal from Australia.

You might read into the conditions of the ETA or eVisitor that you can pretty much stay in Australia for an entire year if you leave and re-enter the country every three months. In the early stages of my relationship with my husband, I had come to Australia on an ETA to be with him and check out the country for the first time. At the end of the three months, we hopped over to the Fijian islands for a few weeks. On our way back into the country, we went through immigration and customs at the Brisbane airport. John had gone through the line for Australian passport holders while I stood at the end of a very long line for everyone else.

When I finally got to the counter, I was asked to stand to the side and wait for an immigrations officer to come over and speak to me. I noticed that a few other people had been asked to do the same. I had wondered about how re-entry would go, since it seemed too easy to just come in and out of the country. But the language of the ETA conditions said "multiple visits of up to three months at a time for a 12-month period."

A serious-looking officer came over and asked to see my passport and documents and wanted to know why I was back in Australia so soon. I told him I was travelling with my boyfriend and pointed over to John, who was standing sheepishly off to the side. We hadn't yet had a talk about our next steps at that point. We both knew we wanted to stay together, but figured we had a little more time to figure all that out.

"Are you two in a relationship?" the officer demanded.

We looked at each other. I think it was John who said, "yes" first. My heart was pounding in my throat by that point.

"You can't just keep coming in and out like this. You need to figure out what you're doing. I'll allow it this time, but this is the last entry on this visa."

I remember being pretty freaked out at the time. Sure enough, I was allowed in. Standing on the other side of the customs barriers, John and I just looked at each other in bewilderment. Talks about our relationship followed soon after but in that instant I remember tears. I felt shaky, worried and very distressed. It is the feeling that you have put yourself in a position where someone else (a very powerful, Western country-sized someone else) has control over your life and your future. When I looked on the ETA website a few days later to check my status, sure enough, my visa's expiry date had been moved forward by six months. We had to make a plan.

The lesson here is that you can't use your ETA as a longer-term option just by leaving and re-entering the country. As tempting as it is given the close proximity of Australia to New Zealand and

Southeast Asia, it is not a solution to your problems and you may not have as kind an immigration officer as I did in Brisbane. Fortunately, there are plenty of visa options for you to choose from if you are eligible.

ETA Eligible passports: Brunei, Canada, Hong Kong SAR, Japan, Malaysia, Singapore, South Korea, United States of America

eVisitor Eligible passports: Andorra, Austria, Belgium, Bulgaria, Cyprus, Czech Republic, Denmark, Estonia, Finland, France, Germany, Greece, Hungary, Iceland, Ireland, Italy, Latvia, Liechtenstein, Lithuania, Luxembourg, Malta, Monaco, The Netherlands, Norway, Poland, Portugal, Romania, Republic of San Marino, Slovak Republic, Slovenia, Spain, Sweden, Switzerland, United Kingdom - British Citizen, Vatican City

Cost: AUD 20 (FREE for eVisitor)

Wait time for ETA: 12 hours maximum, usually approved within 30 seconds

Tourist Visa (Subclass 676)

This visa has the same conditions as the ETA or eVisitor, however it also allows for study for up to three months and may be available for three, six or 12 months. The big difference here is that you must apply for this visa and receive a label in your passport like any other visa aside from the ETA or eVisitor, and it will take longer to process.

Cost: AUD 105

Wait time for Tourist Visa: Approximately 10 business days

Working Holiday Visa (Subclass 417)

The Working Holiday visa is for citizens of Belgium, Canada, Republic of Cyprus, Denmark, Estonia, Finland, France, Germany, Hong Kong, Republic of Ireland, Italy, Japan, Republic of Korea, Malta, Netherlands, Norway, Sweden, Taiwan and the UK who want to travel and work in Australia for periods of up to 12 months. You must be at least 18 but have not turned 31 years of age when you apply, and you can do this program twice if you work in a specified industry[3] for at least three months (88 days) during your first working holiday. The intended purpose of this visa is to allow you to supplement your holiday costs with short-term employment. If what you really want to do is to move to Australia as a full-time employee or come to the country to stay and work long-term, this really is not the visa for you. The reason for this is that you can only work with each employer for a period of up to six months. You can also study for up to four months and leave and re-enter Australia as many times as you want for the 12-month period.

For people from the following countries: Belgium, Canada, Republic of Cyprus, Denmark, Estonia, Finland, France, Germany, Hong Kong, Republic of Ireland, Italy, Japan, Republic of Korea, Malta, Netherlands, Norway, Sweden, Taiwan and UK

Cost: AUD 235

Wait time for Working Holiday Visa: Approximately 4 weeks

---

[3] A list of specified occupations is provided here: http://www.immi.gov.au/visitors/working-holiday/417/specified-work.htm

Work and Holiday Visa (Subclass 462)

This visa is a version of the Working Holiday Visa for people from Bangladesh Chile, Indonesia, Malaysia, Thailand, Turkey and the US. The conditions are the same. Applicants from the US can apply online.

Your employment options will be limited, meaning you can expect to be hired through temporary agencies or for casual shift work such as food service or working in a shop. There are also plenty of regional opportunities available. Fruit picking is a popular choice for some working holidaymakers who want to extend their visas for another year. There is nothing to say that you will not be able to find work in your chosen career field. But I would not come to Australia on a working holiday visa with the high expectations that you'll find a job in your industry and magically get sponsored for a longer stay. It does happen, but it does not happen very often. You are better off applying for a work visa in the first instance.

For people from the following countries: This visa is for people from Chile, Indonesia, Malaysia, Thailand, Turkey and the US. The arrangement with Bangladesh has been signed, but was not yet in effect at the time of writing.

Cost: AUD 235

Employer Sponsored Work Visas

Business (Long Stay) Visa (Subclass 457)

This is the Standard Business Sponsorship Visa, the most commonly used program for Australian or overseas businesses to sponsor a person from overseas to work in Australia for up to four years. The overseas worker can bring any eligible secondary applicants with them to Australia and those applicants can work and study as well. Holders of this visa can enter and leave Australia as they please.

Employers must apply to sponsor and recruit workers from overseas and nominate the occupations they want to fill and whom they want to fill those positions. These visas are generally for people who have found an employer to sponsor them already or who work for a foreign company that wants to send them to Australia for a position within their Australian offices. The company must demonstrate that they have trained Australian citizens and permanent residents and that they have a strong record of hiring local employees and engaging in non-discriminatory hiring practices. This is all too complicated to get into in this book, but basically it means that the company needs to prove that local talent cannot be reasonably sourced to fill the roles it is looking to fill. The employee must be demonstrated to have the specific skills, qualifications and experience to fulfil the position and speak English to a certain standard.

Secondary applicants must be the primary applicant's spouse or partner, dependent child or a dependent relative with special circumstances. Partners in Australia can include de facto partners (including same-sex partners).

Registered nurses can work in Australia for an approved business sponsor for up to four years and bring their family members with them to work and study in Australia under the Temporary Business (Long Stay) visa (subclass 457). There are permanent options for qualified overseas nurses under 45 years of age. If you are interested in a nurse visa, be sure to check with regional employers as well. Nurses can also come to Australia on working holiday visas if they are under 30 years of age and can work as a nurse for one employer for up to six months.

Usually employers will provide support to employees coming to Australia under this visa, including the help of a migration agent.

Cost: Application charge AUD 265 Nomination Charge AUD 70 Sponsorship Charge AUD 350

Wait time for 457 Visa: Approximately three weeks

Employer Nomination Scheme (Subclass 121/856)

This visa allows Australian employers to sponsor employees who are foreign nationals as well as temporary Australian residents for a permanent visa. It allows the employee and any dependent family members included in the application to live as permanent residents in Australia. Permanent residents can remain in Australia permanently to live, work and study and are eligible for social security benefits, healthcare and eventually citizenship.

The employee eligibility requirements are similar to those for the 457 visa, however the eligible position must be full-time, ongoing and available for at least three years, have satisfactory working conditions and be a highly skilled occupation on the Employer Nomination Scheme Occupation List (ENSOL). At the time of writing, this list was available for download via http://www.immi.gov.au/skilled/sol/

Regional Sponsored Migration Scheme (Subclass 119/857)

This is for employers in regional areas looking to sponsor employees as with the 121/856 visa. A Regional Certifying Body will determine whether an Australian employee can fill the position before the visa process can go ahead. The position must not be one that can be filled by an Australian employee and must be available for at least two consecutive years.

Cost for both 121/856 and 119/857 visas: Nomination (ENS only) AUD 455, 1st instalment (outside Australia) AUD 1,735; 1st instalment (within Australia) AUD 2,575; 2nd instalment for primary applicants with less than functional English AUD 7,165; 2nd instalment for dependents 18 and over with less than functional English AUD 3,575

Wait time for 121/856 or 119/857: Approximately two weeks

Skilled Migration Visas

If you don't have a company to sponsor you, you may still be able to migrate to Australia if you have skills in an occupation for which workers are in demand in Australia. These are listed on Australia's Skilled Occupation list (SOL).[4]

There are a variety of options for people wishing to migrate to Australia as a skilled worker under these visas. If you are an independent migrant, meaning you don't have a relative to sponsor

---

[4] At the time of writing, this list was available for download via http://www.immi.gov.au/skilled/sol/

you, you will have the least number of restrictions placed on you. Those choosing the sponsored option will need their sponsors to fulfil several obligations on their behalf.

I am going to assume that you are outside Australia and not a New Zealand citizen because there are a number of visa options unique to citizens of New Zealand and those who are already in Australia that I will not cover in this chapter. For a list of these, please see the section at the end of the chapter titled 'Available visas not discussed in this chapter.' These mostly apply to holders of skilled provisional visas or overseas students who are looking to stay in Australia and work after they graduate.

Skilled – Independent (Migrant) Visa (Subclass 175)

If you are under 45 years of age and have skills and qualifications in an occupation that is in need of more capable people in Australia along with good English language skills, you may be able to migrate to Australia as a skilled worker without any requirements for sponsorship. This visa uses a points test to determine if you have the characteristics needed in the labour market. Once again, we refer to the SOL.[5] You and any dependent family members included in the application will be able to live as permanent residents in Australia. Permanent residents can remain in Australia indefinitely to live, work and study and are eligible for social security benefits, healthcare and eventually citizenship.

So what is this points test? Australia is very big on points checks for assessment, where each item presented is worth a certain number of points. If you get here and try to open a bank account, for

---

[5] At the time of writing, this list was available for download via http://www.immi.gov.au/skilled/sol/

example, you will be asked for 100 points of identification. A passport is worth 70 points, a credit card 25 points, a rates notice 35 points and so on. The skilled points test works the same way.

For this visa, the points test pass mark is 120 points. Here are the criteria under which you will be assessed:

Age: Points in the age category are determined by your age on the day you make your application. Points are assigned as follows:

18-29 years of age	30 points
30-34 years of age	25 points
35-39 years of age	20 points
40-44 years of age	15 points
45 years of age or older	ineligible

You will be required to submit a certified copy of your birth certificate with your application.

English Language Ability: If you are a citizen of or hold a valid passport from the UK, Canada, New Zealand, US or the Republic of Ireland, you will automatically receive 15 points. If you want to prove proficiency (for 25 points instead of 15) or if you are not a citizen of one of those countries, you will need to have your English language skills tested before you lodge your application.

A level of 'Proficient' and 25 points are awarded to applicants providing an English for International Opportunity (IELTS) Test[6]

---

[6] English for International Opportunity website: http://www.ielts.org/default.aspx

Report Form (TRF) Number to show you have a band score of at least seven on each of the four components (speaking, reading, listening and writing) OR evidence of having achieved a score of ´B´ or higher on each of the four components of the Occupational English Test (OET). A level of 'Competent' and 15 points are awarded to those with an IELTS TRF Number showing a band score of at least six on each of the four components.

A higher level of English is required for certain occupations where it forms part of the skills assessment. You can find out if your occupation requires a higher level of English by contacting the assessing authority for your nominated occupation. These are located at the bottom of the SOL.

Nominated Skilled Occupation and Skills Assessment: You must obtain a positive skills assessment for your nominated occupation before you apply for your visa. The assessing authority is listed next to each occupation on the SOL. Your chosen occupation must be on the list at the time you lodge your visa application so be sure to proceed in a timely fashion.

For most occupations where training is specific to the occupation, you'll receive 60 points with a positive skills assessment. In most cases you will have a qualification (such as a degree or trade qualification) and experience that meets the relevant Australian standards. In some cases, experience without formal qualifications may also be acceptable. For more general professional occupations, 50 points are awarded. You must have a qualification equivalent to an Australian bachelor degree or a higher qualification. For other general skilled occupations, 40 points will be granted to applicants with a positive skills assessment. You must have a qualification equivalent to an Australian diploma or advanced diploma. The SOL indicates the number of points your occupation is worth.

You can only nominate one occupation in your visa application and you must provide a suitable skills assessment for that occupation to be granted a General Skilled Migration visa. However, prior to lodging your application, you may apply to any number of skills assessing authorities until you obtain a suitable skills assessment.

You will be asked to include the following in your application to satisfy that your skills are sufficient to receive points for your nominated profession:

- A certified copy of a completed skills assessment document, which confirms that your skills have been assessed as suitable for your nominated occupation

AND

- One of the following:

    Either a certified copy of your post-secondary qualifications, such as your degree or diploma certificate and your transcripts or mark sheets

    Or

    Certified copies of your work references provided by your employers that detail the position/s you held and the duties you performed (if you have worked in an occupation where substantial work experience may be accepted instead of post-secondary qualifications)

Recent Work Experience or Australian Study Requirement: You will have to demonstrate that you have been employed in your nominated occupation for at least 20 hours a week in a paid position for at least 12 of the 24 months immediately preceding your visa application lodgement date. Alternatively, you will need to have completed either a single qualification requiring at least two academic years of study in Australia at an Australian educational institution (full-time) or more than one qualification resulting in a total period of at least two academic years of study in the 16 calendar months prior to your application. This study must be related to your nominated application.

Documentation for your experience or study will need to be provided as follows:

Recent work experience requirement

- Certified copies of work references on official company or department letterhead (specific conditions apply)
- A payslip from your current employer
- You may also include additional documents as supporting evidence including contracts, payslips tax returns, group certificates or retirement account information.

Australian study requirement

- A certified copy of your completion letter from your educational institution (specific information required)
- Certified copies of your transcripts

You do not receive any points for satisfying this requirement.

Specific or Australian work experience: You receive bonus points if you have been employed in a paid position for three of the last four years in your nominated occupation, or a closely related occupation on the SOL for at least 20 hours a week at a skilled level. You will receive 10 points if your occupation is worth 60 points and five points if your occupation is worth 40, 50 or 60 points and you've been employed in any occupation on the SOL for three out of the last four years. You must prove this by submitting evidence as described above.

You can also receive 10 extra points for working in Australia (on an Australian visa that allows you to work) for at least one year in the past four years immediately before you submit your application. If you have completed a recognised Professional Year in Australia in the past two years, you can receive 10 points as well. A Professional Year is a development program in Computing Science, Accounting or Engineering that has been approved by the minister.[7]

Australian qualifications, regional study and fluency in a 'community' language: You may receive between five and 25 points for completing an Australian qualification such as an undergraduate, master's or doctorate degree for a certain number of years. You may also receive points for studying in a regional area in Australia. If you can provide evidence of a university degree in one of the following languages (or pass a test by an accrediting body[8]), an additional five points are yours as well.

---

[7] For more information, please visit
http://www.immi.gov.au/skilled/general-skilled-migration/professional-year.htm

[8] Not available for languages designated with a (*) symbol

Afrikaans*	Danish*	Japanese	Romanian
Albanian	Dutch	Khmer	Russian
Arabic/Lebanese	Estonian*	Korean	Serbian
Armenian*	Fijian	Lao	Sinhalese
Bangla (Bengali)	Filipino (Tagalog)	Latvian*	Slovak
Bosnian	Finnish	Lithuanian*	Slovene*
Bulgarian	French	Macedonian	Spanish
Burmese	German	Malay	Swedish*
Chinese – Cantonese	Greek	Maltese	Tamil
Chinese – Mandarin	Hebrew*	Norwegian*	Thai
Croatian	Hindi	Persian	Turkish
Czech	Hungarian	Polish	Ukrainian
	Indonesian	Portuguese	Urdu
	Italian	Punjabi	Vietnamese
			Yiddish

Partner skills: If your non-Australian partner (Australian permanent residents don't count either) who is also included in your application also satisfies basic age, English language, qualifications, nominated occupation, recent work experience and skills assessment requirements, you can claim five points just for your intention to migrate together.

Location, Health and Character: You must be outside of Australia when your visa is granted. Additionally, you and all applicants will be required to have a health examination, which includes a medical examination by a panel doctor in your home country, a chest x-ray to ensure you do not have Tuberculosis and a HIV/Hep B/Hep C test. These test results are only valid for a limited period of time (generally 12 months) so you should wait until you are advised by the Department before proceeding with a health examination. Additionally, you will be asked to provide police certificates for each country in which you have lived for 12 months or more over the last ten years since you turned 16 years of age. You will also have to sign an Australian Values Statement, which demonstrates that you agree to respect Australian values outlined in the *Life in Australia* book, which is a publication of the Australian Government. You do not receive any points for satisfying these requirements.

Here are the website addresses of the most common assessing authorities listed on the SOL at the time of writing:

Architects Accreditation Council Of Australia
http://www.aaca.org.au

Australasian College of Physical Scientists and Engineers in Medicine http://www.acpsem.org.au

Australasian Veterinary Boards Council http://avbc.asn.au

Australian Institute of Quantity Surveyors
http://www.aiqs.com.au

Australian Psychological Society http://www.psychology.org.au

Australasian Podiatry Council http://www.apodc.com.au

Australian Association of Social Workers
http://www.aasw.asn.au

Australian Computer Society http://www.acs.org.au

Australian Dental Council (ADC) http://www.dentalcouncil.net.au

Australian Institute of Management (AIM)
http://www.aim.com.au

Australian Institute of Medical Scientists (AIMS)
http://www.aims.org.au

Australian Institute of Radiography http://www.air.asn.au

Australian Maritime Safety Authority http://www.amsa.gov.au

Australian Nursing and Midwifery Council
http://www.anmc.org.au

Australian Pharmacy Council http://www.pharmacycouncil.org.au

Certified Practicing Accountants of Australia
http://cpaaustralia.com.au

Council of Occupational Therapists Registration Boards
http://www.cotrb.com.au

Council on Chiropractic Education Australasia
http://www.cea.com.au

Dietitians Association of Australia http://www.daa.asn.au

Engineers Australia   http://www.engineersaustralia.org.au

Institute if Chartered Accountants Australia
http://www.charteredaccountants.com.au

National Accreditation Authority for Translators and Interpreters   http://www.naati.com.au

National Institute of Accountants   http://www.nia.org.au

Optometry Council of Australia and New Zealand
http://www.ocanz.org

State Legal Admission Authority (SLAA)
You must be assessed under the state or territory in which you want to practice:
>   New South Wales and Australian Capital Territory
>   Legal Practitioners Admission Board
>   http://www.lawlink.nsw.gov.au/lpab
>
>   Northern Territory Legal Practitioners Admission
>   http://www.supremecourt.nt.gov.au/lawyers/index.htm
>
>   Queensland - The Secretary, Barristers and Solicitors Board
>   http://www.qls.com.au/lwp/wcm/connect/QLS/About+QLS/Our+Structure/Related+Organisations/Legal+Practitioners+Admissions+Board

South Australia - The Registrar, Legal Practitioners Registry
www.lawsocietysa.asn.au/other/registry.asp

Tasmania - The Secretary, Board of Legal Education
http://www.supremecourt.tas.gov.au/practice_and_procedure/board_of_examiners/overseas_applicants/overseas_applicants_2

Victoria - The Secretary, Council of Legal Education
http://www.lawadmissions.vic.gov.au

Western Australia - The Secretary, Legal Practice Board
http://www.lpbwa.org.au

State/Territory Medical Boards[9]

Australian Capital Territory
http://www.medicalboard.act.gov.au

New South Wales Medical Board
http://www.nswmb.org.au

Northern Territory Medical Board
http://www.health.nt.gov.au/Health_Professions_Licensing_Authority_HPLA/Health_Registration_Boards/Medical_Board/index.aspx

Medical Board of Queensland
http://www.medicalboard.qld.gov.au

Medical Board of South Australia
http://www.medicalboardsa.asn.au

Medical Council of Tasmania
http://www.medicalcounciltas.com.au

Medical Practitioners Board of Victoria
http://www.medicalboardvic.org.au

---

[9] Please read the specific information provided by DIAC regarding migration as a Medical Practitioner here:
http://www.immi.gov.au/skilled/general-skilled-migration/migration-medical.htm

Medical Board of Western Australia
http://www.wa.medicalboard.com.au

Teaching Australia   http://www.teachingaustralia.edu.au

Trades Recognition Australia (TRA)
http://www.deewr.gov.au/TRA

Vetassess   http://www.vetassess.com.au

If you score less than 120 points but more than 100 points, your application will be placed in a reserve (called the 'pool') and will remain in the pool for two years after assessment. If the pass mark is lowered at any time during that two-year period, and your score is equal to or higher than the new pass mark, your application will then be processed further.

If you score less than 100 points, your application will be refused.

As I mentioned earlier, you are able to include secondary applicants in your visa application if they qualify as your partner or dependent children or relatives. These secondary applicants must meet the location, English language ability, health, character and eligibility requirements as well as sign the Australian Values Statement.

Cost: 1st instalment AUD 2,575; 2nd instalment (for dependents aged 18 years or over with less than functional English) AUD 3,575

Wait time: Varies, however wait times of around six months from lodgement of visa to approval were reported at time of writing

Skilled – Sponsored (Migrant) Visa (Subclass 176)

This is a similar permanent visa to the 175 but with one important difference: it is for people unable to meet the Skilled – Independent pass mark. These applicants, therefore, must be either sponsored by an eligible relative living in Australia or nominated by a participating State or Territory government. They must pass a points test lower than that for the Skilled – Independent visa.

Your sponsor must be an Australian citizen or permanent resident or an eligible New Zealand citizen who is a non-dependent child or stepchild, a parent or step-parent, a sibling or step-sibling, a niece or nephew (including step-nieces and step-nephews) or an aunt or uncle (including step-aunts or uncles).

This eligible relative sponsor must sign an agreement to provide:

- Adequate accommodation and/or financial assistance as required to meet your living needs during your first two years in Australia

- Other support, such as child care, to enable you to attend English language classes

- Information and advice (including information about employment in Australia) to help you settle in Australia

The two-year period starts from the date the applicant enters Australia as a holder of this visa.

State or Territory Government nominations are usually provided for those who have an occupation that is in shortage in their particular State or Territory. If you are interested in this scheme, check the websites of each State or Territory government to see if your occupation is on their skills shortage list. If it is, contact that State or Territory government. These governments will also be able to provide you with information relating to employment, housing and schools in the region you may wish to live in.

A great resource is the free Skill Matching Database[10]

Here is a list of relevant websites for the States and Territories:

Australian Capital Territory	http://www.business.act.gov.au
New South Wales	http://www.business.nsw.gov.au
Northern Territory	http://migration.nt.gov.au
Queensland	http://workliveplay.qld.gov.au
South Australia	http://immigration.sa.gov.au
Tasmania	http://development.tas.gov.au
Victoria	http://liveinvictoria.vic.gov.au
Western Australia	http://migration.wa.gov.au

Cost: 1st instalment AUD 2,575; 2nd instalment (for dependents aged 18 years or over with less than functional English) AUD 3,575

Skilled – Regional Sponsored (Provisional) Visa (Subclass 475)

This is a three-year provisional visa for people who can meet the lower pass mark for this visa. Applicants must be either sponsored by an eligible relative living in a designated area of Australia or nominated by a participating State or Territory government. After living for two years and working for at least one year in a Specified Regional Area, applicants can apply for a permanent visa.

---

[10] You can access the website via http://www.immi.gov.au/skills

If you don't qualify for one of previous visas, this is a good option for you if you are happy to live in a regional area. Country Australia is beautiful and not to be overlooked if you really want to move to Australia.

Cost: 1st instalment AUD 2,575; 2nd instalment (for dependents aged 18 years or over with less than functional English) AUD 3,575

Your partner, dependent children and other dependent relatives can apply to accompany you in Australia in your original application or afterwards, but you must apply to bring them before your visa becomes permanent. This applies to the following temporary or provisional visas:

- Skilled – Regional Sponsored (Provisional) visa (subclass 487)
- Skilled – Graduate (Temporary) visa (subclass 485)
- Skilled – Regional Sponsored (Provisional) visa (subclass 475)
- Skilled – Recognised Graduate (Temporary) visa (subclass 476)
- Skilled – Independent Regional (Provisional) visa (subclass 495)
- Skilled – Designated Area Sponsored (Provisional) visa (subclass 496)

The length of time it takes to process Skilled Migration visas varies. From September 2009, priority processing has been assigned to the following visas: Employer Nomination Scheme (ENS), Regional

Sponsored Migration Scheme (RSMS) and General Skilled Migration (GSM) visas (except for 476, 883 and 887 visas).[11]

Skilled visas can be very tedious and time consuming to apply for, with a great deal of paperwork and forms to deal with. They don't necessarily have to take a long time, however and processing times vary widely depending on the circumstances of the applicant(s), how well you put your application together and arbitrary factors such as the time of year in which you apply and departmental priorities. At the end of this chapter I've listed some fantastic online communities where you can read current information about peoples' experiences with different types of visas (and life in Australia and migration in general).

Family Migration Options (including my experience with the Spouse Visa)

If you've fallen in love with an Aussie and want to migrate to Australia on the basis of that fact, you are far from alone. From 2007 to 2008, 39,931 people were granted permanent visas on the basis of being the partner or spouse of an Australian citizen or permanent resident.[12] I was one of those people. Family visas can be obtained if you are the partner, parent, child or dependent family member of an Australian citizen, permanent resident or eligible New Zealand citizen.

---

[11] You can read more about the order of priority here:
http://www.immi.gov.au/skilled/general-skilled-migration/updated-priority-processing-arrangements.htm

[12] From the Australia Bureau of Statistics website:
http://www.abs.gov.au/AUSSTATS/abs@.nsf/Lookup/3416.0Main+Features22009

The definition of a partner is different from the one generally understood by law in the US. In Australia, you are considered the legal partner of an Australian citizen or permanent resident if you are married to that person or if you are living in a de facto relationship. De facto partners, for the purposes of a visa, are defined as two people who have been living together for the twelve months immediately before lodging their visa application and who are in a loving, committed, genuine and continuing relationship. This includes people in a same-sex relationship.

The procedure for applying for this visa will differ depending on your circumstances. If you are already married, a significant part of your work has been completed. This is not to say that every married couple gets through the immigration process without any problems. You will have to provide evidence of your relationship regardless of whether you have a marriage certificate. This includes an interview and supporting documents. We've all seen the movie *Green Card*, right? I do not suggest that you marry someone just to get a visa to come to Australia. Chances are, you will not get past the scrutinising gaze of your Case Officer (CO). But being married means that you can go ahead and apply for your visa if you can support your claim of being a legitimate husband and wife.

What if you aren't married? There are a couple of scenarios here:

If you are in Australia already and have been in a relationship and living with your partner for at least one year as a de facto, and he or she is an Australian citizen or permanent resident or an eligible New Zealand citizen, you can apply for a visa to remain in Australia and work and study on the basis of that relationship.

The one-year requirement[13] for a relationship will challenge you to prove that you have a monogamous, mutual relationship that is both genuine and ongoing. You must live together and show that you share a commitment and are not just roommates. DIAC will make exceptions to the cohabitation requirement in certain compelling and compassionate circumstances, generally those that involve a child from the relationship or where same-sex cohabitation is illegal in your country of residence, but in most cases, unmarried couples who aren't living together will have a hard time fulfilling the one year relationship requirement.

This is not to say that the requirement does not allow for somewhat unusual circumstances. John and I fulfilled the one-year relationship requirement simply by being together for an entire year, living in different places and travelling together. John got a career opportunity in a foreign country and I lived with him during that period of time. We travelled together to visit my family and friends in the US. We lived in Australia for several months together as well. By the time we applied for my spouse visa, we had been together full-time, probably spending less time apart than most married couples, for more than twelve months. But we truly did share commitments and expenses. We had a joint bank account. We kept records of everything and had a stockpile of cards, letters, emails, ticket stubs and airline tickets that accounted for each day, showing that we were together in the same place (if you are at the start of your journey together, you should get into the habit of being meticulous about saving *everything*). Between the time we lodged our application and the day of our interview with our CO we bought a house together. It wasn't that we didn't want to be married. We later had a beautiful wedding in the Whitsunday Islands with our family and friends surrounding us. We just didn't want to have a rush wedding just to get a visa. It didn't feel right to us. So don't

---

[13] You can read all about this here:
http://www.immi.gov.au/media/fact-sheets/35relationship.htm

feel that if you don't want to be married right away that it won't work out for you. But you must not kid yourself that you can have what will be viewed as a casual relationship and prove to DIAC that you are a genuine de facto couple.

The example above illustrates that if you are offshore, with or without your Australian partner and you have no children or special circumstances, you may need to get creative to fulfil your one-year relationship requirement. But if you love each other and want to be together, you will figure out a way. We were fortunate enough to have financial resources, mobile careers and adventurous spirits allowing us to be a bit nomadic and still happily together.

If you are in more of a hurry and you are offshore, you may wish to go ahead and get married. If you do that, you should still be keeping evidence of your relationship from the time you met. If you have not been together very long before you got married, the Department will want you to prove that yours is a genuine relationship. You will eventually need to submit a statement or statutory declaration regarding the history of your relationship, along with evidence demonstrating it to be true.

This may sound like a lot of burden on the applicants, but remember that your CO will not know you personally and it is his job to ensure that people do not receive a visa for residence in Australia by claiming a fraudulent relationship. He will want to know how, when and where you first met, how your relationship developed and progressed and at what point you decided to marry or enter into a de facto relationship. You application will need to outline your domestic arrangements, how you support each other financially, physically and emotionally and at what point that level of commitment began. DIAC will ask about your future plans together and will also ask you to explain any periods of separation and how you maintained your relationship through that period.

Prepare to be thorough and utterly pedantic about every little detail of your relationship. There's a silver lining here: you'll know your partner (and your partner will know you) inside and out. And at the end of it all, when you have your permanent visa attached firmly onto a page in your passport, you'll have a marvellous little collection of minutiae that you might not have saved otherwise. I'm still in the habit: to this day, we save every movie ticket stub, boarding pass and business card from our favourite restaurants in giant shoeboxes stuffed into the back of our closet. They're like time capsules and absolutely precious to us. I can't wait to look through them in thirty years.

You can find more information on evidence and the four categories that DIAC CO's look for here:
http://www.immi.gov.au/migrants/partners/evidence-of-relationship.htm While the website tells you that you only need to submit one type of evidence in each category, you can and should send in as much evidence as you have. It is better to have too much than to allow any doubt into the mind of your CO. I will tell you more about what we included with our application later on in this section.

If you've decided to get married and you are outside Australia, you will need to decide where you want to get married and take care of that little detail first. If you want to get married in Australia instead, you can apply for a Prospective Marriage Visa.

Prospective Marriage Visa (PMV) (Subclass 300)

This visa will allow you to enter Australia, work or study in Australia and leave and re-enter Australia as many times as you wish before your visa expires. Your fiancé(e) will have to sponsor you and you must marry *and* submit an application for a partner visa within nine months of *being granted* the PMV. You can get married inside Australia or outside of Australia as long as you enter the country once before the wedding.

Your sponsor must be an Australian citizen, permanent resident or eligible New Zealand citizen who wants to sponsor you as his or her partner in Australia. He or she must (generally) be 18 years of age or older and be known personally to you, and you must have met in person as adults. Your sponsor must not have previously sponsored two other partners for migration to Australia (including withdrawn sponsorships) or sponsored another partner within the last five years, or been sponsored him or herself within the last five years. Your sponsor must also not be the holder of a Woman at Risk visa (Subclass 204). These rules may be flexible in certain compelling circumstances. There are also restrictions placed on sponsors holding a contributory parent category visa. Additional requirements are placed on applications that include a dependent family member under the age of 18.

Your sponsor will agree to provide for you financially and will become responsible for all financial obligations to the Australian Government that you may incur. He or she will be obliged to support you so that you may attend any required English classes (including childcare if necessary) and provide you with information and advice to help you settle, including about employment. He or she will be required to notify DIAC if your relationship breaks down or if he or she withdraws support before the application is finalised. He or she may be required to provide evidence that he or she is able to provide for you financially, including an Assurance of Support (AoS)[14]

You and your partner must advise the department of any break down in your relationship between the time you apply for the PMV and the date that you receive your Permanent Residency visa (in most cases, around two years after you lodge your initial application for the partner visa). You must also advise them to changes in your circumstances, such as if you and your fiancé (or spouse) have a child.

Cost: AUD 1,735

Wait time: Varies, however wait times of around one to three months were reported at time of writing

Onshore Partner temporary visa (subclass 820) and permanent visa (subclass 801) AND Offshore Partner Temporary Visa (Subclass 309) and Permanent Visa (Subclass 100)

If you are already married or eligible to apply for a partner visa on the basis of your de facto relationship as outlined earlier in this section, whether you live in or outside of Australia, or if you have married while holding a PMV, then you will be applying for one of these visas. They work pretty much the same way except that it costs more to apply from onshore, and offshore applications tend to be processed a bit more quickly.

There are two stages to this visa. In the first stage, you are applying for both the temporary and permanent visas at the same time. You will then wait for your interview and if your application is

---

[14] You can read about AoS here: http://www.immi.gov.au/media/fact-sheets/34aos.htm

approved after the interview, you will receive temporary residency in Australia. You'll be able to live in Australia with your partner, work, study, receive Medicare benefits, etc. About two years after you lodge your application, you will fill out more paperwork demonstrating that your relationship is still in good shape, and then you will receive permanent residency, which is permanent, no matter what happens (within reason). You do not need to apply all over again for the permanent visa as this application is included in your original application (though it may feel like you are re-applying for all the second stage paperwork).

If you have been married or in a de facto relationship with your partner for five years or more or if you have been in the relationship for two years or more and have dependent children, you may be granted the permanent visa right away without having to spend two years on the temporary visa. You may also waive the temporary visa requirement if your partner was granted a Protection or permanent visa under the humanitarian program and you were in a declared relationship before this visa was granted.

You should generally be living with your partner when you apply for the visa. Your partner will have to sponsor you as outlined in the PMV section above. As with other permanent visas, you will be required to submit evidence of your marriage or de facto relationship (outlined earlier in the chapter). You will also have to pass a health examination, including a chest x-ray and HIV/Hep B/Hep C blood test. Finally, you will be asked to provide police clearances and sign the Australian Values Statement.

You are allowed to include your dependent children and relatives in your application provided they meet health and character requirements.[15]

The forms for the visa are relatively straightforward. As with any other visa, the burden here is to prove the legitimacy of your relationship. Whether you are legally married or applying as a de facto couple, you will have to provide evidence of your relationship. You will also be asked to have your friends and/or family provide statutory declarations describing how they know you, your partner and your relationship, and stating why they believe your relationship is genuine and ongoing. Here is a list of items we included in our visa application in order to provide evidence of our relationship:

- Statements from joint bank accounts, including mortgage accounts
- Financial records showing the origin of funds deposited into those accounts (to demonstrate both of our financial contributions and responsibilities in the relationship)
- Leases and tenancy agreements for rented properties where we lived together
- Photographs of us together and with friends and family members together as a couple
- Evidence that we were listed as beneficiaries on each others' accounts
- Evidence of our purchase of a home together

---

[15] You can learn more about eligibility requirements for your dependents here:

http://www.immi.gov.au/migrants/partners/partner/820-801/eligibility-dependent.htm

- Envelopes addressed to us at the places where we lived together
- Airline boarding passes
- Hotel confirmations
- Ticket stubs for movies, concerts, plays, mini-golf, sporting events and other forms of entertainment such as zoos and museums
- Invitations to weddings and other events addressed to us both
- Cards, emails and love letters to one another

The other part of this process is the interview. Once you lodge your application, you will receive a letter advising you of your interview date and time sometime in the distant future. Everyone stresses about the interview and it is hard to say how it will go because it all really depends on your CO. If you are genuine and have put together a solid application, you usually have nothing to worry about. I can only share our interview experience because it is the one interview I have been involved in.

Our CO was a pleasant woman who welcomed us in and went through our application. She asked us to tell her our story and asked a few questions about our relationship. It was nothing too personal. I remember one of the questions was whether we fought at all during our travels. We answered truthfully that, on travel days when things were hectic, we'd snap at each other a bit. And then later on we'd get over it and apologise when we were on the train or had finally reached our destination. She smiled and we ended up having a good chat with her. It was nerve-wracking, of course, because this person sitting across the table from you is judging everything you say in order to make a determination about your future. It's serious business! But they do not go out of their way to invade your privacy and our CO was very professional throughout our entire experience. We mentioned that we'd included our cards to each other (birthday, anniversary, etc.)

"Oh, I only read the cards if I have serious doubts about the couple being genuine," she said.

And that was that. She finished going through everything, closed our file and told us that she intended to approve our visa. We had to wait about six weeks for the actual letter, but we left the interview and treated ourselves to wine and lunch at one of the nicest restaurants in town. Believe me, you will feel like celebrating too.

If you are offshore, you will be able to enter Australia once your temporary visa is granted and remain in Australia for the two-year period until a decision is made on your permanent visa. You will have to enter Australia by a specified date once your visa is granted.

Cost: If lodged outside Australia AUD 1,735

If lodged within Australia and you hold a Prospective Marriage visa (subclass 300) and have married your spouse AUD 840

If lodged within Australia and you entered Australia as a fiancé(e) and do not currently hold a substantive visa but married your spouse/sponsor while your Prospective Marriage visa (subclass 300) was valid AUD 1,060

If you hold a Transitional (temporary) visa AUD 300

If you hold any other visa AUD 2,575

There is no cost if you hold a subclass 445 Dependent Child visa.

Wait time (temporary visa): Varies, however wait times of around three months were reported at time of writing. When I applied in Perth, it took about six months to receive my temporary residence visa. Applications are usually processed faster offshore.

Parent and Child visas

There are a number of visas available to parents and children of Australian citizens, permanent residents and eligible New Zealand citizens. These are:

Parent (Migrant) visa (subclass 103)

Aged Parent (Residence) visa (subclass 804)

Contributory Parent (Migrant) visa (subclass 143)

Contributory Parent (Temporary) visa (subclass 173)

Contributory Parent (Migrant) visa (from subclass 173 to subclass 143)

Contributory Aged Parent (Residence) visa (subclass 864)

Contributory Aged Parent (Temporary) visa (subclass 884)

Contributory Aged Parent (Residence) visa (from subclass 884 to subclass 864)

These visas can cost thousands of dollars. If you would like more information about any of these visas, please visit the DIAC website: http://www.immi.gov.au/migrants/family

Student visas

Becoming a student in Australia is a popular pathway to residency for thousands of people around the world. Importing international students is big business for Australian universities due to the higher fees they command. I did my master's degree in Australia, the time spanning both my time on the temporary residency visa and also once I became a permanent resident. I was thrilled to be able to pay the local student fees once my permanent visa was granted.

Australia has world class educational and student facilities and faculty. More than 320,368 student visas were granted in the 2008-09 program year, representing more than a 15 per cent growth in the student visa program in one year. If you are interested in studying in Australia, there are a number of visa options for you.

Part of your visa application will involve an objective measure of immigration risk for each of 190 different countries called 'assessment levels.' These determine visa requirements. There are five assessment levels in the student visa program, with Level 1 representing the lowest immigration risk and Level 5 the highest. The higher the assessment level, the more evidence you will be required to submit to demonstrate support of your claims made in the application. These levels are determined by each student group's compliance with their visa conditions and other indicators in the previous year. Levels are raised and lowered based on these factors. So the behaviour of your country's student group from last year will affect your visa requirements this year.

The number of combinations of visa types and assessment levels makes describing them all here prohibitive. Your first port of call should be the Overseas Student Program – Assessment Levels information sheet found here: http://www.immi.gov.au/students/student-visa-assessment-levels.htm Australia offers student visas for programs from English Language Intensive Courses for Overseas Students (ELICOS) to primary and secondary courses to vocational and sponsored training to university study at all levels. You should first think about what you might want to study and then proceed to determining your eligibility and choosing the visa that most closely matches your needs. Your family members may be eligible to apply for a visa to accompany you to Australia while you study and they are subject to the same assessment level as you are, regardless of the passport they hold. You may also be eligible to work during your studies (restrictions apply).

Cost: AUD 550 plus AUD 75 for permission to work; you will also be responsible for your course fees at international student rates. The only way to pay local student rates is to become a permanent resident of Australia. Holders of temporary visas, even if you are on the path to permanent residency as was the case with my partner visa, will still have to apply as an overseas student and pay overseas fees.

Wait time for student visa: From one to six weeks

Available visas not discussed in this chapter

This is not intended to be an exhaustive list. Please consult http://immi.gov.au for a full listing and detailed information about all of the available visas.

Business Development (Provisional and Permanent): A number of visas exist for people to establish or manage businesses in Australia or invest in Australia. Most offer pathways to permanent residency.[16]

Exchange Visa (Subclass 411): This is a maximum two-year visa allowing skilled people and their eligible secondary applicants to come to Australia to broaden their work experience and skills under exchange arrangements.

---

[16] For more information, visit
http://www.immi.gov.au/skilled/business/visa-options.htm

Investor Retirement Visa (Subclass 405): This is a temporary visa for people over the age of 55 who are self-supported and able to make a significant long-term financial investment in Australia. This visa does not lead to permanent residence.

Labour Agreements: Formal arrangements for Australian industry groups or employers to recruit a specified number of skilled workers over several years

Medical Treatment Short Stay (Subclass 675) or Long Stay (Subclass 685) Visas: For travel to Australia for medical treatment or consultations for up to 12 months

New Zealand Citizen General Skilled Migration Visas: You are advised to apply for the offshore visa, regardless of whether you are in or outside Australia. Available visas: Skilled – Independent (Migrant) Visa (Subclass 175), Skilled – Sponsored (Migrant) Visa (Subclass 176), Skilled – Regional Sponsored (Provisional) Visa (Subclass 475), Skilled – Recognised Graduate (Temporary) Visa (Subclass 476)

Refugees: Australia has an offshore Humanitarian Program for people seeking protection. Please refer to the DIAC website for more information.

Service Sellers: For representatives of overseas suppliers working on agreements to supply services in Australia

Skilled – Graduate (Temporary) Visa (Subclass 485): This is an 18-month temporary visa for overseas students who have obtained an Australian qualification in Australia as a result of at least two years study. This allows applicants who are unable to pass the points test to remain in Australia for 18 months to gain the skills and experience needed to apply for a permanent or provisional General Skilled Migration visa.

Skilled – Independent (Residence) Visa (Subclass 885): This is a permanent visa for eligible overseas students who have obtained an Australian qualification in Australia (at least two years study) and for holders of certain temporary visas with skills in demand in Australia. Applicants are not sponsored and must pass a points test. For applicants not able to meet the Skilled – Independent pass mark, who have either a relative in Australia to sponsor them or a nomination from a State or Territory government, the **Skilled – Sponsored (Residence) Visa (Subclass 886)** is available.

Skilled – Recognised Graduate (Temporary) Visa (Subclass 476): This is an 18-month temporary visa for Engineering graduates of recognised overseas educational institutions who have skills in demand in Australia. There is no points test for this visa.

Skilled – Regional (Residence) Visa (Subclass 887): Permanent visa for eligible provisional visa holders who have lived for at least two years and worked for at least one year in a Specified Regional Area in Australia.

Skilled – Regional Sponsored (Provisional) Visa (Subclass 487): A three year provisional visa for eligible overseas students and holders of certain temporary visas who can meet the lower pass mark for this visa. Applicants must be either sponsored by an eligible relative living in a designated area of Australia or nominated by a participating State or Territory government. This can lead to a permanent visa.

Specialist entry visas: If you are an internationally recognised professional, artist, athlete or scholar, you may be eligible for a permanent visa based on that qualification alone. Similarly, entertainment professionals, religious workers, foreign government staff and representatives as well as other people undertaking in specified activities (usually related to their craft or profession) can obtain special visas for these purposes.[17]

Sponsored Family Visitor visa (Subclass 679): Requires formal sponsorship by an Australian Citizen or Permanent Resident and allows you to visit family members for up to 12 months

Applying for a Visa

You can apply for many visas online with eVisa[18], attach documents to the application and access information about the progress of your application online as well. Because I used a migration agent for my partner visa, my application was submitted in paper format by the agent's office. I applied for my citizenship online, however, and found the process to be much faster and more efficient for me. If you prefer to use paper forms so that you can see the information all at once while you are completing them, you can always print out the paper application forms for your visa and then apply online, copying the information off the forms you have completed ahead of time. Having the ability to check the status of your application online will come in very handy.

---

[17] For a list of specialist entry visas, please visit
http://www.immi.gov.au/skilled/specialist-entry/visa-options.htm

[18] You can access eVisa information via this link:
http://www.immi.gov.au/e_visa/

If you submit your application the old-fashioned way, here are some tips for what I've heard DIAC CO's like to see when your file hits their desk:

- Do not use binders, folders, clear page protectors etc. for presenting your application.
- You can tape small items to larger full sized sheets of paper.
- Number every page at the bottom and put everything together in order. Include a cover sheet listing the page numbers of important sections.
- Don't laminate anything.
- If you submit loose pages, put a large binder clip on them to keep them together.
- Place passport photos in a plastic sandwich bag, and then tape the sides of that bag to an A4 sheet of paper.
- Do not send electronic or musical greeting cards with your application. Do not include videotapes or photo albums.
- Use a sturdy envelope or packaging so that your materials are not damaged. Large manila envelopes lined with bubble wrap are great for this purpose.
- Use a delivery service that enables you to track the arrival of your package so that you can confirm it was received.
- Include the name of your CO on the outside of the envelope if you know his/her name.

The name of the game is patience. Probably the most frustrating part of your visa application is going to be the waiting time. Some visas can take six to eight months just to get through the first stage of the visa, during which time you will be in a state of limbo, wondering what the future will hold. If you are applying for an Australian visa for family reasons, this can add an extra level of emotion to the entire process. To make matters worse, the more you look on discussion forums and speak to other people about how long they are waiting and how their visa applications went, you will begin to realise that everyone is completely different and most people have experiences with DIAC at varying degrees of pleasantness and this can also fluctuate depending on the stage of the visa.

For us, the most difficult part was stage one of my partner visa. After gathering all the necessary application materials, getting health and police checks and filling out the forms, which had its own special frustrations because of our migration agent (see next section), we lodged the application in Perth in April. Our interview with our CO was not until September. Five months is a long time to wait. I was able to do some temporary work in the meantime because of the conditions on my previous visa, but the time lapse was definitely detrimental to my career. I got through it by telling myself that this was what we needed to go through and that I would get past it. And we did.

A lot will depend on your CO. Some of them are very organised and work quickly, processing applications with efficiency and getting people through the procedure swiftly. Others not so much. And you have no idea about your CO and what he or she is capable of. Even once you meet him, you will not have a full picture of his capabilities, caseload, personal circumstances or your particular office's backlog. We are just outsiders to the Department and have to wait our turns. Just keep repeating that mantra and prepare yourself for aggravation. You may be pleasantly surprised.

In recent years, DIAC has made efforts to be more friendly and human. I first applied for a long-term visa four years ago. So my experience is probably different than people going through the process at this very moment. And the people who apply this year will have a different experience from next year's applicants. This is just the nature of immigration. Visas and priorities change for the government all the time. There are just too many variables to predict anything specifically.

What you can do to help is to prepare your application meticulously. Don't give your CO any need to contact you for further information. Front-load your application where possible.[19] Be neat and organised and clear. If you completed a printed application form, make sure that it is typed or that your handwriting is legible. Read every question thoroughly and ensure you've answered it completely. Be polite in your dealings with your CO and other DIAC staff. Doing these things will not guarantee a fast-track of your application, but they will help prevent your application from being delayed.

Try not to compare yourself to other applicants or other people in general. It is a great idea to join an online community and seek the support of others going through the same process. Other people in your life won't really understand what you are going through. While you delay a year of your life to apply for a visa and make a move to another country, your peers will be going on with their lives as normal. In our case, friends were getting married or advancing their careers while we were wading through bureaucracy and a pile of papers. They didn't really get what we were stressing about or realise how complicated it all was. Other people were tremendously supportive. You have your own circumstances and it will help you immensely to put blinders on to other people's progress. The wait for a visa will probably feel like a pretty stagnant time in your life. But it is not forever.

---

[19] Front-loaded applications contain every piece of documentation that must be included in the application and all evidence at the time you lodge the application.

Don't put too much effort into comparing timelines to other applicants you meet in discussion forums or support groups. You just don't know what their circumstances were. We knew of a couple whose family knew a politician and apparently pulled some strings to get their application fast-tracked. Most people won't admit to things like this for fear of jinxing themselves or instigating a report to the department about the irregularity. You can't possibly know if a person got approval faster because he listed a specialty in his skilled application that was on the priority list for the state he wanted to move to. Or perhaps someone has a compassionate circumstance that got her through faster. You can only worry about yourself and your own situation. This can go the other way as well. Your application may move more quickly than someone else's who applied for the same visa. When I applied for citizenship in Melbourne, I got my approval three days after I took my test. Another woman waited five months. I have no idea why that happened. I know my CO seemed very organised and friendly. Was that the reason? I will never have an answer to that.

Remember the old adage: this too shall pass.

Penal, Character and Health Clearances

Your visa may require you to provide police certificates for each country in which you have lived for 12 months or more over the last ten years since you turned 16. If you are applying offshore, you do not have to provide this information when you apply. You will be advised when it is required. If you are applying onshore, you should provide this information with your application. Australian police checks are conducted by the Australian Federal Police. Instructions and further information for obtaining the required police clearances can be found here:

http://www.immi.gov.au/allforms/character-requirements

At the time of writing, Federal Bureau of Investigation (FBI) checks from the US were taking about 13 weeks to process. You can check the status of your FBI record request by calling +1 (304) 625-5590.

You may also be required to undergo a health examination as part of your visa application, particularly if you are an older applicant. I've discussed these a bit already in an earlier section. Health examinations are designed to ensure that you do not have a pre-existing condition that will cause you to be a significant burden on Australia's public health system. You'll learn more about the Australian health system in chapter six. These examinations consist of a chest x-ray, for which you usually need to get a referral form and then make an appointment with a Panel radiology clinic (nominated by the Australian Government in Australia or your home country) to have the x-ray taken. You will then pick up your sealed x-ray and report and take it with you to your medical examination. If may be possible to attend a Panel clinic that does both the x-ray and the examination.

A Panel doctor conducts the medical examination. In Australia, you will go to *Medibank Health Solutions* for this exam. If you are applying from overseas, you can find a list of Panel doctors here: http://www.immi.gov.au/contacts/panel-doctors I did my health checks onshore before DIAC used Medibank Health and have nothing overtly unpleasant to report about the experience. You'll sit in a waiting room for a while and then have a blood test and urinalysis. A doctor will check you out and talk to you about your medical history. You do not receive your medical reports as those will be sent directly to DIAC. You will be contacted if you are found to have a health problem. A friend of mine was actually grateful for the health examination because her doctor discovered a thyroid problem that she may not have caught otherwise. Just make it your annual physical and get on with it. Further information on the health requirements for migrating to Australia can be found here: http://www.immi.gov.au/allforms/health-requirements

Whether to use a migration agent

To use a migration agent or not: a very important question for anyone considering a visa application. We used one when I applied for my spouse visa. We were very emotional and overwhelmed with the process and the requirements, and wanted to ensure that there would be someone with experience there to hold our hands in case of any complications or delays. We were also in a financial position where we could afford an agent. Their fees can run into the thousands of dollars and if you're applying for a permanent visa, you're probably looking at a couple of thousand dollars for DIAC fees already. Add to that all the little fees along the way for police and medical clearances, certified copies of documents, etc. and you're looking at a hefty bill. It all adds up. We spent over AUD 5,000 before it was all over with.

There were times when we felt that our migration agent wasn't earning her fees. She would return application forms to us with typos and other errors, late and without a sincere apology when we pointed out the mistakes. Sometimes we felt like she cared more about her other, "needier" clients. We were just a couple of middle-class, English-speaking white people, after all. Our application was easy. What about the refugees she was helping? I'm being sincere. This is the attitude we received. Some might say, "fair enough" and get on with it, but when you're paying a couple of thousand dollars to someone who isn't very detail oriented, for something as important as the rest of your life, you get a little cross.

In the end, however, I don't know if we would do things any differently if we had to do it over again (except to use a different agent). It was nice to have someone to answer the barrage of paranoid questions we had and to have another pair of eyes going over all our documents. A migration agent will come in handy when you get to that ambiguous question on page 27 of the third part of the last form in the tall stack that has been sitting on your desk for a week begging for attention. She will draft a lengthy tome of legal mumbo jumbo to slap onto the front of your two-kilo pile of forms and supporting evidence outlining exactly how, when and where you fulfilled all those eligibility requirements. With our migration agent standing between us and the intimidating Department, we felt bulletproof, even as we swallowed the lumps in our throats and hoped that we hadn't missed one of her secretary's little "typo errors."

She did indeed earn every last cent when I begged her for an update on the status of our second stage permanent visa application and four days later received a call from her slightly English language-challenged assistant to tell me that my visa was finally approved. I was now a permanent resident of Australia and I didn't even have to wait for the letter. I could just go right into the DIAC offices and have the label put into my passport. Oh what a feeling! Did our agent know someone in the immigration offices the day she called? Did she charm a case officer on a good day? Or was it just my time already, my application fished from a pile of approved cases waiting for the letters to be sent off? I'll never know – she got the credit no matter what in that instance.

Here are some pros and cons of hiring a migration agent based on my own experience and what I've heard from others:

Pros
- Migration agents handle thousands of cases a year, so they know exactly how to best present your case.

- If you have a difficult or complicated case, I highly recommend using an agent.

- Applying for most visas is a lengthy, time-consuming, energy intensive process and can be emotionally draining as well. An agent will guide you through this difficult time and his or her knowledge and suggestions can assist you in ensuring you haven't missed anything. You wouldn't want to miss an opportunity because you submitted a poor application.

Cons

- You'll probably think it is a waste of money if you have a straightforward case and the time to spend on doing it yourself. Registered migration agent fees can run into the thousands. Do not use an unregistered agent.

- You'll have more control over the process if you do it yourself. I've heard many stories of frustration from people who had a similar experience to ours. Their agent was sloppy and disorganised and caused them a great deal of stress throughout the process. I'm sure there are many quality agents out there but you must choose carefully.

- There is a wealth of free information available on the internet, including several wonderful online communities of other people going through the same experience. You can troubleshoot for free online anytime 24/7.

In Australia, migration agents must be registered with the Office of the Migration Agents Registration Authority (MARA)[20], which regulates migration agents in Australia. You can and should check to

---

[20] MARA website: https://www.mara.gov.au/

ensure that your agent is currently registered and has no complaints against her. A list of sanctioned agents is available on the MARA website.

If you are outside of Australia, MARA also provides information about registered agents overseas. Otherwise, be sure that the agent you use meets any local laws or registration requirements in your country. You can read more information about overseas agents here:http://www.immi.gov.au/visas/migration-agents/using/outside-australia.htm

Once you have the visa

If your residency visa was granted offshore, you will have a date by which you must enter the country for the first time in order to validate your visa. All family members must enter Australia by this date. If you are travelling separately, the primary applicant must enter Australia first or at the same time as the rest of the family. The other applicants must enter Australia after the main applicant (or at the same time) and before the first entry date. Usually this date is set around twelve months from the earliest date of police checks and medicals, but it could be six months as well. Check your visa carefully to ensure that you know the date and that you can make it to Australia by that time. You cannot usually change this date unless there are exceptional circumstances, so if you can't enter by the date you should immediately seek professional advice before you contact DIAC. Otherwise your visa can be cancelled.

Permanent residency visas are valid for five years from the date they are granted (not the date they are validated). You need to remain in Australia for at least two years (730 days) within this five-year period so that you can easily qualify for the Resident Return

Visa (RRV) at the end of this period. The RRV is used to re-enter Australia as a permanent resident if you choose not to pursue citizenship. If you don't meet the requirement but you are in Australia on the visa's expiry date, the visa will not expire until you leave Australia. For more information, read Form 968i thoroughly. Please note that these rules can change at any time.[21]

Australian resources

Australia in Brief   http://www.dfat.gov.au/aib
Information about Australia

AustraliaNZMigrate
http://groups.yahoo.com/group/AustraliaNZMigrate
This is a moderated Yahoo group for questions and answers about immigration issues and is run by a registered migration agent.

Community Legal Centres (CLCs) http://www.naclc.org.au
Provide legal assistance in a wide range of matters

Gay and Lesbian Immigration Task Force
http://www.glitf.org.au
This is the website of the organization in New South Wales. There are similar organizations in other Australian states. The primary aim of GLITF is to assist the foreign partners of Australian lesbians and gay men to migrate to Australia.

Immigration Advice and Application Assistance Scheme (IAAAS)
http://www.immi.gov.au/media/fact-sheets/63advice_providers.htm
Provides free professional assistance to the most vulnerable visa applicants, to help visa applications, liaison with the department,

---

[21] Form 968i can be downloaded here:
http://www.immi.gov.au/allforms/pdf/968i.pdf

and advice on complex immigration matters; also provides migration advice to prospective visa applicants and sponsors.

Immigration Advice & Rights Centre http://www.iarc.asn.au
This website offers free advice to financially disadvantaged potential applicants, sponsors or proposers for an Australian Visa. This site also has comprehensive information packets for most visa applications and covers a variety of special circumstances.

Migrant Information kits from DIAC
http://www.immi.gov.au/living-in-australia/settle-in-australia/beginning-life/booklets/english.htm

Refugee and Immigration Legal Service (RAILS)
http://www.rails.org.au
Provides free legal assistance in immigration and refugee cases to people in need

US resources

Australian Embassy in the USA http://australia.visahq.com

Embassy of Australia in Washington, D.C.
http://www.usa.embassy.gov.au/whwh/Visas_and_Migration.html
Official visa information specifically for applicants in the USA

United States Embassy in Australia
http://canberra.usembassy.gov

UK and Commonwealth Country resources

Australian High Commission in Canada
http://www.ahc-ottawa.org

Australian High Commission in the U.K.
http://www.australia.org.uk

British High Commission in Australia
http://www.ukinaustralia.fco.gov.uk

Canadian High Commission in Australia
http://www.canadainternational.gc.ca/australia%2Daustralie

Expat and migrant communities and other international resources

British Expats website   http://britishexpats.com/forum
If you're from the UK, this website covers migration and other information for expats to not only Australia, but other countries as well. I've linked to the forum here so that you may participate in the online community. But be sure to check out the home page for other resources as well. People migrating from other countries may also find useful information and help here as well since the community is so large.

Expat Forum   http://www.expatforum.com
Online community of around 60,000 members who have either moved abroad or wish to emigrate; features articles and a forum with Australia specific information

Federation of American Women's Clubs Overseas
http://www.fawco.org
An international network to support American women living abroad with over 75 member clubs worldwide, including Australia

Go Matilda   http://gomatildaforums.com
Online discussion community for people moving to Australia; includes forums for each part of the country

Life in Australia
http://www.immi.gov.au/living-in-australia/index.htm
Australian Government information on working and living in Australia

Living in Australia   http://www.livingin-australia.com
A website about migration and living in Australia

PomsinOz   http://www.pomsinoz.com
This is an online discussion community for English people (and an excellent resource for everyone else as well) considering a move to

Australia, migrating to Australia or who are already here. This forum is really well organised by subject so you'll be able to find discussion topics and get your questions answered quickly and easily. I've found the information here to be really specific and covers a wide variety from places to live to moving and job issues and all other aspects of life down other; definitely worth a look even if you aren't English.

Working in Australia.com
http://www.workingin-australia.com
Dedicated to information for those wanting to come to Australia for work

Yanks Down Under   http://yanksdownunder.net
This is an online community with an active forum for Americans living in Australia offering excellent support for migrants and Americans living in Australia.

2.

Chapter Two: What happens when you assume? That's right...common misperceptions of Australia and living overseas

Moving to another country, especially when you're doing it because you've fallen in love with a foreigner, can seem so romantic. We lived in Paris for awhile before settling in Australia and it was just so exotic and exciting to be in a place that was different from what I was used to. Of course, I loved the city already and spoke a little bit of high school French so I could get by. But it wasn't easy. John and I really only had each other and a few fellow expat friends to hang out with. The language and culture barriers were confronting every day. And it got a little lonely for both of us. We never really felt that we were part of the culture there.

So I thought that moving to Australia permanently would be a breeze. The culture seemed somewhat similar to that of the US and we speak the same language, after all. But the reality, and this rings true for many English-speaking expats in Australia, is that things aren't easy. I'm not saying this to scare you, but I definitely moved here under a lot of false assumptions and, while I have no regrets, I wish I'd known more. I'm a very adaptable nomadic person by nature and I've been able to cope better than I think some people would. I don't think anyone should move here expecting it to be simple and without complications. So I've identified some of the things that you might be thinking or expecting when you imagine your new life in Australia and laid them out here, with my thoughts on what you need to be prepared for. Everyone has different experiences and you might not have any of the problems I mention. You may be older, wiser and have such talent and drive that nothing gets in the way of your career or social aspirations no matter what country you're in. If so, that's wonderful. But for the rest of us, here are some assumptions to watch out for.

Myth number 1: Australia (and Australians) will be pretty similar to people in [insert the name of your English-speaking country].

Australia has its own history and Australians have their own unique viewpoints, backgrounds, opinions and ways of doing things. Aussies have an international reputation for being friendly, laid-back people. I'm not saying that they aren't. But the problem with stereotyping, as you'll soon find out, is that it goes both ways. As an American, I sometimes come across people who have very strong opinions about the country that I came from. While I would argue that Aussies are exactly like Americans in many important ways, most of them don't see it that way. I don't even try to argue the point. I had one really upsetting encounter with another guest at a close friend's birthday party once, which perfectly illustrates this example. I was standing at the bar when the drunken guy approached John and me, looked at me, turned to John and said, "Don't go with the Americans, man. They're the ones that got us into the financial crisis." He was drunk, yes, but this was pretty inappropriate behaviour. Incidents like this have happened more times than I would like to remember, and I've been on the receiving end of plenty of snide little comments. Most of my encounters with Aussies have been positive, but these incidents do occur and you have to know how to handle them. British expats have reported similar negativity towards them from Aussies. I don't ever take it personally when a nasty comment is made about my being American, but it is disquieting the first few times you encounter it.

You will also notice subtle differences that you may or may not like and adapt to. Businesses, banks and government-run organizations may function differently here than in your home country. Service in shops and restaurants will usually surprise Americans. Products and the food you will be eating are going to be different. If you come from the northern hemisphere, the seasons are reversed. This means Christmas comes in the summer. And Australians celebrate their own special holidays. There is no Thanksgiving and Halloween isn't really observed here either. I can continue to list the differences but hopefully you get the idea: you're going to have to adapt if you want to get along here. Australia is not going to change for you.

Myth number 2: I have what it takes to be an expat.

I've intentionally tried to stir you here. Maybe you do have what it takes. I certainly don't know. You should try to take stock before you proceed any further.

Are you flexible, open-minded, a fast learner and a diplomat? Can you stand being away from your family and friends for years at a time? Will you be able to handle losing some friends who aren't interested in keeping up long-distance relationships? Are you adventurous and willing to try new things? Is your relationship with your partner secure? These are all questions to ask yourself because, as I pointed out in the first myth, Australia is not necessarily going to be just like where you came from (or like it at all).

Myth number 3: My career and financial situation won't change.

This is a hard one to swallow. When I first came to Australia, I thought everyone would be keen on my US work experience. I'd studied at the best advertising portfolio school in the world and the most talented Aussies in my field practice their craft overseas. I'd worked in New York City and was feeling pretty confident about my prospects. But no one in Melbourne really cared about that. My portfolio impressed potential employers in Sydney, but in Melbourne I felt it was almost a drawback to be foreign (or maybe it was that I was American). And Melbourne was the place I needed to make it work because it was where my partner's job was.

I'll discuss this issue more in the section on work and employment, but you need to know that it isn't always easy to find a job in your chosen industry, and many migrants to Australia get stuck taking jobs they are way overqualified for. It's going to depend on your specific experience and where you live, but Australian employers look for specific qualifications and local experience. John, who is Australian by birth, faced this problem as an *engineer* (mathematics and science are the same everywhere, right?) when he returned to Australia after working overseas for a few years. Some employers cared more about the work experience he did in Australia as a graduate after university than his later jobs in the UK and France. You may also find that not all overseas degrees and qualifications automatically convert to Australian versions. This can be very frustrating; especially for people whose career is everything to them.

Your lifestyle and financial status may also change. Salaries in Australia can be lower, taxes are high and the Aussie dollar, while currently having a good run, is not always strong in relation to other currencies. The cost of living is high in Australia. There is not as much competition among companies here and you'll find that certain items are very expensive. Real estate is also very expensive to purchase and rents can be extremely high. These are all things to be prepared for.

Myth number 4: Moving overseas will clean the slate.

If you're running away from anything in your life, moving to another country is not going to solve all your problems. You'll still be you no matter what country you put down when writing your address on a form. If you have personal problems or a bad relationship, moving may actually make things worse because of all the stress you will pile onto pre-existing conditions. Putting a bandage on problems and hoping they will go away, especially when there are issues of mental health involved, is not a solution. This does not mean that you can't or shouldn't move if something is unsatisfactory in your life, but just know that you're better off dealing with the issue (with professional help if necessary) than running from it.

Myth number 5: I've always been social and had lots of friends so it will be really easy to meet people and make new ones.

Being a person that people tend to like and get along with will go a long way, and will definitely be an asset to you here in Australia. It is certainly better to be this way than the opposite. But don't assume that your personality alone will do the job. You're going to have to be very pro-active and determined to make friends with Australians. I've had plenty of fleeting friendships with Aussies but I can count on my hand the number of them that I consider to be real friends. Australians, especially women tend to make friends when they're young and stick with those friends for life. The Australian (male and female) friends that I have are all fellow travellers. They've spent lots of time abroad and most of them have foreign-born partners, and I feel certain that this is the reason why they have friends who are foreign as well. This doesn't mean that I don't meet and have lots of fun with Aussies. We just don't usually become close friends.

3.

Chapter three: And where will you live? Six states and two territories to choose from

Australia conjures up many different images depending on who you are across the world. When I first told my American friends I was planning to move here, several sniggered and brought up *Crocodile Dundee*, and one actually thought that Perth was some kind of outpost where I would be catching my own dinner and fighting off kangaroos in the garden. Actually, kangaroos do graze on domestic gardens in parts of Perth, but that's generally something that would happen in the hills, not the inner suburbs where we lived. But I'll forgive my American friends. After all, we get very little news of Australia in the US media. And I'm always appalled at the way Australia allows itself to be consistently portrayed as a jungle full of crocodile wrestling larrikins. The customs video you'll be shown as you land in the country is a perfect example.

For other people, Australia is a land of oceans and surf, with beautiful beaches and a sun-drenched lifestyle you couldn't imagine in most parts of Europe or Canada. The truth is, you will have quite a different experience of Australia depending on where you choose to live. If you are moving here on a regional skilled visa or for a specific job in the Australian branch of your current company, or to live with a partner who is already established in one location, you may not have much of a choice as to where you land. But if you have the freedom to pick anywhere you like, I will now go through all the possibilities with you.

Australia is a huge country, the sixth largest in the world. But it also has the lowest population density, with only two people per square kilometre of land. Climates and geography change from region to region, with different temperatures in each part of the country at any given time. Australia is also the driest inhabited continent, with poor soil (only six per cent is suitable for agriculture). You will hear about droughts in many of the states and water restrictions apply throughout most parts of Australia.

I've divided each section into city and country, with the capital city highlighted and some notes about the regional areas. Country Australia is really beautiful and, though we've always lived in a major city, we make an effort to visit places in the country. I love the people and the wonderful fresh food and wine you can find in Australia's regional areas. Aussies there are famously friendly and country towns have a level of sophistication that I haven't seen in most other countries. I certainly wouldn't compare them to country towns in the US. There is something magical about a day in country Australia (and I'm a city girl at heart).

Let's look at each state and territory individually.

New South Wales (NSW)

New South Wales is home to Australia's largest city, Sydney. With so much diversity in landscapes, NSW has something for everyone. From beaches to skiing to rainforests to Outback to city, you'll find what you're looking for in this exciting state.

Sydney

Built around one of the world's most magnificent harbours, Sydney houses all the typically Australian icons you've probably seen on postcards and in travel articles. The world-famous Opera House, Harbour Bridge and Bondi Beach can all be found here.

You can pick up any travel guide to learn about all the sights you will see in Sydney, but you're probably not going there to sightsee in the long-term. So what can you expect as a resident of this beautiful city? I've only visited Sydney and absolutely love it there. Sydney-siders probably wouldn't live anywhere else. How could you want to if you already have so many amazing beaches, coastal walkways, vibrant restaurants and nightlife, brilliant shopping and such a beautiful setting to experience it all in?

For one thing, Sydney can be prohibitively expensive. It is a large major city on par with New York, Paris and London. If you can afford to live near the water and have an international, big city background, I can hardly imagine that you'd want to settle anywhere else in Australia, unless you're looking to make a great change. If you live away from the central business district (CBD), you're looking at a very long commute, either in car or bus traffic or by train or ferry. The problem with public transport is that, unlike New York, Paris or London, it won't get you everywhere. I have never met anyone who lived in Sydney and did not have a car, unless he lived and worked in the CBD, which for most people is financially impossible.

We always talk about living in Sydney someday and it would have been much better for my career because that is where the best jobs are in my field. But my husband could not possibly find a job there because of his specialty. We settled for Melbourne instead (I just got a mental image of thousands of Melburnians raising canned tomatoes to throw at me in hatred – there's a strong rivalry between the two). But sorry Melbourne, Sydney's got it all. I love the combination of mansion-topped hillsides next to the gorgeous harbour with all the little coves and inlets. It's the big city I'm used to, having lived in Miami, San Francisco and New York prior to migrating to Australia. And it's warmer than Victoria.

Around Sydney, you have Botany Bay, Parramatta, Penrith, Camden and the five 'Macquarie Towns' of Windsor, Richmond, Wilberforce, Castlereagh and Pitt Town. The Blue Mountains begin 65 kilometres (km) inland from Sydney, with the highest mountains reaching 1100 metres (m). The area between Broken Bay and the very liveable city of Newcastle to the north is considered the Central Coast.

If you want to learn more about Sydney, here are some great places to start:

Australian City Life Sites: Sydney City Life
http://www.bcl.com.au/sydney

City of Sydney
http://www.cityofsydney.nsw.gov.au/AboutSydney/Default.asp
Information direct from the city council

The Daily Telegraph (tabloid newspaper)
http://www.dailytelegraph.com.au

Department of State and Regional Development information
http://www.sydneyaustralia.com/en

Stuck in Sydney   http://www.stuckinsydney.com
Information on areas in Sydney, prices and articles to help you get started.

The Sydney Morning Herald (broadsheet newspaper)
http://www.smh.com.au

Country New South Wales

If you continue north from Newcastle, you'll reach the North Coast, home to Hunter Valley, which is wine country and numerous coastal towns such as Port Macquarie, Coffs Harbour and Byron Bay. Here you will find exceptional beaches, forests and wildlife. These are the beautiful and relaxing places Aussies go for a beach holiday in NSW. There is also the New England region, which has a bit of a Scottish feel to it. Much further inland, 400 km west of the Blue Mountains, is the Central West, which has a goldrush and bushranger history. You'll also find vineyards and other agriculture here. Go far west and you'll hit the Outback, which contains mining towns and wilderness.

Other parts of regional NSW include Lord Howe and Norfolk Islands, the Northwest and the South Coast. The South Coast is similar to the North Coast, except it is much less busy and developed. On the Victorian border, you'll find the Snowy Mountains, wonderful for winter skiing, as well as the Southwest region, which is mostly a farming area and home to the Murray River. Towns in this area include Albury Wodonga (Wodonga is actually in Victoria) and Wagga Wagga (the largest inland city in NSW).

If you want to learn more about New South Wales, here are some websites that may interest you:

Department of State and Regional Development information
http://www.sydneyaustralia.com/en/regional.asp

Discover NSW tourism site http://www.discovernswaustralia.com

Fairfax Community Newspapers for NSW
http://www.adcentre.com.au/fairfax-community-newspapers-nsw.aspx

Information from the NSW government
http://www.business.nsw.gov.au/investment/living
Regional profiles:
http://www.business.nsw.gov.au/investment/regional

News Limited Community Newspapers
http://www.newsspace.com.au/communitynews/cumberland

New South Wales tourism site http://www.visitnsw.com

Victoria (VIC)

The smallest of the mainland states, Victoria offers a variety of lifestyle options from country to coast to vibrant city life. Victoria is leading Australia in terms of population growth. According to the Bureau of Statistics, 70 per cent of the state's growth came from overseas migration in 2009.

Melbourne

Melbourne is the second largest city in Australia and often considered the most European of Australia's major cities. It has a thriving café, restaurant and bar scene with, arguably, some of the best restaurants and coffee in Australia. Melbourne is also the capital of sports and a vicious rival to Sydney for the best arts, culture and festivals. Its reputation for shopping is renowned (though you will be disappointed if coming from Sydney or another major international city), though the variety of boutiques and funky neighbourhoods is competitive.

While this is not the city to live in if you want to spend your days on Australia's most beautiful beaches (Port Phillip bay is no match for the ocean) or bathed in perennial sunshine, Melbourne has much to offer singles, couples and young families alike. Melbourne is growing rapidly, attracting people due to its reputation as a liveable city because of its multicultural mix and affordability compared to Sydney. There is talk that Melbourne's population may outnumber that of Sydney's in ten years. Judging by the development going on around the CBD in the past few years alone, one can see how this could be possible.

The weather is a common griping point for most Melburnians and visitors alike. I've lived here for the past three years and we really do experience four seasons in one day. As long as you learn to dress in layers and don't mind a few Indian summers, you'll be okay. In my opinion, Melbourne tries to do too much – it hosts every type of festival imaginable each year as well as several major sporting events annually including the *Australian Open* tennis, *Formula One* racing, cricket, most of the Australian Rules football games, soccer, basketball, netball and rugby. The good thing about this is that there's always something going on. And Melburnians do go out for things. A sleepy, lazy city this isn't. But the crowds and traffic can be tiring.

I am in the minority when I complain about life in Melbourne. Everyone I know, from former Sydney residents to foreign expats to visitors from the rest of Australia rave about the city. It is an affordable capital that is very easy to navigate on public transport or bikes and it has a great cultural atmosphere. My favourite aspect of the city is the plethora of different restaurants at all price levels, a brilliant bar scene and access to pretty much any show you want to see on any given night. Melbourne has the best casino in the country, world-class shopping and entertainment and you don't have to travel very far to get out of the city and to relaxing country getaways and spas, or down to the coast for a drive to the Mornington Peninsula or along the Great Ocean Road.

If you want to learn more about Melbourne, here are some websites providing more information:

The Age (broadsheet newspaper) http://www.theage.com.au

Australian City Life Series: Moving to Melbourne
http://www.bcl.com.au/melbourne/movetomelbourne/default.htm

Destination Melbourne http://www.destinationmelbourne.com.au

Herald Sun (tabloid newspaper) http://www.heraldsun.com.au

Information especially for migrants (government)
http://www.liveinvictoria.vic.gov.au

Information from the Melbourne City Council
http://www.bcl.com.au/melbourne/movetomelbourne/default.htm

Visit Melbourne tourism guide http://www.visitmelbourne.com

What's on Melbourne   http://www.onlymelbourne.com.au
Local event guide for the city

White Hat Guide for Melbourne
http://www.whitehat.com.au/melbourne.asp
"Informed, Intelligent, Independent and (sometimes) Irreverent" coverage of Melbourne events, things to do and places to visit.

Country Victoria

Heading southwest along the coast of Port Phillip Bay, the next major town you come to is Geelong. Further along, you'll reach the Bellarine Peninsula. On the other side of the bay, southeast of Melbourne, lies the beautiful Mornington Peninsula, which is a favourite holiday getaway spot for Melburnians. The combination of wine country and beaches is truly unique and its location less than an hour's drive from the capital is an added bonus. Surrounding Melbourne to the northeast, you'll find the Yarra Valley, another popular wine region. To the west, are the Dandenong Ranges.

Further away from Melbourne, you can head south to the Great Ocean Road, a magnificent stretch of coastline leading you to the country towns of the southwest and eventually South Australia. This is another popular holiday destination for Melburnians, who can choose from several towns along the coast. Inland lies the Wimmera, a large province of wheat fields and farms that also includes the Grampians. If you head to central Victoria instead, you'll find the Goldfields, with many towns and an attractive countryside. In the winter, some Victorians trade the beaches in the south for the spa country towns of Daylesford and Hepburn Springs. Skiing enthusiasts can opt for a trip to the High Country instead. Yet another region of Victoria is the southeast Gippsland region, with forests and interesting scenery. The Mallee region is Victoria's Outback. So as you can see, despite its small size, there are a variety of landscapes to choose from if you decide to live in Victoria.

If you want to learn more about Victoria, here are some websites that may interest you:

Fairfax Community Newspaper network for Victoria
http://www.fcnonline.com.au/vic

Information from the Victorian Chamber of Commerce
http://www.victoriachamber.ca/moving_victoria

Information from the Victorian Government
http://www.provincialvictoria.vic.gov.au

Leader Community Newspapers for Victoria
http://leader-news.whereilive.com.au

Visit Victoria Tourism Guide   http://www.visitvictoria.com

Queensland (QLD)

Queensland is the second largest state in Australia. Famous for the Great Barrier Reef that runs along its coastline, Queensland is also home to many islands, tropical rainforests, temperate coastal areas and an often-dry inland area. Sunny weather and phenomenal beaches are the big draws here, though its residents put up with a great deal of humidity and are subjected to cyclone season each year from January to April. There are only two real seasons: Wet and Dry.

Brisbane

Australia's third largest city, Brisbane is a very desirable place to live. It is cosmopolitan, with an excellent café and cultural scene, beautiful parks and great nightlife. The Brisbane River runs through the city and there are excellent bike tracks and gardens to explore. Immediately east, Moreton Bay offers beaches, islands and boat races. Just south of Brisbane lays the infamous Gold Coast, a 35 km stretch of over-developed waterfront that attracts millions of visitors a year. Inland, you'll find beautiful national parks and mountains.

Being one of the smaller major cities in Australia, Brisbane is very laid back, with a sub-tropical climate and the typical infrastructure and cultural scene of a medium-sized city. Housing prices are generally more affordable here than in cities like Sydney, Melbourne and even Perth, though Perth is about the same size. If you are young and single and want a big-city nightlife or don't like heat and humidity, Melbourne or Sydney might be more your scene. But if you have a family and don't go out a lot, plan to live in the suburbs and enjoy spending time in the outdoors, I'd seriously consider Brisbane. Yes, you can do all of these things in every Australian city, but most young families take affordability into consideration, so this is something you should look at. Affordable housing in Melbourne and Sydney can see you living much farther from the CBD than you intended. It's just something to think about.

If you want to learn more about Brisbane or the Gold Coast, here are some websites for you to check out:

Australian City Life Series: Brisbane City Life
http://www.brisbanecitylife.com.au/bcl

Brisbane Courier Mail newspaper http://www.couriermail.com.au

Information from the Brisbane City Council
http://www.brisbane.qld.gov.au/BCC:BASE::pc=HOME

Our Brisbane   http://www.ourbrisbane.com
Guide to Brisbane events, dining, real estate and more

Beyond Brisbane

More resort than traditional countryside, the rest of Queensland's cities and towns lie along the coast as well as inland. The beautiful Fraser, Sunshine and Capricorn Coasts are less developed than the Gold Coast, with stunning coastline. In southern QLD, west of the Great Dividing Range, you'll find Darling Downs, which is more typical country. The area away from the coast is commonly known as hinterland. Queensland also has its own Outback as well as many islands including Fraser Island, the Whitsunday Islands and Magnetic Island. Farther north, Townsville and Cairns are small cities with even more tropical climates. At the very top, you have Cape Tribulation and the Cape York Peninsula, which are wild, with crocodile-infested rivers and estuaries and probably not on your list of places to settle. The Torres Strait Islands rest right at the top. Generally, the further north you go in Queensland, the hotter and more humid the climate and the greater the chance of being affected by cyclones and the rainy season.

If you want to learn more about Queensland, here are some resources:

Information from the QLD Government
http://www.workliveplay.qld.gov.au/dsdweb/v4/apps/web/content.cfm?id=4045

http://www.qld.gov.au/about-queensland/moving.html

QLD Tourism sites   http://www.queenslandholidays.com.au
http://www.tq.com.au

Quest Community Newspapers
http://quest-news.whereilive.com.au

Western Australia (WA)

The largest state, Western Australia is dramatically different from east to west, with both desert and rich agricultural areas. This is the home of large mining projects and gorgeous beaches as well as a fashionable wine region and more than its fair share of the country's Outback.

Perth

Perth has exploded in recent years; the population and home price increases are largely attributable to the mining boom but also to a surge in migrants from the eastern states, who decided to sell their overpriced homes in cities like Sydney and head out west. When I think of the expression "way out west," WA pops into my mind before the usual images of cowboys and ranches in the western parts of the US. Because Perth is out there. Alone in the southwest of Australia's most sparsely populated state, the city catches a lot of abuse from its neighbours to the east. But, having lived in Perth and being a frequent visitor there due to our family and friends calling it home, I can tell you that Perth is a beautiful place to live. If you can afford it. And if you are prepared to spend a small fortune and a day's travel any time you want to visit the rest of the country.

That said, Perth is an excellent place for families, but probably not the best bet for the young and single. It is pretty much a big country town, despite its population and, aside from outdoor pursuits, of which you can take your pick, there is not much to do there. But it is an attractive, clean city, set on the Swan River, with amazing parks and an extremely laid-back atmosphere. I always enjoy visiting there and feel certain it will be a wonderful place to retire someday. If your job centres on natural resources, you will probably find the best job opportunities here and the quality of life is pretty incredible if you aren't looking for a bustling nightlife scene or the quantity of festivals and cultural events that you'll find in the east. That isn't to say that Perth has nothing going on. In recent years we have noticed more festivals and events happening around town. There just won't be something big on every night.

Perth's many beaches are gorgeous and there are a number of national parks around. The city also has its own holiday destination just to the south in the Margaret River region. Here you'll find wineries, remarkable surf beaches, national parks and a relaxing country atmosphere. It is a bit of a drive (around four hours) from the city centre, more if there is a lot of traffic, but it is an option if you want to get away.

If you want to learn more about Perth, here are some websites that may interest you:

Australian City Life Series: Moving to Perth
http://www.bcl.com.au/perth/movetoperth/default.htm

Information from the City of Perth
http://www.cityofperth.wa.gov.au

Move to Perth   http://www.movetoperth.com
Offers information on relocating to Perth and furnished rentals.

Perth Now (online news) http://www.perthnow.com.au

Perth's tourism website   http://www.experienceperth.com

This Perth Life http://www.thisperthlife.com

A blog written by a British expat about moving to Perth and life there

The West Australian newspaper
http://au.news.yahoo.com/thewest

Regional Western Australia

WA is huge. Massive, in fact. If you want to go anywhere in the north, you'll probably want to fly or hire a campervan. Aside from the region directly south of Perth (described above), there are a few more areas of the state that you could consider for a place to live. To the east of the Margaret River region is an area known as the Great Southern, which is a natural wonderland of spectacular beaches and smaller towns. The southern Outback town of Kalgoorlie-Boulder is surprisingly well-populated considering its isolated location. If you're a miner, you might find yourself there.

North of Perth, along the Central West Coast, you'll find more towns, the largest of which is Geraldton. Further north lay the Coral Coast and Pilbara regions, which are tourist destinations of their own, containing the world's largest west-coast reef, Ningaloo, a rival to the Great Barrier Reef. There are many resort towns along this coast. Miners may also find themselves in Karratha or one of the surrounding towns. Finally, at the top, is the Kimberley region and the attractive town of Broome, which is a popular tourist destination in its own right. The region of northern WA is tropical, with wet and dry seasons and plenty of saltwater crocodiles in its river systems.

If you want to learn more about Western Australia, here are some websites that may interest you:

Information from the WA Local Government
http://dlg.wa.gov.au

Information from the Western Australia State Migration Centre http://www.migration.wa.gov.au

Western Australia tourism
http://www.westernaustralia.com/au/Pages/Welcome_to_Western_Australia.aspx

South Australia (SA)

South Australia is celebrated as wine country, with fame for its many major wine regions being world-renowned. The state also boasts the beautiful rugged southern coastline. Most of the state's population lives in Adelaide and a few rural centres. SA has hot, dry summers and cool winters and it can become very hot there, especially between October and April. It is also the driest state, receiving less than 250mm annually in most parts. In spite of this, parts of SA are very green. You'll find over 300 parks, wildlife reserves, waterways and regional reserves.

Adelaide

Similar in size to Perth, Adelaide is cultural and green, with beautiful beaches and the famed wine country a short drive away. There are plenty of cultural events and festivals to enjoy if you are a resident as well as sporting events, beaches and parks. Thirty minutes away are even more nature parks in the Adelaide Hills.

If you want to learn more about Adelaide, here are some places to begin:

Adelaide Bound   http://www.adelaidebound.com
Written by two migrants to Adelaide, this site contains comprehensive information to make your move easier.

The Advertiser newspaper   http://www.adelaidenow.com.au

Australian City Life Series: Moving to Adelaide
http://www.bcl.com.au/Adelaide/movetoadelaide/default.htm

Information from the Adelaide City Council
http://www.adelaidecitycouncil.com/home.html

Country South Australia

The Outback takes up over 75 per cent of the state's area. The rest of the land makes up for it with incredible wine regions and lovely small towns. South of Adelaide, the Fleurieu Peninsula offers the medley of uncrowded beaches, rolling hills, national parks and wineries, including the celebrated McLaren Vale wine region. Only 55 km to the north of Adelaide lays the most famous wine region in all of Australia: Barossa Valley. There are a few different townships here and the countryside is breathtaking. The Clare Valley lies further north (another wine region) and the surrounding towns are steeped in history. The southeast portion of the state, known as the Limestone Coast, leads you to Victoria and has some pretty little towns and fishing communities. More towns lie along the Murray River and through the agricultural areas of the Yorke and Eyre Peninsulas.

If you want to learn more about South Australia, here are some websites that may interest you:

Information portal for the SA Government
http://www.sacentral.sa.gov.au

Messenger News Community newspapers
http://messenger-news.whereilive.com.au

Migration information from the SA Government
http://www.southaustralia.biz/Living-Working-in-SA.aspx

South Australia immigration website
http://www.migration.sa.gov.au/sa/home.jsp

South Australia Tourism site http://www.southaustralia.com

Tasmania (TAS)

The smallest state, situated across the Bass Strait from Victoria, is Tasmania. Made up of mostly unspoilt wilderness, Tasmania is pretty much all country, even in its major cities. However, the people there are friendly, the national parks and scenery gorgeous and the gourmet offerings outstanding. It can get quite cold here compared to other parts of Australia, but that is no reason not to give Tasmania a look.

Hobart

Australia's second-oldest city is one of hills and a harbour, with a compact city centre and a very laid-back atmosphere. This is not the place to come if you're looking for a happening nightlife or lots of different things to do every week. But if you like nice markets and a small-town feel in a very pretty setting, you will enjoy it here. It is small enough to be friendly but still large enough to have all the amenities of a blooming capital city. The city centre sits at the harbour's edge while the suburbs lie to the north and south along the Derwent River, to the east towards superb beaches and west to Mount Wellington. There is a vibrant arts community here and many festivals.

Country Tasmania

The other major town in Tasmania is attractive Launceston in the north. The rest of the state largely consists of farmland, tiny towns and national parks. Most of the population lives on the north and east coasts and in between Hobart and Launceston. The southwest section of the state is wilderness, home to Tasmania's largest national park.

If you want to learn more about Tasmania, here are some websites to begin with:

Australian City Life Series
http://www.bcl.com.au/hobart/movetotasmania/default.htm

Australian City Life Series: Hobart City Life
http://www.bcl.com.au/hobart

Department of Economic Development, Tourism and the Arts website
http://www.development.tas.gov.au/migration/living_in_tasmania

The Mercury newspaper   http://www.themercury.com.au

Tasmania tourism website http://www.discovertasmania.com

Australian Capital Territory (ACT)

Similar to Washington, D.C. in the US, Australian Capital Territory is home to the country's important national institutions and national government headquarters. ACT is only 2,366 square kilometres in size, is surrounded completely by NSW, and is full of pretty parks, hills and areas of bushland. The territory has plenty of museums, theatres and galleries, interesting architecture and a large lake. Aside from the central district of ACT, the rest of it is suburban. Most people in Canberra (the major city's name) actually work in the private sector. It is relatively serene, orderly and basically unexciting.

If you want to learn more about ACT, here are some websites that may interest you:

Government's relocation website
http://www.liveincanberra.com.au

Information from the Canberra tourism website

http://www.visitcanberra.com.au/en/Visitor%20Info/Moving%20to%20Canberra.aspx

Out in Canberra   http://www.outincanberra.com.au
Local dining, arts and event guide for the city

Northern Territory (NT)

With a tropical north and desert south, Northern Territory conjures up images of the Australian Outback, crocodiles and red sands. It has a very small population, most of it situated along the main highway between Darwin and Alice Springs and in Darwin itself.

Darwin

A small city, situated right at the top of Australia, Darwin is a long way from all the other major cities. It sits on a pleasant harbour and is quite liveable if you can stand the heat. However, it is a fairly transient place, with around a third of the population comprised of military service people and their families. Many others who give the city a try often move on after a few years because of its isolation and the weather. This can provide opportunities for newcomers, but it can also be frustrating for long-term residents. Additionally, the cost of living in NT is very high.

Regional Northern Territory

Many small towns dot the landscape of the NT, however these are truly isolated and probably not your best choice if you are a newcomer to Australia without a good reason to be in them. Alice Springs is the other modern town to look into if you are migrating and want to live in NT. This is still a very small town, however, but not too small to mention.

If you want to learn more about the NT, here are some websites that may interest you:

Australian City Life Series: Darwin City Life
http://www.bcl.com.au/Darwin/movetodarwin/default.htm

NT Tourism site   http://www.tourismnt.com.au

Additional relocation resources

CityHobo   http://www.cityhobo.com
Provides information about several Australian cities including selecting the right city for you, what suburb to live in, maps, schools and more.

4.

Chapter Four: Exit strategy - How to close up shop at home, relocate to Australia and answer questions like "You're doing what?!"

Prior to making the big move to Australia, I had relocated several times to different houses and apartments, even across the entire US. But nothing prepared me for moving to the other side of the world. You can expect to pretty much shut down your life in your home country before leaving and then start up an entirely new life (with different rules and ways of doing things) in Australia. If you've gotten to this point, you've already had some practice being organised and meticulous, and these skills will come in handy over the next few months or weeks.

The first step in the process is to evaluate your current situation. Where are you living? Do you own or rent? Do you have dependants? Will you be leaving right away? If you are renting, have no children or pets and you're pretty flexible with your schedule for getting to Australia, you're in an enviable position. I was in this kind of lucky shape when I moved here, but I was in my mid-twenties and pretty nomadic to begin with. I think this is the type of person that has the easiest time with a move like this. If your situation is more complicated, don't fear. You'll make it over; it just takes a bit more planning. That's what this guide is intended to help you do. Some of the things in this chapter may sound like the regurgitation of common sense, but you'd be surprised at how many people forget details when they're facing a major change, so I've been sure to mention every last detail.

The first two most important things to think about are your employment situation (not a big worry if you have ample reserves of cash) and your current housing. In this chapter, I'm assuming you have your visa organised: either you've received approval and now have a date by which you must enter Australia or you've applied for the visa and done such a wonderful job lodging it, as I discussed in chapter one, that your approval letter should be arriving any day.

Preparing to leave your current country of residence

Your employment and financial situation

If you're transferring to a new office within your current company, this will take care of itself. I trust that you've negotiated a good expat deal for yourself and hopefully included some moving expenses, assistance with temporary housing until you find a permanent place to live and professional help with your visa. If you are being sponsored by a company in Australia that is bringing you overseas and this means a change of employer, be sure to give your old employer ample notice under the terms of your contract.

If you are moving to Australia on the basis of a skilled visa qualification or because you're the partner of an Australian, the employment situation is less clear. You will have a date under the terms of your visa by which you must enter Australia. This will dictate how long you can continue working in your current job. Your savings account balance will likely determine the date you can quit your current gig. It can take several months to find a job in

Australia and employment can be difficult to line up before you arrive. Most companies will want to see your visa and meet you, and the interview process here can be long and involved. It is worth your while to look before you arrive, but you will probably have better luck searching for a job once you get here. This works to your advantage as well. You should meet your prospective employer in person and see where you'll be working before you accept a position. Starting your life in Australia with a job you end up hating isn't ideal.

So the remaining question is: how much money do you need to have in reserve for your move to Australia? The figure will be different for everyone depending on the lifestyle you're used to. Naturally frugal people can get by with less cash. But you should not assume that you will find a job right away. If you have a family to support or are moving to an expensive city like Sydney, your cash needs will increase. I'm a cautious person, so here is what I recommend:

1. Keep track of your spending for at least two months. Write down everything you purchase, from your morning cup of coffee to the daily newspaper to your spending on things like internet and movie tickets. Don't assume that you won't pick up your normal routine once you arrive in Australia. If you're looking for a job, you're going to have even more free time on your hands and your minor leisure and entertainment purchases might actually increase.

2. Calculate the amount of money you will receive from lease deposits, sale of property and any other miscellaneous income you have coming to you before the date you have to enter Australia. Add that to the total of your bank account balances.

3. Examine your debts such as credit cards and loans. You should pay these off before you leave if you can. If you will be penalised financially for breaking any leases you hold, you should also factor in those costs.

4. Start getting quotes for your moving expenses and add up the costs for known expenditures in the first 90 days of arriving in Australia. These could include airfare, transportation to the airport, shipping, storage and moving costs and hotels.

5. Anticipate and estimate costs for things you will have to pay for to establish your new life in Australia. Some of these will be:

    - Mobile (cell) phone if you do not have a GSM 900 or 1800 that is compatible with Australian mobile phone operators
    - Deposit and first month's rent for accommodation; deposits in Australia (called 'security bonds') are usually four week's rent but can be up to eight week's rent
    - Deposits or set-up costs for utilities such as gas, electrical, water, telephone, cable television, internet and insurance
    - Food, toiletries and other essentials
    - Car and petrol (gasoline) costs if you will not be living in a place with adequate public transportation
    - Bus, train and tram fares if you will be using public transport

6. Determine, from adding up all of your anticipated costs, debts and known expenses, how much money you will need for the first six months, assuming you will not find a job right away and will not have any income. You can subtract any anticipated income from item number two from this total as long as that money is guaranteed. This is the amount of money you need in your savings account prior to departing.

You can't count on welfare in the public system in Australia unless you are a permanent resident. So if you're coming up short on funds, consider delaying your journey to Australia and start cutting back on your expenses. I do not recommend making rationalisations with yourself that you won't spend as much money as you currently are in your home country. We tend to act more frivolously when in a new place and you will likely also need to purchase some new things.

If you have your target amount already, congratulations. You can leave your current job whenever you want. But if you need to keep working for a little while longer, it is advisable that you keep up your current standards of work and not tell everyone in the office that you're about to take off. If you depend on your job to be able to finance the move, you don't want them to prematurely hire your replacement.

Current housing

If you're renting and still have time left on your lease, you may need to look into breaking it. Landlords are often willing to negotiate with their tenants in these situations. They may let you out of your rental obligation without penalty if you assist them in finding a suitable tenant to replace you. Otherwise, you may face fees and the loss of your security deposit. It is always worth asking whether you can work something out.

If you have roommates, the situation will probably be quite similar. If your name is on the lease then you will have legal obligations in a shared living situation. If your name isn't on the lease and you have not signed any legal documents, you are pretty much a free agent and your conscience will dictate how much notice you give your flat or housemates. These situations are rare, however, and you're probably bound by something you signed before moving in.

If you are a property owner and you live in your property, you have two choices: sell your place and bank the money or rent your house or apartment to someone while you're away. There are a number of things to consider here. If you live in a place where the cost of a purchasing property is prohibitive (such as in Australia, where the taxes you pay on settlement are very high), you will probably want to be sure that you've held your investment long enough to break even or turn at least a small profit. One of the nice things about the US is that there are no irrecoverable stamp duties and people often buy and then sell houses within a few years. There are many things that will factor into your decision about whether or not to sell, including property values and prices at the time, your emotional attachment to the property and how long you plan to be in Australia.

If you choose to rent out your house instead of selling it, you can always sell at a later date. You'll need to think about whether you want to deal with managing the property yourself from another country in order to save a little money or hire a property management company to handle those details. Remember that just because you find tenants for your house before you leave does not mean that they will stay in the property forever and the money you save on management fees could just end up being used for a plane ticket to come home and deal with finding new tenants or any problems that may occur. You'll also need to think about your action plan should anything happen to the house while you're on the other side of the world. If you have a willing family member close by who is happy to assist you with looking after the property, and he is someone you trust, then it may be feasible to manage it yourself. Just be aware of the hassles and all of the things you have to look after as a property manager. We own a house in Perth and have tenants living in it, and we have to look after the following on an ongoing basis:

- Ensuring rent is paid on time
- Monitoring rental rates in our area and ensuring our rent keeps up with market rates; administration of rent increases
- Finding tenants for the property and associated administrative work (security deposit administration, screening potential tenants, advertising, open houses, confirmation of identity, etc.)
- Payment of bills and insurance associated with the property
- Handling of both non-urgent and emergency maintenance items and repairs
- Responding to enquiries from our tenants, the council and neighbours
- Dealing with our tenants when issues occur such as their failure to pay rent, damages to the house and other problems
- Annual inspections of the property

We're lucky that John's parents look after the property for us when issues arise that we are unable to deal with from afar. But if we did not have them to help us, we would definitely have the property managed through an agent. Be sure to change your home insurance to a policy that is for landlords to protect you from special circumstances. You will also no longer need to cover as many contents on the policy if you're leaving the property unfurnished so be sure to re-evaluate the value of the contents within your property. Landlords usually only insure contents such as blinds, fixtures and carpeting. Your tenants will take out their own renters insurance to cover their own belongings.

If you decide to sell your property, contact a real estate agent as soon as possible and discuss your situation with her so that you may move forward and discover all your options. In many cases, you might be able to move to Australia while your house is still on the market and handle all of the settlement details remotely. This could help you get more money for your house because you are not in a rush to sell it. As with everything else in your move, the more options you are aware of, the better off you'll be.

People moving with you

If you are migrating with a partner and/or children or dependent relatives, this will be a stressful time for them as well. It is important to communicate with your loved ones and support each other. Your partner will also be dealing with his or her employment situation and you will need to work together to balance everything and make it work.

If your visa was granted offshore, you will have a date by which you must enter the country for the first time in order to validate your visa. All family members must enter Australia by this date. If you are travelling separately, the primary applicant must enter Australia first or at the same time as the rest of the family. The other applicants must enter Australia after the main applicant (or at the same time) and before the first entry date. Usually this date is set around twelve months from the earliest date of police checks and medicals, but it could be six months as well. Check your visa carefully to ensure that you know the date and that you can make it to Australia by that time. You cannot usually change this date unless there are exceptional circumstances, so if you can't enter by the date you should immediately seek professional advice on contacting DIAC. Otherwise your visa can be cancelled.

Moving to another country can be particularly difficult for children, whatever their ages. They may be leaving friends behind and the familiarity and comforts of home. They may not understand why you want to move and feel conflicted and angry about it. Perhaps they are excited and have no negative feelings about the move. Even if this is the case, they will still be managing a great deal of stress, especially if your family does not normally move around a lot. You will also be leaving behind your support network of family, in-laws, close friends and neighbours who previously helped you with the children. It will be especially important for families to meet other expats and form a new network once you've settled into your new home in Australia.

The phenomenon of the 'trailing spouse' or 'accompanying partner' is common in expat circles. This occurs when one partner has given up his or her career or put that career on hold in order to follow his or her partner overseas to a new country. This can be stressful for the partner who has left her career because she will be struggling to find a new identity and her place in not only the home but in a new environment as well. This can be particularly stressful when there is a language barrier because the working partner will be surrounded by colleagues at work and will have people to communicate with, while the other person is often alone at home.

If you are the partner of an Australian citizen and you are applying for a visa offshore while your significant other is waiting for you in Australia, you may be in the most stressful situation of all. It can be very difficult to be separated from your loved one for any length of time, even more so when you are waiting for a decision from DIAC. There isn't really any way around this if the person is not able to join you, as you must be outside of Australia when the decision is made. Keeping the lines of communication open is very important as is being patient and understanding with each other through this difficult time. It will help you to stay focussed on a positive outcome and working proactively on your moving preparations so you keep looking forward and feeling emotionally well.

Resources to assist you:

Please also refer to the online community and meet-up sites in chapter one and the online parenting communities in the appendix.

Location Independent Parents
http://locationindependentparents.com
This blog offers some great tips and resources for parents looking to travel and work with their children in tow.

Pets

It would be unthinkable for most people to move to another country and leave their beloved pets behind. Luckily, you probably don't have to. It is not as simple, however, as putting your dog, cat or other pet into a carrier onto your flight. Australia Quarantine and Inspection Service (AQIS) has strict guidelines for the importation of animals into the country in order to limit the risk of diseases being brought into Australia. This can be an expensive process, but it is the only way for you to make your move to Australia with your pet(s) in tow. Generally, you can bring dogs, cats and horses from a number of countries, however pets such as hamsters, guinea pigs, ferrets, birds, etc. are usually prohibited. Be sure to check with AQIS for your specific type of pet. Your costs will include the airline ticket for your pet (usually much more expensive than tickets for humans), quarantine costs and the costs of any required treatments, permits and condition compliance.

Your first stop will be the AQIS website.[22] Here you will find all the rules for bringing your pet into Australia depending on what country you are coming from. There are different rules for disability assistance dogs.[23] You'll find that your pet's breed will be taken into

---

[22] AQIS 'Bringing cats and dogs (and other pets) into Australia' web page http://www.daff.gov.au/aqis/cat-dogs

[23] Rules for bringing disability assistance dogs to Australia: http://www.daff.gov.au/aqis/cat-dogs/assistance

consideration, dogs and cats must have a microchip and your pets may have to receive vaccinations, treatments and blood tests prior to travelling. Depending on the country of origin, a determined quarantine period will apply. You will have to pay for your pet's accommodation while it is in quarantine.

Once you have read these rules and decided whether it is financially feasible to bring your pet along, you may wish to recruit some professional assistance. Here are some companies that can help (please note that I have not used any of these services and can not personally endorse them; they do come recommended, however):

From the US

All Pet Travel   http://www.allpettravel.com

Animals Away   http://www.animalsaway.com

Happy Tails Travel   http://www.happytailstravel.com

International Pet Transportation
      http://www.iptlax.com/index.htm

Jet-A-Pet   http://jet-a-pet.com

Pet Express   http://www.petmove.com

Puppy Travel
http://www.puppytravel.com/transport_relocation.html

Worldwide

Animal Land Pet Movers
http://www.petmovers.com/site/index.htm
Animal Land has offices in Atlanta, Hong Kong, Johannesburg, London, Los Angeles and Sydney.

Checklist of things to do before you leave

- Make your travel arrangements.
- Ensure you have at least a year of validity remaining on your current passport (and your family members' passports if they are migrating with you).
- Organise for the termination of insurance policies you no longer need in your home country (be sure that you no longer need them first). Ask for a copy of your 'no-claim' bonus from your insurance company if you have one.
- Terminate subscriptions (newspapers, magazines, book clubs, Netflix, etc.)
- Arrange for your gas, water, telephone, internet and electricity to be turned off on your move-out date.
- Close any bank accounts you no longer need. It is a good idea to keep at least one bank account open in your country of origin but make sure you change it to one with low or no monthly fees.
- Visit your safety deposit box if you have one and stash away valuables that aren't coming with you (if applicable). Make sure it is paid for at least a year and that you know when your next payment is due. Empty and close it if you no longer need it.
- Submit a statement to your state, locality and/or national tax office to let them know that you are ending your residence in that area. This is a good idea for US citizens who are liable for state income tax in order to avoid any residency disputes later on.
- If you own a business, ensure that you have finalised anything you need to and tied up loose strings before departing. If you are moving your business to Australia, check with the government of the state or territory to which you are moving to find out what you need to do.

- Speak to your attorney about the impact your move has on your will.
- Obtain your records from doctors, dentists and opticians.
- Forward your mail to your new address in Australia if you have one already. If not, forward it to a family member until you have a permanent address in Australia.
- Try to open a bank account in Australia. *Australia New Zealand Bank* (*ANZ*: http://www.anz.com.au) has branches throughout Australia and allows overseas residents to open an account prior to arriving in Australia (restrictions apply). Some Australian banks also have branches in London (see chapter five in the banking section).
- Request credit records from your bank or lending agent as well as letters of reference from current and previous landlords and employers.
- Provide your overseas contact details to your property manager or real estate agent. Be sure to give him a phone number or email address that you have regular access to in order to avoid communication delays.
- Notify your local elections commission of your relocation. Apply for an absentee ballot if applicable.
- Provide your employer with details for deposit of your final paycheque and address for forwarding tax information.
- Cancel your health insurance.
- Advise DIAC and your migration agent of your new details (if applicable). Use form 929 for providing this information to DIAC.[24]

---

[24] Download this form here:
http://www.immi.gov.au/allforms/pdf/929.pdf

- Cancel your library card, video store and other memberships.

- Advise retirement account providers of your new details. Find out how to forward any pensions or distributions you are entitled to (if applicable).

- Close your credit card accounts or update your details with them and organise electronic payment access so that you can pay them off. It can be difficult to get credit as a newcomer to Australia so I recommend that you leave one account active (see chapter five). Another option is to get an *American Express* card or a credit card with *Citibank* as far in advance as possible before you leave your home country. This way you can change to the Australian version of the card when you move to Australia. Destroy your old cards.

- Speak to a local accountant about your tax liabilities once you move.

- Advise frequent flyer memberships and other incentive programs of your new details.

- Keep your driver's license because you will need it to get a new one without hassle in Australia.

- Speak to your children's schools and ensure that you have transcripts and any other information they will need to make a successful transition to a new school system. Obtain your children's immunisation records as well.

- Advise friends and family of your move.

- Book accommodation for the first few weeks you are in Australia (longer if you are planning to purchase a property to live in). I've provided some tips on this in 'Finding a Place to Live' later on in this chapter. Book a rental car if you will need one.

- Start thinking about suburbs and looking for a place to live in Australia (resources listed later in this chapter).

- Make sure you have original copies of birth certificates, marriage certificate, medical and work records, your university or trade papers and your passport together and ready to go with you (and your family's documents as well). You will need these documents often when you first arrive in Australia so do not ship them separately.

- Organise birthday cards and presents for the next few months as you will probably be too busy to think about such things.

- Ensure all of your accounts are paid and up-to-date.

- Transfer funds to Australia if you've already opened an account there; ensure you have access to plenty of cash otherwise.

- Apply for a Tax File Number (TFN) if you are able to. You will need to do this before you can receive any income in Australia such as wages, salary, government payments and investment income. This is your identification number for tax purposes. You can apply online at the Australian Taxation Office (ATO) website: http://www.ato.gov.au This can take up to 28 days to process.

- See your doctor for any prescriptions you may need and a check-up before you go. Make sure you have adequate supplies of any medication. It may take you a little while to find a new doctor in Australia and you won't be able to have foreign prescriptions filled in the meantime.

- Stock up on things you may not be able to find in Australia (as long as you are allowed to bring them through customs). I've listed some of these in chapter seven.

❏ Organise a going away party so that your family and friends can give you a proper farewell.

Packing, selling, moving, storing and shipping

Ah, the fun part. Kudos if you can afford to pay someone else to come and pack up your entire house. I've moved over 15 times in my adult life and I dread even the thought of it. If you're doing it yourself, grab your boxes, newspapers, bubble wrap, heavy-duty markers and masking tape and let's get started.

You can buy boxes from your moving company or storage facility, or you can do it the fun, hobo way that I do: make your rounds to the local supermarkets and beg for them. When we moved into our current place, I was so tired of box collection that I just stacked them all under the bed in the guest room once we'd unpacked and there they sit until our next adventure. Good packing is an art form I have perfected over the years. My top five tips are:

1. Pack heavier items in smaller boxes. Those extra-large boxes are for items like blankets, pillows and towels, not ceramic cookware and books. Help save your removalists from crippling back injuries. Those support belts they wear only help so much.

2. Put like with like. Pack glassware with other glassware and clearly mark the boxes 'fragile' with heavy-duty marker or 'fragile' stickers. Don't mix appliances with your candle collection or silverware with your clothing. For an overseas move, you should put everything that you will declare to quarantine (such as wooden items) together in a few clearly labelled boxes.

3. Number your boxes and create a master list indicating what each box contains. This is a good habit for any time you move but is especially important when moving overseas for three reasons. First, you will want to insure your goods against loss or damages and most international shipping companies will want an itemised account of what is in each box and the value of its contents when they put together your insurance statement. Second, customs and immigration will want to know what is inside each box and doing this as you pack is the easiest way to preserve your sanity. Third, after a long move, when your goods might take months to reach you, labelled boxes make the chore of unpacking much easier. Some items will be high priority for unpacking and you will want to be able to find those quickly and easily. Be sure you keep a copy of your itemised box contents list with you. Label every box with your name, phone number and final destination directly on the box with heavy-duty marker (even if the moving or shipping company places their own labels on your boxes). AQIS provides specific information about how to label your boxes on its website (see the 'importing personal effects' link in the resources section at the end of this chapter).

4. Reinforce boxes well with good quality packing tape as you put them together. You can get away with folding the box tops closed with a local move, but for international moves you must seal and secure your boxes. If something will be destroyed by moisture, you can line its box with plastic to help preserve it. Your boxes probably won't get wet but don't assume anything.

5. Don't skimp on packing materials for breakable items. International moves put much more stress on your boxes than local moves. The boxes will be moved from your home to a temporary storage facility to a packaging facility to a container on a ship to another temporary storage facility to

your new home. Things will be stacked haphazardly on top of each other and pushed and compressed into tight spaces and your packing has to stand up to all of this. Framed photos and artwork with glass should be wrapped in layers of bubble wrap and placed in a box on their ends back to back, so that nothing can shift and crack the glass. Wine glasses should be stored in the boxes you purchased them in if possible or stuffed with packing material and wrapped in bubble wrap before being placed in a box with packing material lining it. Styrofoam peanuts may be bad for the environment but you can put an ad on the internet to give them away for free once you get to your destination. Don't be afraid to use too much packing material because it can always be recycled through sharing.

First, however, you have to figure out what you're packing. I always trim the fat first. Give your favourite charity that collects household goods a call for a pickup date, and then raid your cupboards and closets for anything you aren't using anymore. I've never been a hoarder so this step is easy for me. If you tend to hold onto things, remember that you may not be able to use all of your things in Australia or even bring some of them into the country. You'll need to examine the voltage requirements for all of your appliances and determine if they will be compatible with Australia's 220-240V AC, 50Hz electricity supply. You could ship all that heavy furniture, but it may be cheaper to just buy new pieces. You can always give sentimental pieces to a friend or family member. Again, it pays to investigate all your options before deciding anything.

Once you've decided what is staying behind and what will come with you, you'll need to sell, store or give away the former and arrange to ship the latter. Before you can finalise your list of items to come with you, you need to confirm that you can, in fact, bring the items into Australia to begin with. Customs is concerned primarily with ensuring that dangerous or illegal goods don't enter the country. When I say 'dangerous', you're probably thinking of weapons or explosives. While these are included, dangerous can also mean food, plant material and animal products.[25] Please see the resources links at the end of this section for a list of what you are allowed to bring into Australia.

Selling items is free and easy to do online. If you have a number of items to sell, the easiest way to get rid of them is as follows.

> 1. Think of people who might want to purchase everything you are selling all at once and approach them first. Do you rent an unfurnished apartment? Try approaching your landlord to see if he wants to buy all of your furniture and rent the place out as a furnished or partially furnished property going forward. Furnished properties generally attract much higher rents and chances are the landlord will make his money back in the first few months of renting out the property. Furnished properties are also harder to come by so it makes the property more attractive.

> 2. If your offer is declined, create a single web page that you can modify easily and list your items, prices, photos and terms and conditions for sale. If you are web-savvy, you can do this easily with a program such as *Dreamweaver* (or just regular HTML coding if you know how) and upload it to the free web space that probably comes with your internet service. Or you can host the page on your pre-existing website. If you do not have web space, a website and/or software/coding ability, you can start a free blog with *Blogger* (http://www.blogger.com) or *Wordpress* (http://www.wordpress.com) and make this

---

[25] A list of common items of concern among personal effects can be found here on the AQIS website: http://www.daff.gov.au/aqis/travel/entering-australia/moving-emigrating/items_of_quarantine_concern_in_personal_effects

119

content your only post. Just create a free account with one of these providers and add a new post. The key is to have a single page listing the items you are selling and for people to be able to access it easily online.

When you are creating your terms and conditions for sale, be sure to think about all the practicalities and be clear about what you are offering. Do you live in a second story apartment with no elevator and no intention of assisting buyers with that three-piece sofa set down to their vehicles? Stipulate that the purchase price is for 'move-it-yourself' transportation of the goods in your advertisement. Is there a large dent in your washing machine? Even if it works perfectly fine, you should mention the condition in your ad. You don't want to waste time and miss out on other buyers because someone passes on the goods due to your offer misrepresenting the item.

Pricing is another important factor to consider. You don't want to price your items too high or too low. Try searching websites such as *Craigslist* for items that are similar to the ones you are selling. If you're unsure of what you should ask for an item, put your higher price on the ad and write 'or nearest offer' or just 'ONO.' This indicates that you are willing to negotiate a price.

3. Post the URL for the site on all of your online social networks such as *Facebook*, *Twitter*, *Myspace*, forums you belong to (only if they allow private sales links in their guidelines) and any other online property you own. You can also place a free listing for each individual item on websites like *Craigslist* (http://www.craigslist.org), *Gumtree* (http://www.gumtree.com) or *Free Ads* (http://www.freeads.co.uk). You should list items individually in separate ads because people often search and scan the

headlines of online sites for the specific item they are looking for. Be sure to include a line in each ad that says "For a list of all items for sale, visit: http://YOURURL so readers can find the other goods you are selling. You can also include your website address on any paper flyers that you post on supermarket, gym or office bulletin boards, building lobby walls or in newspaper ads.

4. If you have to sell an item or items that you need up until the time that you vacate your home, you can still put it up for sale now. Just note in your terms and conditions or item description that the item is available for pickup on a specific date, and that you will accept a deposit to reserve the item for pickup until that time.

5. As your items sell, don't delete them from the page. Just put 'SOLD' next to each item in red. This increases your credibility as a seller and improves the perception of quality in what you are selling.

If you are storing items, you will still have to pack them up and hire a moving company, unless your storage facility includes a free move-in service. All of the same packing rules apply. Your challenge is to find the best deal on a storage facility that you can. If you live in a big city, try looking a bit further from the city centre. You can often find out everything you need to know about a storage facility on the internet ahead of time, minimising site visits prior to moving your goods into the facility. Storage rates may be cheaper the farther from the city you go. After all, you won't need to visit your stuff every day. I stupidly used a mini-storage facility on the Upper East Side of Manhattan when I moved to Australia. Surely I could have gotten a better deal in New Jersey or Queens. Laziness costs you money.

You will need to ensure that your storage facility is reputable, secure and in good condition and you will need to protect your goods with comprehensive insurance. You will also need to organise a payment plan via direct debit of your credit card or bank account and ensure the facility knows that you will be living overseas and how to contact you. You should also discuss the possibility that you might need to send for your goods one day and find out their policies for allowing access to your unit (authorised by you via fax or mail, of course), and subsequent termination of your account should you decide not to return to your previous home in the future. This access will need to be possible without your physically returning to the storage facility.

Finally, you will need to arrange to have your goods shipped to Australia. Immigration laws stipulate that you can bring your personal property that you owned while living overseas. You will need to confirm that everything you are bringing is acceptable for importation into Australia and some items will need to be cleaned up before you pack them. Be sure to read every page of the resources below and if there is anything you are uncertain about, check the AQIS website specifically for that item. If you ship something that isn't allowed (or try to carry it in with you), you could be required to pay for the item to be buried or destroyed (around AUD 75). This applies even to simple food items. So be sure to check your shipment carefully for banned items to prevent unnecessary fees.

Customs is also concerned with preventing people from purchasing large quantities of new items and bringing them into the country without paying the appropriate amount of duty. Therefore, you will need to be careful about items you've owned for less than 12 months. You may have items you've had for a longer period of time but haven't used. You should remove these from their packaging and/or provide receipts showing the date you purchased them. Don't buy a lot of new items and throw them into your shipment with the tags still on them. You can find out more about this by visiting the websites in the resources section below.

You will most likely use a moving/freight forwarding company if you are bringing all of your items with you. You'll need to find a company that specialises in overseas relocations. These companies can often pick up your goods from your home, store them until you are ready to ship, ship them to Australia, hold them again in Australia if you require, and then deliver them to your new home. Shipping can take several months, so speak to the company you choose as your service provider about timing and all the details. Ensure that they have a reputable delivery service in Australia to receive your goods and transport them to your new home. If you are unsure about any part of the process, be sure to ask questions.

If you are only sending a few items aside from the luggage you will take with you on the plane (be sure to check baggage allowances for your airline), you may just want to ship your boxes overseas. You will need to fill out a customs declaration form when you post them. Generally you may ship your personal items that you've had for more than 12 months; you just need to indicate that they are personal items on the declaration form. Otherwise, duties will apply to new goods being shipped over a certain value as I mentioned above. You can find out more about this by visiting the websites in the resources section below.

If you need to ship your car or motorcycle, you will need to contact a company that specialises in automobile shipments overseas. You'll need to do a cost analysis to ensure it is worth it. Cars are generally much more expensive in Australia than in the US, for example, but you will also have to pay conversion costs to right-hand drive as well as the shipping costs. Another thing you should know about cars in Australia is that leasing an automobile, which is common in the US, is not popular here and you do not usually have the option to buy the car at the end of the term. You can learn more about bringing your car to Australia on the Australian Automobile Association website: http://www.aaa.asn.au/touring/bringing.htm

Resources to assist you

AQIS
What can't I take into Australia?
http://www.daff.gov.au/aqis/travel/entering-australia/cant-take

What can't I mail to Australia?
http://www.daff.gov.au/aqis/mail/cant-mail

Bringing your household goods and personal effects, furniture, etc. into Australia
http://www.daff.gov.au/aqis/travel/entering-australia/moving-emigrating

Expat Exchange   http://www.expatexchange.com
Expat community site with articles and information, including a resource guide, global forum and job and property listings

General customs info for travellers to Australia (duty-free, etc.) Travelbug.gov.au   http://www.travelbug.gov.au

Moving Scam   http://www.movingscam.com
A consumer advocacy website in the US that will help Americans find a reputable mover and avoid fraudulent or unsatisfactory companies

Redbook – car prices and values in Australia
http://www.redbook.com.au

Voltage Valet   http://www.voltagevalet.com
What you need to bring and whether it will work overseas

Will your gadget work in Australia?
http://www.avalook.com/newsite/?page_id=47

Those you leave behind

If you have lived in the same place for many years and have a strong network of family and/or friends in your local area, many of them will probably be surprised, even shocked, at your decision to move so far away from most of the rest of the world. To some people facing such a loss of closeness to you, this may feel like an act of betrayal or at least rejection. Why would you want to leave us when we're all having such a good time here?

If you're leaving for an amazing job opportunity or a loved one who lives in Australia, people are likely to be more understanding than if you're just looking for a change or a new adventure. People may well be happy for you and excited for a new place to visit. But be prepared for all kinds of responses and try not to take them too personally. People, especially those who have lived in one place their entire lives and can't imagine ever leaving, will not understand your decision, may take it personally and may not make the same effort to keep in touch with you as you are willing to make for them. In life, people and situations change, and you will have to live with the consequences of your decision.

I got all kinds of reactions when I decided to move to Australia. There were the people who knew me well, were a bit nomadic themselves, knew John and completely understood my decision. Then there were the friends who were bewildered, shocked and surprised, even amused, family members who were angry and plenty of people who couldn't have cared less. The latter just removed me from their social calendars and mailing lists and got on with it.

Those are not the people you want to worry about. I got reactions like, "You're really a free spirit, aren't you?" or "You're doing what?!" followed by a chuckle. Keep in mind, I was living in New York City, where many people, like Parisians or Londoners, can't imagine what life is like off the island of Manhattan. As with everything else in your move, it's going to depend with your own personal set of circumstances, lifestyle and the people you call friends.

I've found that the best way to deal with comments and reactions from people, good or bad, is to be honest, unapologetic and positive about your decision. We can make no guarantees in this life that we will be around forever and moving is just another one of those things that happens. Reactions from people whose opinion you care about may make you think twice about your decision to relocate. You should not be afraid of this happening. It's okay and actually good to be faced with challenges when making such an important decision. But you should always consider the source and the context. You'd feel pretty sad if no one cared that you were going away, but don't let people's feelings and objections stand in the way of what you want for your life.

Some of your friends and family members may take it very personally that you are leaving. You should reassure them that you aren't leaving to get away from them or because you are necessarily unhappy with your relationships or support network, but because [insert your reason] and your decision is not a reflection on them. Try to emphasize the positive aspects of your move. Reassure them that you will still keep in touch (if you will) and that you'll visit them (if you will). With really close friends and family, it can help to make specific plans for when you will see them again. This forms a concrete impression in their minds that they are not losing you forever and that they will see you again soon.

And then you must just get on with it. We experienced similar separation stress when we decided to move from Perth to Melbourne. John's friends and family will probably never leave Perth. The friends who had gone away and worked overseas or interstate for several years all returned home and were starting families of their own. Everyone else was back in Perth so why shouldn't John be back too? It was incomprehensible for some friends and family members that we would want to leave. Never mind that I wasn't from Perth and that it's probably the most isolated city in the world, which is not very attractive if you aren't used to it. Four years later we still get comments like, "So when are you coming back to Perth?" (as in, to live in Perth permanently). Well, we aren't…maybe ever. This can be frustrating and even angering. It is like no one is listening to you or considering your feelings and can feel like a question of your decisions or judgement. But this is how people are. They are generally going to see things through their own filter. Some of it is the thought that, "Well if it's good enough for us, why isn't it good enough for you?" or "Why would you want to do your own thing?" But you can't take it personally. People aren't deliberately trying to question you. The motivation behind their comments is probably the fact that they miss you.

Another situation I faced when I moved overseas was the loss of friendships. Many of these friendships were with people I was very close to and always thought would be in my life. I find it is almost easier to keep in touch with the people with whom you had weaker ties. They don't and won't expect as much of a time commitment to you and this makes it easier to keep up friendly banter over email. The friends I lost were ones I was really close to, which is devastating, really. We never had any major fights or confrontations about anything, but they just stopped responding to my emails and requests to arrange a time for me to call them, and after awhile I gave up. With the friends and family that I do still keep up with, it is very clear that I am the one who has to make the most effort to visit them, call them and write to them. My family are better at keeping in touch, as you would expect, but there is no way they are getting on a plane to come and visit us, even for important events.

I'm certainly not saying that this is going to happen to you. But I also don't want to give you a false sense of security that you can just leave your home country and expect everything in your life to be maintained remotely via electronic communications. With *Skype*, which wasn't as popular when I left the US as it is now, there's really no excuse not to speak with people. But for some, it may just not be enough. Memories and friendships can fade if not nurtured and some people are more needy than others. Disagreements tend to intensify when long distances are involved. You won't always be able to come back for weddings or to visit new babies. They may not be able to afford to come and visit you or even want to come to Australia in the first place. The only reassuring fact that I can share with you is that, in my experience, your true friends will still be there. I am still close to many of my good friends; with some friends, our relationships are even stronger than they were before.

The bright side of all of this is that you are going off on a new adventure. You'll need to make room in your life for new people. The other thing that I have experience with is living in the past. I did this in the first couple of years I was away. I stayed in touch with my old friends at the expense of meeting new people and forming new relationships. I'd say I had an 80/20 ratio, where I was focussing eighty percent of my efforts on my old friends and twenty percent of my attention on my new home. Now it is more like 30/70. I still spend a third of my time keeping up with my old friends. But the vast majority of my life is spent in the present, enjoying the new relationships that I've formed and my life in the present, which also includes meeting new people and pursuing new opportunities. I still have professional interests back in the States and friends and family there that I still care about. But early on I recognised that if you're ever going to have a chance at being happy in your new life, you need to let go of the past. After all, you made a decision to come to Australia for a reason. And you should embrace it.

Here are some sites to help you stay in touch:

Facebook http://facebook.com

Skype http://skype.com
Voice over internet service allowing you to talk for free by using a headset from one computer to another and cheaply from a computer to a telephone; you can also use Skype for instant messaging

Geni http://geni.com
This is a great site for families, even older relatives who are online. It is a social networking site somewhat similar to Facebook, however it creates a family tree and is easy to use. Build your genealogy records while keeping in touch with relatives. You can share photos, messages, timelines of family history and more.

Arriving in Australia and the first 60 days

Entering Australia

Your arrival in Australia will be similar to your arrival in any other foreign country. You'll get off your flight and line up at immigration in the queue for people with non-Australian passports. On the plane, you will have been handed an Incoming Passenger Card, which you will need to fill out before you reach the immigration desk. Be sure to answer all the questions honestly and accurately to avoid any delays. When it is your turn, present your passport with your visa and the Incoming Passenger Card. The immigration official will process your paperwork and then return your papers to you.

You will then collect your checked baggage and proceed through customs. If you have nothing to declare, as you have indicated on your Incoming Passenger Card, you can proceed through the exit gates for people with nothing to declare. If you have items to declare, you should queue and exit through the appropriate exit gates. No matter what exit you choose, the Australian Customs and Border Protection Service officers may check your baggage and this can include passing your bags through an x-ray machine or an actual physical inspection of your items. They are looking for prohibited goods or items that have not been declared. You can be fined if you do not declare an item that is included in the checklist of items to declare listed on your Incoming Passenger Card. Items, including cash over AUD 10,000 can also be confiscated if you do not declare them. So be sure you calculate the currency conversion rate to determine how much cash you are carrying in Australian dollars and declare it if you are carrying over this amount. You can bring as much money as you want into Australia as long as you declare it.

Once you are through Customs and Immigration, you will find yourself in the arrivals hall, where family, friends, sponsors or pre-arranged drivers can greet you. There will also be facilities for changing money, arranging transport and booking short-term accommodation. If you have any questions, there should be an arrivals information desk where you can get assistance.

Finding a place to live

Assuming you have already booked temporary accommodation for your first few weeks in Australia, you'll probably be spending a great deal of time looking for permanent accommodation. Most capital cities in Australia have competitive rental markets and it can take some time to find exactly what you're looking for. If you are looking to purchase a home, you'll be in for even more fun. I've had experience with purchasing a property in Perth, one of the hottest real estate markets in the country, and I will discuss property purchases in detail in chapter nine.

When choosing temporary accommodation for your first few weeks in Australia, try to select a place where you will be able to extend your time easily if you need to. It could take you a month or more to find a rental and you should be prepared for this. If you are coming to work on an employer sponsored migration visa, ask your company to help you choose an executive rental. Most companies are happy to help their employees with temporary housing when they are moving to a new country and some even have special apartments that they own for this purpose.

If you are a single person, you might want to try shared housing, especially if you are young and want to meet new people right away. You'll also save a lot of money doing this, as it can be expensive to live alone. If you want to go solo, you'll need to find a property in a price range that property managers will deem your salary sufficient to afford (usually your rent must not be more than one-third of your salary). You may also encounter some private listings when you look through the newspapers or online. Renting a property through a private individual can be a more flexible experience than renting through a real estate agent. We do not use a property management company or real estate agent to manage our rental property and I can assure you we are much more lenient with our tenants than the property agents managing the apartments we have rented over the years. Each state has laws that govern professional agents and independent landlords equally, and you will be protected under the same rules and provided with the same rights and obligations as if you rent from a professional agent.

Each state has different laws and different governing bodies that enforce housing rules. You will be provided with the rules in your state once you sign a rental agreement. I've listed the most popular websites used to find properties available for sale or rent in the resources section below. Properties are available for viewing either by appointment, at 'open for inspection' times or by picking up the keys from the leasing agent's office (a deposit may be required and conditions will apply). Once you find a place that you're interested in, you can ask for a residential tenancy application. The landlord or agent will ask for formal identification such as a driver's license or passport, your employment details and references. You may also have to provide bank statements, birth certificates, a rental history and a mortgage statement from your last country of residence if applicable. Most properties will allow children except under certain specific conditions. If you are successful in your application for a rental property, you will be asked to sign a standard tenancy agreement, which may include a supplementary annexure covering additional conditions you must agree to as a tenant.

There are two types of tenancy agreements in Australia. The first type of agreement is a fixed-term agreement, which is set for a specific period of time (usually one year). The second type, a periodic or month-to-month agreement, goes from week-to-week or month-to-month. The primary differences between the two are the ability of the landlord to raise rent (usually only after the fixed term ends and only every six months for a periodic agreement) and the notice periods required for certain actions during the tenancy such as terminating the agreement. You usually must give a certain number of weeks' notice before vacating your property at the end of a fixed-term agreement, even if the agreement ends on a specific date. Please check the details of your particular lease agreement if you have questions about anything.

Before you commence a rental tenancy, you will also be asked for a security bond, which is money to cover any damage to the property or loss of rent that the landlord may incur during your tenancy. Usually the amount of the bond is equal to one month's rent, however, under certain circumstances, the landlord can ask for more than one month's rent. The bond cannot be used towards any part of your rent. You will also be asked to provide one month's rent in advance. Before you move in, you will fill out a condition report that notes any pre-existing damages or irregularities to the property prior to moving in. Be sure to keep a copy of this report so that you have evidence to show that you did not damage the property if there are any disputes about the bond at the end of the lease.

If you decide to purchase a property, know that it can take some time to transfer ownership of the property. 'Settlement' is when the exchange of money and property between the owner and the buyer (and the bank if the buyer is taking out a mortgage) takes place. So you will need to allow more time before you are able to move into a purchased property. The Foreign Investment Review Board (FIRB)[26] must make a decision on any proposed purchases by non-citizens or non-permanent residents of Australia. These decisions can take thirty days. As I mentioned earlier in this chapter, it can be cost prohibitive to purchase property in Australia due to the high cost of Stamp Duty, a non-refundable tax paid by buyers of properties. The tax is based on a percentage of the purchase price of your home so it can become very expensive if you are buying a pricey place to live. If the FIRB requires that you sell your home when you leave Australia, you may want to determine whether it is in your best financial interests to purchase a property for such a short amount of time. If you are planning to stay permanently, this becomes less of an issue.

You may wish to enlist the assistance of a buyer's agent if you plan to purchase a property and would like help to get the best deal. You can find a list of reputable buyers' agents through *The Property Buyer's Agents Association of Australia* (http://www.pbaaa.com.au)

---

[26] FIRB website: http://www.firb.gov.au/content/default.asp

or *Real Estate Buyers' Agents Association of Australia* (http://www.pbaaa.com.au). Your buyer will probably be able to start assisting you before you arrive in Australia.

Resources

Allhomes (listings)   http://allhomes.com.au

Domain (listings)   http://www.domain.com.au

Easy Roommate   http://au.easyroommate.com
Share accommodation and flatmates ads

Flatmates.com.au   http://www.flatmates.com.au
Australia's largest free website listing flatmates, share houses and shared accommodation in Sydney, Melbourne and Brisbane

Gumtree ads   http://gumtree.com.au
This link will take you to the Sydney listings, but you can just change city to go to your own local listings.

Hospitality Exchange   http://www.hospitalityclub.org
Free accommodation worldwide

Housemates.com.au   http://www.housemates.com.au
Free share accommodation ads with articles and noticeboards

Housepals   http://www.housepals.co.uk/index.php?cid=3
This is a British-based house and flat share website with listings in Australia.

Local Voices   http://localvoices.realestate.com.au
Check out reviews from locals before you sign that lease.

RealEstate.com.au   (listings)   http://www.realestate.com.au

Real Estate View (listings)   http://www.realestateview.com.au

Sleeping With The Enemy   http://www.sleepingwiththeenemy.com
Short to medium term accommodation

Moving in and Settling in

Once you find your place to live and have all the paperwork sorted, you'll have your keys and you can move in. Australia is no different than any other place in the world in this respect. Here are some listings that will help you find items for your new home:

Freecycle http://www.freecycle.org/group/AU
You can find things that people are offering for free here and also list your own.

The Good Guys http://www.thegoodguys.com.au
Discount warehouse specialising in appliances and electronics; you can pay less when you pay with cash

Gumtree http://gumtree.com.au
This link will take you to the Sydney listings, but you can just change city to go to your own local listings. You'll find everything from home wares to furniture to jobs to cars.

JB Hi-Fi http://www.jbhifi.com.au
This nationwide chain usually has the best prices on DVDs, music, games and electronics.

Trading Post http://www.tradingpost.com.au
Online classifieds

In addition to setting up your home with furniture and appliances, you will also need to organise services like telephone, internet, utilities and a mobile phone. Your landlord will usually advise you of the local utilities companies to call. Just ask them if they forget to provide you with a list. For internet and mobile phone information, here are some places to start researching the best plan for you:

Broadband Guide http://www.broadbandguide.com.au
Compare broadband providers and internet plans, from ADSL to cable to satellite mobile to wireless.

Whirlpool http://www.whirlpool.net.au

Australian broadband news and information, with a popular online community, including job boards for IT

As you will notice, the main service providers are *Telstra*, *Optus* and *Three*. Each of these providers makes different claims about its coverage areas and offers different products. If you are purchasing a mobile phone in Australia, you can buy an unlocked phone, which is a phone that allows you to choose any service provider you want. I highly recommend that you do this so you are not tied to any one service. All you will have to do is change the SIM card in your phone to a new provider and you can make the transition to a new service (and a new phone number), assuming you didn't sign a contract.

Most internet and mobile phone plans have fixed-term contracts of 12 to 24 months to get the best rates. You can also use prepaid mobile and internet, which I find work just fine and can be very cost effective. Mobile phones in Australia can be expensive to use. You spend available minutes or credit if you make a call as well as if you receive a call. It is also much more expensive to call a mobile phone from a fixed line telephone than to call another fixed line telephone. If you do decide to enter into a mobile phone contract, it is important to do all of the following:

>1. Find out exactly what your standard call rates will be; the store representatives have a legal requirement to tell you. Ask if there are any special promotions in effect, allowing you unlimited calls to a designated phone number or at certain times of day, for example.

>2. Have the billing procedures explained to you and make sure you understand what they are.

>3. Do your research on all the phone models available. Find out if you can use an unlocked phone.

4. Know what the penalties are for breaking the contract early. Be sure you are aware of the different types of contracts available and how the rates change depending on the contract.

5. If you have credit on an existing mobile account, either from a previous carrier or for another contract/pre-paid account with the carrier that you're interested in signing a new contract with, you will usually lose it. Be sure you ask and are aware of how much credit you will be losing.

For fixed line telephones (landlines), *Telstra* is the main service provider. You can find information on their website: http://www.telstra.com.au The subscription television service in Australia (cable TV) is provided by *Foxtel* (http://www.foxtel.com.au/default.htm) and *Austar* in regional and rural areas (http://www.austar.com.au). You can usually bundle your telephone, cable and broadband services and save some money that way.

For long distance calls overseas, I highly recommend purchasing a calling card as there are many inexpensive providers. I call the US for about two dollars an hour and you will find that you can get similar rates for most countries. You can find these cards at newsagents, *Australia Post* outlets and online.[27]

Checklist for after you arrive: Days 1 to 15

- Apply for a TFN.

---

[27] Try this website: http://www.telephonecards.com.au

If you haven't done this already, you will need to do so before you can receive any income in Australia such as wages, salary, government payments and investment income. Your TFN is your identification number for tax purposes. You can apply online or in person or you can have a TFN application form mailed to you by calling the ATO. This can take up to 28 days to process. Further information about this can be found on the ATO website: http://www.ato.gov.au

- Open a bank account if you have not done so already.

    You will need only your passport for identification if you open an account within six weeks of your arrival in Australia. After six weeks you will need additional identification to open your account. Australian banks are discussed further in chapter five.

- Register with Medicare.

    Medicare is the Australian Government health care scheme that provides financial assistance with basic medical expenses. You may be eligible to join Medicare and receive access to the health services and programs such as free public hospital care, partial payment of your out-of-hospital expenses and subsidised prescription medication. You'll need to go to a Medicare office seven to ten days after you arrive and bring your passport, travel documents and visa with you. For more information, visit the Medicare website: http://www.medicareaustralia.gov.au

    If you meet all the requirements, you may be given your Medicare card number right away to use until your card arrives in the mail. If you need to see a doctor urgently, you can register with Medicare without waiting the seven to ten days and ask for an interim number.

- Enrol your children (if you have any) in school. Australian law stipulates that children must attend school from age five until they are 15 years old. This may vary slightly in some states. Both public and private schools are available. Here is a list of websites for education systems in each State and Territory:

    NSW   http://www.schools.nsw.edu.au

    QLD   http://education.qld.gov.au

    VIC   http://www.education.vic.gov.au

    SA   http://www.decs.sa.gov.au

    WA   http://www.det.wa.edu.au/education

    TAS   http://www.education.tas.gov.au

    ACT   http://www.det.act.gov.au

    NT   http://www.det.nt.gov.au

- Apply for a driver's license and register your vehicle if you have one.

    You'll need to obtain an Australian driver's license from your state or territory government in order to drive in Australia. If you hold a permanent resident visa and have a current driver's licence from another country, in English or with an official translation, in most states and territories you are allowed to drive for your first three months after arrival. In WA, the three-month period begins when you are granted your permanent residency visa, not when you arrive in Australia.

You will most likely be able to transfer your license from your last country of residence over to an Australian license, though you may be required to pass tests for knowledge, practical driving and eyesight. Here is a list of the websites for the licensing authority for each state and territory. The websites will tell you everything you need to know about obtaining your license.

    NSW http://www.rta.nsw.gov.au

    VIC http://www.vicroads.vic.gov.au/Home

    QLD http://www.transport.qld.gov.au/Home/Licensing/Driver_licence

    SA http://www.transport.sa.gov.au/index.asp

    WA http://www.dpi.wa.gov.au/licensing/566.asp

    TAS http://www.transport.tas.gov.au

    NT http://www.nt.gov.au/transport/mvr

    ACT http://www.rego.act.gov.au

Once you have your new license, remember to advise the department that issued your last license that you have transferred the license so that they can cancel it. This will protect you against someone else renewing your old license or receiving your renewal paperwork with identifying details inadvertently in the mail. It is important that you do so to protect yourself from identity theft.

- Register with Centrelink.

    This is a government agency that provides assistance to those in need. You may not need to register here (I never have), however, you may want to use Centrelink to help you find a job, arrange for skills and qualifications recognition or enrol in some courses. Centrelink can also assist you in applying for your TFN. You may also be eligible for Family Assistance payments from the government to help with the costs of raising children. New migrants are not immediately eligible for social security or the full range of government employment services, however, permanent residents, refugees and humanitarian entrants may be eligible to access some services.[28] There is usually a two-year waiting period for payments once you arrive in Australia. You can find all the information on their website:

http://www.centrelink.gov.au/internet/internet.nsf/home/index.htm

Information in languages other than English is found here:

http://www.centrelink.gov.au/internet/internet.nsf/languages/index.htm

- Enrol in an English language course if you do not already speak the language.

    You may be entitled to receive free English language tuition of up to 510 hours, but you need to register as soon as possible or you can lose this entitlement. You can find out more and register with the Adult Migrant English Program here: http://www.immi.gov.au/living-in-australia/help-with-english/amep/learning-english

---

[28] Here is the web page for new arrivals:
http://www.centrelink.gov.au/internet/internet.nsf/individuals/settle_index.htm

Information in non-English languages: http://www.immi.gov.au/living-in-australia/help-with-english/amep/other-languages

- Choose a private health insurance fund (if you plan to do so) and enrol.

    Private health cover is discussed in further detail in chapter six. Medicare doesn't cover you for things like dental care, optical care and ambulance services, and waiting lists can apply for certain procedures in the public system. Private cover often has waiting periods for certain items after you enrol, so I encourage you to look into this right away. You will also need to take into account the Medicare levy surcharge (MLS) if you earn over AUD 73,000 (AUD 146,000 for couples and families). If this applies to you, you should take out private insurance cover because otherwise you will be taxed an additional one per cent of your taxable income. If you're paying the extra money anyway, you might as well reap the benefits of private cover and spend that money directly on yourself.

- If you signed a Health Undertaking (Form 815) at the request of DIAC, you need to call the Health Undertaking Service. They will advise you of the nearest Health Authority Clinic where you can have your follow-up medical checks. The phone number is 1800 811 334.

- Arrange for homeowners, renters and/or auto insurance along with any other policies you may need.

- Organise for all of your utilities to be connected and switched on at your new home (see last section).

- Unpack any major appliances and electronics you may have shipped and ensure they are working properly as you may have a limited amount of time to make a claim with your insurance provider.

- Have your mail forwarded from your old address. You can contact the post office servicing your last address and enquire about this. Alternatively you can use a mail forwarding service. Just type 'international mail forwarding' into a web search engine to find a list of providers.

- Familiarise yourself with emergency services contact details. In Australia, you can dial 000 on any telephone to reach the police, ambulance or fire brigade. These calls are free and you will be asked for your name, address and telephone number. If you do not speak English, you will have to tell the operator what kind of help you need (Police, Ambulance or Fire) and then say your language. He will connect you to the Translating and Interpreting Service (TIS National) directly so don't hang up.

For non-urgent police matters, ring your local police station. You can find these details in the *White Pages* telephone directory. Police and fire services are free, however the ambulance is not unless you have a special concession or pension for this. These services can be very expensive so it is recommended that you take out ambulance cover with a private company or become a member of your state's ambulance service. A specified number of ambo rides are usually included per year with private health insurance policies but you usually must be admitted to hospital to be able to claim for them. Check with your insurance provider. You should make sure that you are covered for ambulance services.

- Get out there and explore your new surroundings. Locate service providers you will use frequently such as your local *Australia Post*, a chemist (pharmacist), grocery stores and a dry cleaner. Choose a local café or pub to frequent. Begin to establish a routine. You will probably be doing a lot of running around during your first two weeks in Australia, but it is important to start making your new neighbourhood feel like home. This will seem silly if you are in temporary accommodation because you will just have to do it all over again when you move into your permanent place. However I recommend that you do it anyway, just in case your temporary accommodation ends up being your home for longer than you anticipated.

Checklist for after your arrivev: Days 15 to 30

- Find a new doctor (see chapter six), dentist, medical specialist (physiotherapist, chiropractor, etc.), veterinarian, etc.

- Subscribe to your local newspaper or start reading the local news online. This will familiarise you with what is going on in your area. The Saturday paper is especially useful because it has listings of events and feature articles that will help you find things to do in your new city. You'll start to get a feel for the Australian lifestyle. You can usually subscribe to only the weekend papers if cost is an issue.

- Purchase a car and insurance if you do not plan to use public transportation.

- You may wish to register with the embassy of the country to which you are a national.

- Purchase a street directory for your city or a GPS unit.

- Download the settlement information kit for your state here: http://www.immi.gov.au/living-in-australia/settle-in-australia/beginning-life/booklets/english.htm

Checklist for after you arrive: Days 30 to 60

These are mostly ideas and may not apply to everyone.

- Review your financial situation and cash flow, transferring more money if you need it.

- Speak to your children's teachers to ensure they have settled in and are adjusting well at school.

- Find reliable service tradesmen in your area (electrician, plumber, mechanic, etc.)

- Evaluate your will and have a new one made if necessary.

- Sign up for a library card at your local branch.

- Say hello to at least one or two of your neighbours. Simple questions about the area can be a great icebreaker.

- Subscribe to magazines or transfer old subscriptions.

- Join a local gym or fitness class (yoga, pilates, etc.)

- Get a membership card at a local video library.

- Attend some networking functions or meet-up groups. Here are a few to check out:

    American Chamber of Commerce in Australia (AmCham)
    http://www.amcham.com.au
    Regularly hosts events for members and non-members in NSW, VIC, WA and SA

    Network Canada   http://www.networkcanada.com.au/
    Professional networking group based in Sydney that is open to everyone, not just Canadians

    Schmooze   http://www.schmooze.net.au/site/
    Network with a diverse range of professionals at over 80 events a year. Schmooze also offers seminars and workshops.

    Women's Network Australia
    http://www.womensnetwork.com.au
    Membership-based organization that empowers and encourages women to reach their full potential in business

    Please also find more groups in the resources sections at the end of chapters one and eight, as well as in the appendix section on parenting.

5.

Chapter Five: Money in, money out: Working, spending and where to put the rest

Prepare yourself. The cost of living in Australia is high. How expensive you find it to be will depend on where you are coming from. If you come from one of the US states where things are very cheap (pretty much everywhere except for places like California, Hawaii, Alaska and New York City), you will find prices to be astronomical. If you're like me and the last two places you lived were San Francisco and NYC, things will seem about right. Western Europeans will probably find the cost of living to be similar to their home countries as well. Despite its geographical proximity to Asian countries, where you can buy most things for a fraction of what they cost here, Australia is a relatively expensive place to live.

In this chapter, I'll discuss the practical aspects of working in Australia as well as the costs of living and some tips for saving money. I'll also discuss banking and investments, taxes and other financial aspects of your life in Australia.

Working in Australia

You'll need the appropriate permissions to get a job in Australia, which are provided to you when you obtain the appropriate work visa (see chapter one to learn what visas are available). This is not something that you should mess around with as DIAC is very strict when it comes to people working without the correct visa, and you will be deported if you're caught working without one. You may also be subjected to an exclusion period from the country (usually three years), which will make it hard for you to obtain a working visa in the future.

You will need to obtain your TFN (see previous chapter) and a bank account before you start working. Your employer will require paperwork for you provide your TFN, bank account details, Superannuation (see later section) and other personal information when you start work. I can't comment on the differences in workplace culture in Australia compared to other countries. There are too many variables and occupations; this is something you will have to discover for yourself. I've spoken to many other expats about the subject and heard a variety of opinions. Naturally, it's something you are going to be curious about but I encourage you to make your own judgments about your workplace. If you have permission to work in Australia and you already have a job, you can move on to the next section of this chapter.

If you don't have a job, you'll want to start looking for one right away, especially if your savings are running low. Even if you have plenty of cash, I encourage you to start working as soon as possible so that you can get settled in your new life, begin to meet people and become involved in Australian society. There are several ways to go about your job search but you are likely to feel quite limited in Australia because of a very important factor: you are in a strange country and your network of friends, family and associates probably doesn't extend to your new home. These days most people find the best jobs through people they know and through contacts in their networks, which they've probably spent a lot of time and effort building. This is likely to be your number one frustration in the job hunt.

But this shouldn't discourage you. Looking for a job in Australia is still very similar to looking for a job anywhere else and most of the same rules apply. If you're looking for shift work or a low-skilled job, you will fill out job applications at the places you are interested in working and you may or may not need a resume. If you are going for an office job or have a professional career, you will definitely need a resume.

Your resume and the job search

As this book is not intended to be a job search guide, I will not be giving you resume tips and suggestions. What I will tell you, however is that resumes in Australia (also known here as Curriculum Vitaes, or 'CVs') are generally expected to be longer and more detailed than those in the US. This is changing for some industries and I recommend that you familiarise yourself with the standards in your field. You can look at the professional association websites for your industry for referrals to more information. Be sure you look at the Australian professional associations so the information is specific to this country. I've listed a portal for these in the resources section. You may also wish to join these associations so that you can attend their networking events. You can check out the tips and suggestions provided by the websites I've listed at the end of this section for more information as well.

Getting your resume in shape is the first step to projecting the best possible image of yourself to potential employers. But your personality will also count for a lot in the interview process. It's very important in Australia and I recommend that if you see a listed job that you're really interested in, just call the contact person and have a chat with him before you send a resume. You will still need to submit a formal application in most instances, but this is a great way to convey your personality in the hiring process before you send through a faceless resume listing your skills and qualifications, no matter how good that resume may be.

Finding a job

The job search process may take months (over a year in some cases, I'm sorry to say) or just a few weeks. A lot will depend on your specialisation (if you have one) and your previous experience. Overseas experience and education doesn't always count for as much as local experience, so don't get too cocky about your fancy degree from a top tier school or all the big names you've worked for. Obviously these things will matter more for certain occupations, but don't count on them.

I want to caution you about your job search and prepare you for the reality that it can be heard to get a break in parts of Australia as a foreigner. Plenty of people have no problems and make an easy transition. But as I mentioned in chapter two, others have had to take a step back in their careers when they came here. Women should know that the Australian workplace does not typically treat the two genders equally. According to a recent special report in *The Age*, women in Australia do not hold the majority of senior job positions in any industry in Australia and not a single industry pays women more than they do men (most of them pay less and the gap is around 17 per cent).[29]

---

[29] You can learn more about this issue at Equal Opportunity for Women in the Workplace: http://www.eowa.gov.au

Australia's job market is heavily dominated by recruiters (or 'head-hunters' as you may know them). If you have a few years of experience under your belt, it's a good idea to initiate a relationship with one or two of the best ones in your field. The top recruiters are usually specialised and if you look on the job boards of your professional or industry association you will start to get a feel for which recruitment firms are central in your field. You can make an appointment with them to discuss what you are looking for or simply apply to jobs they have listed.

You can also search online job websites for openings. You should be aware that many of the ads posted on these sites attract hundreds (sometimes thousands) of applicants, so this is probably not the most efficient way to get a job and you can waste a lot of time preparing cover letters and sending out your resume. The best way to use these sites is to call the contact person and speak to her about any jobs you see listed. This at least gets you some top-of-mind awareness with the hiring manager and distinguishes you from other applicants. You can also use the job sites to see what companies are hiring in general. Then you can contact the appropriate persons at these companies about what they might have available for a person with your skills and qualifications, and you can sell yourself to them based on that. If you're looking for jobs in the printed newspaper, most of these will be advertised on Saturday. The better jobs may have ads in the first main news section as opposed to the employment classifieds section.

Centrelink has a Career Information Centre and all Australian residents can use the services provided there. You may want to give this a try if you're having great difficulty getting an interview. The Job Network is another government option, which has job search support services, training in interview skills and job searching, help for starting your own business and assessment fee subsidies for overseas trained residents. Centrelink has Job Network Access facilities that offer the use of telephones, photocopiers, fax machines, touch screens, computers and internet to eligible job seekers. Your state government may also be able to provide you with job search assistance.

When going for interviews, the same rules apply as everywhere else in the world. You should dress professionally and appropriate to the job. Be polite and courteous and thank the person for her time after the interview (I always send a handwritten note after an interview). Be sure to bring any documentation you may need such as qualifications and your passport/visa. You might notice that Australian employers tend to get a bit more personal when they interview you than you might be used to. While this is against the law, many still do it and you should be prepared. You should also try not to get discouraged if your search is taking longer than expected. This is common for expats (and Aussies too). You may get no response to your applications, which usually means that you were not on the short-list of candidates, but you can always call and enquire. I've had actual interviews and never heard from the company again afterwards. When the job market is tight and there are many applicants, you may notice rude behaviour like this. Try not to take it too personally and move on to the next job prospect. Good luck!

Job search resources

Australia's government-run job board http://jobsearch.gov.au

CareerOne   http://www.careerone.com.au
CareerOne recently partnered with Monster and is another large, popular job board in Australia. You can also get career advice here including tips on preparing your resume and searching for a job.

Department of Education, Employment and Workplace Relations   http://www.deewr.gov.au/Pages/default.aspx

Job Network   http://www.jobnetwork.gov.au

Mumbrella   http://mumbrella.com.au/jobs
I've included this one for my fellow media professionals as media is a tough nut to crack when it comes to job hunting. This is usually an exhaustive list of all the media (and many marketing) jobs, which are often underrepresented on the major job boards.

MyCareer   http://www.mycareer.com.au
This is Fairfax Digital's job board (the media company that publishes the Sydney Morning Herald). You'll find tools and salary information as well as advice and research here as well.

Now Hiring   http://nowhiring.com.au
Yet another job board, which is quite popular with certain industries

Professional Associations
https://careers.vu.edu.au/Content/Students_and_Graduates/Job_Hunting/Professional_Associations/Associations_List.chpx
An outstanding list of professional associations by industry provided by Victoria University

SEEK   http://www.seek.com.au
This is probably Australia's largest and most popular jobs site. It also has other information such as salary information, advice and education information.

Taxes

Once you're working, you'll notice that your employer withdraws taxes from your income automatically. Australia has a PAYG (pay as you go) tax system, which deducts the appropriate amount of tax before distributing your net income to you. You must apply for a TFN before you can legally work in Australia. If you operate a business, you will need to apply for an Australian Business Number (ABN). Every business in Australia must have an ABN and if you work as an independent consultant you will need one as well.

The rate of tax in Australia is quite high in order to pay for all of the public services provided to its citizens and residents. The tax rates are progressive, meaning that the higher your income, the more tax you pay. At the time of writing, the tax rates for residents were as follows:

Taxable income	Tax (does not include Medicare levy)
$1 - $6,000	Nil
$6,001 - $35,000	15 cents for each $1 over $6,000
$35,001 - $80,000	$4,350 plus 30 cents for each $1 over $35,000
$80,001 - $180,000	$17,850 plus 38 cents for each $1 over $80,000
$180,001 and over	$55,850 plus 45 cents for each $1 over $180,000

The Medicare levy is an additional 1.5 per cent of your taxable income and it applies to everyone unless you qualify for an exemption. The three categories of exemptions are medical, foreign residents and residents of Norfolk Island, and those not entitled to Medicare benefits. You will be entitled to a reduction on the levy if your taxable income is equal to or les than your lower threshold amount[30] or greater than your lower and less than or equal to your upper threshold amounts. You may also be eligible if your taxable income is over your upper threshold amount but you had a spouse or de facto partner, had a spouse that died and you did not have

---

[30] Thresholds can be found here: http://www.ato.gov.au/individuals/content.asp?doc=/content/40500.htm&page=2#P27_2049

another spouse before the end of the year, are entitled to a child-housekeeper or housekeeper tax offset or were a sole parent and had sole care of one or more dependant children. If you make over AUD 73,000 as a single person or AUD 146,000 as a couple or family, you will also be taxed an additional 1.5 per cent of your taxable income for the MLS (see last chapter) if you do not take out private hospital insurance.

The Australian tax and financial year starts on 1 July and runs through 30 June. Most people are required by law to lodge tax returns with the ATO between 30 June and 31 October each year. If you are senior, on low income, have a disability or fall under another special category, you can seek free assistance from Tax Help. Otherwise you can complete your tax forms yourself or hire an accountant. Accountant's fees are tax deductible and I highly recommend using one in Australia if your taxes are at all complicated. Being an expat usually means that they will be. As a resident of Australia you are generally required to disclose all income received from inside or outside Australia, as Australian residents are taxed on their worldwide income. You should consult the ATO website for more information about your tax obligations.

The other type of tax you will encounter day-to-day is the Goods and Services Tax (GST), which is 10 per cent on most items. The GST is included in the price you are asked to pay. Basic food, most education and health services, eligible child care and nursing home care are GST-free.

If you are a citizen of a country that still requires its citizens to file and pay tax on worldwide income, such as the US, you might assume that since you have no income in your country of origin, are not in the country of origin and don't plan to return to your home country, that you will never have to pay your tax debt. However, tax treaties between Australia and other countries provide a mechanism by which foreign tax debts are effectively converted into Australian tax liabilities, in relation to which the ATO may enforce its debt collection powers.

So your foreign tax debt could conceivably catch up with you here in Australia and you could find yourself being subject to the recovery of your debt. This is something to keep in mind and factor into your expectations of relocating to Australia. Your country of nationality may have a foreign tax credit and/or income exclusion scheme in place, where you have a tax-free threshold for income earned overseas if you are a bona fide resident of your country of residence for tax purposes. This is to prevent double taxation. The US, for example, excludes foreign earned income from taxation up to USD 91,400 per person. You should check with an accountant in all countries where you are a citizen or resident to determine your specific tax liabilities.

You will have to declare taxable income from overseas on your Australian tax return even if tax was taken out in the country where you earned the income. If the foreign income is taxable in Australia and you paid foreign tax on it, you may be entitled to a foreign tax credit. Taxes for which credit is allowed are called creditable taxes. You must also declare foreign income that is exempt from Australian tax because this income may be taken into account when determining the amount of tax you owe on your assessable net income from both Australian and foreign sources.

Tax resources

ATO International Tax Essentials
http://www.ato.gov.au/individuals/pathway.asp?pc=001/002/012

Australian Tax Office website   http://www.ato.gov.au

Business and GST enquiries   13 2866

International Comparison of Australian Taxes 2006   Treasury report
http://comparativetaxation.treasury.gov.au/content/default.asp

Personal Tax Information Line 13 2861

Tax Act Online http://www.taxactonline.com
Free online software to file your US federal return and one of the few online tax prep services that takes overseas credit cards; I've tried a few different online tax services over the years and keep coming back to this one.

Tax File Number Helpline (within Australia)   13 2861

Tax information from American Citizens Abroad (ACA)
http://www.aca.ch/joomla/index.php?option=com_content&task=blogcategory&id=32&Itemid=84
There's some really useful tax information here for American expats including IRS forms you should look at and a list of articles answering commonly asked questions.

TFN online registration   http://www.ato.gov.au/individuals

Banking, loans and Investments

Banks in Australia

Australian banks are comparable to banks anywhere else in the developed world and several international banks are represented here. The banking system is sound and in October 2008, the Australian Federal Government announced that it would guarantee bank deposits held in Australian banks, credit unions and building societies as a response to the global financial crisis. Therefore, total deposit balances up to AUD 1 million are guaranteed for three years. Most banks will offer an 'opt-in' option to the scheme for customers with over a million dollars.

You'll find all of the regular banking services that you would find in the US or the UK and similar types of accounts. Most people apply for their credit cards through their banks in Australia, however you may notice that there aren't very many 'no fee' credit cards, which is something I miss from the US. You should enquire with a few different banks to find the best interest rates and account types for your needs. Australian banks also provide mortgages, loans and investment services. I'll discuss home loans and purchasing property a bit more in chapter nine.

Here is a list of the major banks (retail and business) in Australia as well as a few of the major investment service providers:

Australia New Zealand Bank (ANZ) http://www.anz.com.au
Has branches throughout the country; overseas residents may open an account (with restrictions) prior to arriving in Australia; has branches in London and New York City

Bank of Queensland http://www.boq.com.au
Has branches and ATMs nationwide

Bank of Western Australia (Bank West)
http://www.bankwest.com.au
Has branches in every region except TAS and NT, with ATM machines in *7-11* stores

BankSA http://www.banksa.com.au
Has branches in every region except ACT, QLD and TAS

Bendigo Bank http://www.bendigobank.com.au
Has over 530 branches across Australia

Citibank Australia http://www.citibank.com.au
International bank with a few branches in NSW, VIC, QLD and WA

Commonwealth Bank http://www.commbank.com.au
This is the largest bank in Australia with branches nationwide and it owns *Bank West*; has a branch in London.

Credit Suisse   https://www.credit-suisse.com/au/en
Offers private and investment banking and asset management. Offices in Melbourne and Sydney

Deutsche Bank   http://www.deutschebank.com.au
Investment banking, asset management and private client services

Goldman Sachs JB Were   http://www.gsjbw.com
Offices in Melbourne and Sydney

HSBC   http://www.hsbc.com.au
British bank with branches nationwide and in the US as well

ING Direct   http://www.ingdirect.com.au
Bank online or over the phone only; ING is a global bank.

Macquarie Bank   http://www.macquarie.com.au
Investments & funds management (based in Sydney)

National Australia Bank (NAB) http://www.nab.com.au
Has branches in all states and territories

St. George Bank   http://www.stgeorge.com.au
Has branches in all capital cities.

Westpac   http://www.westpac.com.au
Bank with branches Australia-wide and also has one in London

Other useful financial resources

Banks.com.au   http://www.banks.com.au
Independent reviewer of the Australian banking industry and its products

CANNSTAR Cannex   http://www.canstar.com.au
Compare interest rates and star ratings for loans, cards, accounts, insurance and investment products.

FX Converter   http://www.oanda.com/convert/classic
Currency converter (features interbank, credit card, and cash rates)

InfoChoice   http://www.infochoice.com.au

Compare home loans, savings and term deposits, personal loans, credit cards, transaction accounts, investments and brokers, small business banking and life insurance products.

Travelex   http://www.travelex.com.au
Offers global cross-border payment services, money transfers, currency services, traveller's cheques and money cards.

XE   http://www.xe.com
Currency conversion
X-Rates   http://www.x-rates.com
Currency converter featuring rate history

Yahoo Currency Converter
     http://finance.yahoo.com/currency

Superannuation (if you're working, you'll have a fund)

Superannuation (commonly known as 'Super') is a mandatory long-term investment account for retirement, to which your employer will be required by law to make payments if you are between the ages of 18 and 70 and you make at least AUD 450 before tax in a calendar month. The benefits are also available should you become an invalid or to your beneficiaries upon your death. Americans will be familiar with 401K or Individual Retirement Accounts (IRAs). This is a similar scheme. Worldwide, people often know Super as 'pension' or 'retirement.'

You can choose any complying Super fund or retirement savings account you wish, and your employer will generally have a fund they are registered with to suggest to you if you don't have a preference already. As with any investment product, you should be very careful when deciding what super to put your money into. Usually your employer's Super contribution is nine per cent of your earnings. You may also contribute extra money into your Super. Sometimes the government will run schemes where it matches the contributions made by eligible residents so be sure to look into those programs.

There are several independent ratings bodies you can refer to in order to determine what Superannuation funds are performing the best. I recommend that you check on your Super at least every couple of years. We recently noticed that our once top-rated Super fund had suddenly become the worst performing of them all. Treat it like an investment because not only is it an investment, if you work for any length of time in Australia it's likely to become a sizeable one. Superannuation funds will also usually provide life insurance policies, which is something you should evaluate when you investigate a fund.

The ATO Superannuation Infoline can be reached on 13 1020 from within Australia. You can also access information online at http://www.ato.gov.au/super and http://www.fido.asic.gov.au

Super fund evaluation organization websites and governing bodies:

Australian Prudential Regulation Authority (APRA) http://www.apra.gov.au

Australian Securities and Investments Commission (ASIC) http://www.asic.gov.au

Chant West   http://www.chantwest.com.au

SelectingSuper http://www.selectingsuper.com.au

SuperRatings   http://www.superratings.com.au

Superannuation Complaints Tribunal   http://www.sct.gov.au
Should you have any problems with your fund

Australian currency and spending it

Cash

Australian money consists of notes and coins. The notes are colourful, coated paper bills that seem almost plastic. You can scrunch one into a ball and it will unfold nicely by itself right back to its original form. I'm convinced this is so that they are not destroyed when Aussies go to the beach. The coating is also very handy if you accidentally wash your money in the laundry. Australians carry five, ten, twenty, fifty and one hundred dollar notes, all featuring people and icons that are important to the nation. Coins come in five, ten, twenty and fifty cent as well as one and two dollar denominations. As there are no one cent pieces, if your purchase comes to an amount not divisible by five cents, it will be rounded (for example, $2.98 becomes $3.00)

Automatic Teller Machines (and their fees), commonly known as ATMs, can be found all over Australia so you can easily take cash out at any time. You won't find drive-through ATMs here, however. Be advised that you must declare cash amounts over AUD 10,000 to customs when you come into Australia. You may bring in as much cash as you want but you must declare it if it is over AUD 10,000. Customs can confiscate your money if you break this rule so ensure your conversion rate calculation is correct before you travel. If you are concerned about transferring money into the country, you can get a good exchange rate for money transfers by doing some research. I've listed a few good options for transferring money below:

HiFX http://www.hifx.com.au
Foreign exchange specialists for currency transfers

Ozforex http://www.ozforex.com.au

Online foreign exchange dealing and currency transfers with good

Xe Trade http://www.xe.com
Global payments and transfers

Credit and Debit (EFTPOS) cards

Pretty much every establishment accepts at least one of these forms of payment, though you may find that some places pass on credit card surcharges (the fees they pay to the bank for taking credit cards) to you. The most popular credit cards are *Visa* and *Mastercard*, and some businesses accept *American Express*. You can sign for your purchases (most places check the signature so don't put your card away before you sign) or use your Personal Identification Number (PIN) associated with your card. Credit and EFTPOS cards are available at all banks.

EFTPOS stands for 'Electronic Funds Transfer at Point of Sale' and this is basically a debit card, which takes funds directly from your nominated account. Usually you will be required to input your PIN and will be able to get "cash back." When you get cash back with your purchase, the amount you are taking out will be added to the amount charged to your card and the total will be removed from your account. Australians use credit and debit cards often and it is not uncommon for people to use them for purchases under five dollars.

Credit ratings in Australia are separate from credit ratings in other countries such as the US. Your bad (or good) credit rating won't follow you from your previous country of residence. This can be advantageous or disadvantageous depending on your situation. If you apply for a credit card such as *American Express*, where you have a previous credit history, they will take that into account. This will also be the case with international banks. Otherwise you are starting from scratch, and in Australia credit ratings don't exist the way they do in the US. You're either delinquent with your accounts or you aren't. What creditors do take into account are your salary history (it's best if you have a job for at least six months) and your savings. Essentially, if you don't have bad credit in Australia from not paying your bills in the country, and you have a permanent full-time job, you should not have too much trouble obtaining credit. I have heard people say that they had trouble getting a credit card when they were newcomers to Australia. You may want to keep your old credit cards for now just in case.

Resources

Credit Card Finder   http://www.creditcardfinder.com.au
Compare credit cards in Australia.

Credit Card Offers   http://www.creditcardoffers.com.au
Compare credit card special offers and apply online.

Cheques and Money Orders

Personal cheques are not very popular in Australia. One of the first things I noticed when I arrived here is that people take their utility bills to the *Australia Post* and pay them there. Cheque facilities are available from banks, building societies and credit unions, but neither my husband nor I have ever used personal cheques since we've been in Australia.

If you do need to use a cheque to make a payment, a popular way of doing so is to get a Money Order from an *Australia Post Shop*. You can also get a bank cheque from your institution, but the fees for these are usually significantly higher than getting a money order from the Post.

Australia Post

I'm mentioning Australia's postal service here because, as I've just explained, you can do most of your banking activities at any Post Shop (the outlets of Australia Post that double as retail shops and service providers). You can pay your bills, do your personal banking, send money and purchase pre-paid, reloadable *Visa* cards.[31] Australia Post shops are not only the place to go if you want to send letters and parcels, but also where you can go to obtain or renew your British or Australian passport, get passport photos taken, have documents certified or witnessed, purchase *American Express Travellers Cheques* and *Travelex Cash Passports,* and purchase a variety of other products and services.

Shopping

There is nothing particularly special about shopping in Australia. You'll find department stores, nationwide chains, boutiques, convenience stores and some cheaper options such as markets and wholesalers. Online shopping is also popular; though you probably won't find the deals you would in more densely populated countries. The central business districts of major cities have the most concentrated shopping areas, but you'll also find plenty of unique shops in your local suburb or other suburbs as you explore your city more. Generally each suburb has a major shopping street (some of these are better than others). We also have large indoor shopping malls (not the behemoths you may have noticed in the US), outdoor shopping "villages" and outlet shopping plazas. Markets are a great way to find bargains and unique items as well as wonderful produce vendors, delis, butchers, fishmongers and gourmet specialty shops.

---

[31] For more information on these Australia Post services, visit: http://auspost.com.au/personal/bills-banking-sending-money.html

In chapter seven, I've listed the prices of 100 commonly sought-after items so you can start to get an idea of what things cost in Australia.

If you're looking for a product review site, try **Choice** (http://www.choice.com.au), which allows you to compare products and find independent reviews.

Here is a list of the major nationwide supermarket and department store chains. You can find most of the major retailers' catalogues online at *Lasoo* (http://www.lasoo.com.au)

BigW   http://www.bigw.com.au
Discount nationwide department store for clothing, cosmetics and home wares

Bunnings   http://www.bunnings.com.au
Huge nationwide chain for home do-it-yourself builders and renovators with sections for bathroom, kitchen, garden, outdoor and more

Coles   http://www.coles.com.au
Part of the *ColesMyer* group and also offers home delivery in some areas

David Jones   http://www.davidjones.com.au
The other major nationwide department store; this one is quite similar to Myer though it can seem more upscale. It is often referred to as "DJ's."

Foodworks   http://www.foodworks.com.au
Smaller group of independent supermarkets found in seven states and territories.

Harvey Norman and Domayne http://www.harveynorman.com.au and http://www.domayne.com.au
A leading retain chain in Australia, which carries appliances and home ware products; *Domayne* is the furniture, bedding and home wares store.

IGA   http://www.iga.net.au
Group of over 1200 independently owned supermarkets

Myer   http://www.myer.com.au
Nationwide department store with men's and women's fashion, cosmetics and home wares

Officeworks   http://www.officeworks.com.au
Largest supplier of office and stationery products with stores across Australia

RetraVision   http://www.retravision.com.au
Great prices on appliances, audio visual, home entertainment, kitchen appliances, cooling and heating products

Spotlight   http://www.spotlight.com.au
Fabric, craft and home interior superstore

Target   http://www.target.com.au
Target Australia is somewhat different from *Target* in the US, however the offerings are similar. *Target* is a nationwide department store but much less expensive than *Myer* or *David Jones* for clothing, cosmetics and home wares.

Woolworths   http://www.woolworths.com.au
Supermarket chain that also offers home delivery in some area

Gambling

Most forms of gambling are legal throughout Australia and you'll find that punters bet on everything from football to horse racing to ministerial elections. There is a nationwide lottery and licensed betting outlets can be found in pretty much all of the shopping areas and suburbs. Registered clubs, hotels and casinos can host games as well. You'll probably see a 'pokie' (electronic poker machine) at your local pub. If gambling is only legal in certain areas of your home country, as it is in the US, you'll probably be surprised by how much betting goes on here. Obviously I don't recommend that you use gambling as a way to make a living, but it is another option for something to do with your money and most Aussies have a bet at some point, even if its just at an annual horse race or football grand final. Online options are plentiful as well.

The major gaming outlets are listed below. Most of them claim to have the best odds so you'll have to make your own deductions on the subject.

Sportingbet Australia   http://www.sportingbet.com.au
Online licensed and regulated racing, sports and entertainment bookmaker

Sportsbet   http://www.sportsbet.com.au
Online licensed and regulated sports and racing bookmaker

Tabcorp (TAB)   http://www.tab.com.au
Sports betting outlets with online services as well

Tatts   http://www.tattersalls.com.au
Runs Australia's national lotteries with outlets throughout Australia.

Saving money

If you're like me, you love good deals and saving your funds. Here are my money-saving tips for Australia:

> 1. **Get an Entertainment Book.** Every April, companies and charitable organizations sell these books to raise money for their causes. For AUD 65 you can get a book for your city and I assure you that if you go out to restaurants, movies and other forms of entertainment anyway, or if you travel within the country, the book will more than pay for itself. You'll receive a gold *Entertainment Card* to use for discounts (usually 25 per cent) in fine dining establishments, and vouchers for discounts (usually 25 per cent or two-for-one) at

cafes, bistros, casual and fast food restaurants as well as coffee shops and takeaway outlets. The book also contains vouchers for everything from the ballet to sporting events to movie tickets to zoos and tourist attractions. You'll also get corporate-type discounts on hotels and car rentals and discounts on magazines, nationwide florists and many other products and services. http://www.entertainmentbook.com.au

2. **Shop during the sales.** While you will find mid-season retail sales, especially when the economy isn't doing very well, most of the sales occur twice a year: after the Christmas holidays and just before the end of the financial year.

3. **Sign up for your favourite stores' rewards cards.** Many of the large nationwide retail chains have their own loyalty rewards programs. These generally allow you to accumulate points for your spending and earn store gift cards, merchandise and/or other privileges. Two popular programs are *FlyBuys* and *MyerOne*.

4. **Don't forget about your favourite overseas retailers online.** It can often be cheaper to purchase items like books and cosmetics online, despite the shipping fees. I still place orders from *Amazon* and I also order beauty products from a company called *StrawberryNet* (http://strawberrynet.com). If your favourite overseas retailer doesn't ship internationally but they will take your overseas credit card, you can use a service like *vPost* to have your goods shipped to a US, UK or Japan address and then forwarded to your address in Australia (https://www.vpostasia.com/australia/index.html). Another service to consider is comGateway (http://www.comgateway.com).

5. **Look for savings days.** Movie theatres usually have one day a week when ticket prices are significantly reduced. Pubs often have lunch and dinner specials depending on the day of the week. Keep an eye out for these kinds of deals at the places you frequent and take advantage of them.

6. **Shop around.** This tactic works anywhere in the world and it applies to everything from interest and mortgage rates to appliances. Get into the habit of enquiring with at least three vendors before you make a purchase. You can usually use competitors' prices to negotiate deals with other suppliers.

7. **Cut down on little extras.** Pack your lunch when you go to work instead of buying it. Use the library. Take tea and coffee to work instead of buying it at the café. Turn lights off when you aren't using them. Buy generic brands of sugar, flour and other basics. All these extra dollars add up.

8. **Use eBay.** Buy items at low prices and sell your unwanted stuff as well. Australia has its own site: http://www.ebay.com.au

Here are some additional websites to help:

FrugalAussies http://groups.yahoo.com/group/FrugalAussies
Around 300 Australian residents share their tips for saving money

Reward Program Credit Card finder
http://www.creditcardfinder.com.au/australian-reward-credit-cards
Find credit cards with rewards programs.

Complaints

The Australian Securities and Investments Commission (ASIC) recommends that if your complaint concerns a product or service you have purchased, you should first raise your complaint with the business or person who provided you with the goods or services you are complaining about. If the problem can't be resolved, or if your complaint is about misconduct or illegal activity by a company or person, then you should refer to this web portal for government or non-government organizations that can help:

http://www.asic.gov.au/asic/asic.nsf/byheadline/Complaining+about+companies+or+people

6.

Chapter Six: Health - Insurance, Doctors and Medicare

Coming from the US, the healthcare system in Australia was very different to what I grew up with. You can rest easy knowing that you will get good care here, however you should be familiar with how things work before you arrive and prepare yourself for some differences. As I'm not familiar with any other countries' healthcare systems other than the US and Australia, I can't comment on the ways in which these differ. However, I will explain the entire system in detail in this chapter so that you may make your own comparisons.

Medicare

If you completed my checklist in chapter five, you will have either a blue or green plastic card issued by Medicare, the Australian Government's universal health care program. Medicare Australia administers the following health programs:

- **Medicare**

- **Pharmaceutical Benefits Scheme**
  This is the governmental provision of prescription medicines at affordable prices to all Australian residents and those overseas visitors who are eligible under reciprocal health care

agreements. Payments are made to pharmacists to subsidise medicines on the Pharmaceutical Benefits Schedule.

- **Australian Childhood Immunisation Register**
  This is a national online database containing information on the immunisation status of all children living in Australia under the age of seven.

- **Australian Organ Donor Register**
  Australia's only national organ and tissue donor register, ensuring that a person's consent (or objection) to donating organs and/or tissue for transplantation can be verified anytime, anywhere in Australia.

- **Medicare Teen Dental Plan**
  This plan offers assistance to persons aged 12-17 who receive (or whose family receive) tax benefits, ABSTUDY, support payments or disability. You can check with Medicare to learn whether your child qualifies.

- **30 per cent Private Health Insurance Rebate**
  Anyone who pays hospital and/or general private health fund premiums for a Complying Health Insurance Policy to a registered health fund can get a 30 per cent reduction on the cost as long as you're eligible for Medicare. The rebate is not means-tested.

- **General Practice Immunisation Incentives Scheme**
  Provides financial incentive to general practices that monitor, promote and provide immunisation services to children under the age of seven.

- **Practice Incentives Program**

This program aims to improve the quality of care received by Australians from their doctors by offering payments to accredited practices.

- **Rural Retention Program**
  This program offers financial incentives to doctors who remain in eligible rural and remote areas of the country.

- **Claims processing and payments for the Department of Veterans' Affairs**

- **Family Assistance Office**
  You can find Family Assistance Offices at Medicare offices and Centrelink Customer Service Centres across the country and they exist to make payments to support families with the cost of raising children. There are payments available for all kinds of circumstances, so if you have children, you should look into these:
    - *Family tax benefit A:* Payable to a parent/guardian or an approved care organization for a child aged under 21 years or a dependent full time student aged between 21 and 24 years. The payment is made fortnightly or through the tax system as a lump sum at the end of the year. Currently the maximum rate is awarded for family incomes up to AUD 42,559 and the rate is reduced by 20 cents for every additional dollar of income until a base rate is reached. Once the family income reaches AUD 94,316 (plus an additional AUD 3,796 for each additional child), payments reduce by 30 cents for every dollar over that amount until the payment is zero.

    - *Family Tax Benefit B:* available to families with one main income earner, including sole parent families with a dependent full time student up to the age of 18 years.

This is an additional benefit available to families whose sole income is AUD 150,000 or less.

- *Child care benefit:* Available to parents, foster parents and grandparents with a child in your care who is attending child care services approved by, or registered with, the Government. Your child must meet immunisation requirements and you or your partner must meet residency requirements and meet the income test.

- *Child care rebate:* This rebate covers 50 per cent of out-of-pocket child care expenses for approved child care, with a rebate of up to AUD 7,778 per child per year for eligible families.

- *Baby Bonus:* The baby bonus is paid to families following the birth (including stillborn) or adoption of a child. This payment is only available for parents with an adjusted taxable income of less than or equal to AUD 75,000 for the period of six months from the date of birth of the child or six months from the date the child entered your care.

- *Paid Parental Leave:* This is a new scheme, which will come into effect for parents of children born on or after 1 January 2011. It will only be available to those earning less than AUD 150,000 in the previous financial year that worked continuously for at least 10 of the previous 13 months prior to the birth or adoption, and worked at least 330 hours in that 10 month period with no more than an eight week gap in employment. Eligible mothers will receive AUD 570 per week (the National Minimum Wage) for up to 18 weeks. Part or all of the benefit may be transferred to the other parent if there are exceptional circumstances. This scheme will replace the baby bonus for those who are eligible for it. The baby bonus will still be available to those who do not qualify for paid leave.

- *Maternity Immunisation Allowance:* You receive a bonus for immunising your child.

- *Other types of assistance:* Large family supplement, multiple birth allowance, rent assistance, health care cards, double orphan pension, jobs, education and training child care fee assistance, economic security strategy payments and household stimulus package bonus payments. For more information about these or any of the payments described above, visit the Family Assistance website: http://www.familyassist.gov.au/Payments/Pages/default.aspx

- **Special assistance schemes**
  Australians can receive assistance for disasters and other special situations. Recently assistance has been provided to victims of the Mumbai terrorist attacks, drought, the 2005 Bali bombings and the 2004 Indian Ocean tsunamis.

It begins with your either your General Practitioner (GP) or the Emergency Room (ER)

Treatment or preventative care in Australia will start with either your GP or, if you have an emergency, the ER of your local hospital. The GP serves as the centre of your medical care and, unless you have an emergency, you should see her for all of your medical issues. One of the first things you should do in Australia is to find a doctor you like.

If you require any specialty treatment, you will have to get a referral from your GP before a specialist will see you. This was very new for me because in the US we are accustomed to seeing a specialist without a referral (unless your insurance provider requires it). And in Australia, commonly sought practitioners such as gynaecologists and paediatricians are considered specialists. So if you have a child, he will see your GP unless there is a specific problem that causes your GP to refer you to a paediatrician. For women, your GP will conduct all of your normal female check-ups including Pap tests, which are done every two years in Australia unless there is a problem or history requiring you to have them more frequently.

If you have registered successfully for Medicare and you receive treatment by medical practitioners such as GPs, specialists or participating optometrists, Medicare will pay for some or all of your care. It provides benefits for tests and examinations such as X-rays and pathology tests, consultation fees, eye exams, most surgical and therapeutic procedures as well as some surgical dental procedures and other procedures and you can choose your own doctor.[32] You should bring your Medicare card with you when you attend your doctor's practice.

If you have registered successfully for Medicare and you visit the ER and are admitted to hospital, or if your GP or specialist admits you to hospital for surgery or other care, you will receive free treatment as a public patient in a public hospital. Your doctors and specialists will be nominated by the hospital and Medicare will pay for your care and treatment or after-care. When you go to the hospital, you will need to take with you any medicines you are using and also

---

[32] A full list of what Medicare provides for is available here:

http://www.health.gov.au/internet/mbsonline/publishing.nsf/Content/a-z

your Medicare card, private health insurance card and Health Benefits or Pension Concession Card.

If you have registered successfully for Medicare and you are a private patient in a public or private hospital, you may choose the doctor who treats you and Medicare will pay 75 per cent of the Medicare Schedule fee for services and procedures. You will be charged for your hospital accommodation and items such as theatre fees and medicines. If you have private health insurance (see next section), some or all of the outstanding balance can be covered.

Medicare does not cover the following:

- private patient hospital costs (for example, theatre fees or accommodation)
- dental examinations and treatment (except specified items introduced for allied health services as part of the Enhanced Primary Care (EPC) program)
- ambulance services
- home nursing
- physiotherapy, occupational therapy, speech therapy, eye therapy, chiropractic services, podiatry or psychology (except specified items introduced for allied health services as part of the EPC program) or acupuncture (unless it is part of a doctor's consultation)
- glasses and contact lenses
- hearing aids and other appliances
- cost of prostheses (except External Breast Prostheses covered by the External Breast Prostheses Reimbursement Program)
- medicines (except for the subsidy on medicines covered by PBS)
- medical and hospital costs incurred overseas

- medical costs for which someone else is responsible (for example a compensation insurer, an employer, a government or government authority)
- medical services that are not clinically necessary
- surgery solely for cosmetic reasons
- examinations for life insurance, superannuation or membership of a friendly society
- eye therapy

Private health cover can provide for what Medicare doesn't cover if it is included in your extras plan (see next section).

When you visit your doctor, you will need to present your Medicare card and he may either bill Medicare directly (known as 'bulk billing') or charge you the full fee. If he bulk bills, you will only need to pay the difference between the cost of your care and the amount Medicare covers. If you are charged the full fee, you can either make the payment yourself and then claim the benefit from Medicare or claim the unpaid amount from Medicare and receive a cheque made out in the doctor's name, which you can then give to your doctor along with any outstanding balance. Medicare usually pays the full Schedule fee for GP services, 85 per cent of the Schedule fee for other out-of-hospital services and 75 per cent of the Schedule fee for in-hospital services. Many doctors now offer electronic claiming that allows you to pay your claim into your nominated bank account. Consult the Medicare website to register.

If your doctor gives you a prescription, you can take this to any chemist shop (pharmacy). If you have a Health Care Card or Pension Concession Card from Centrelink, you will be eligible for a concession on certain medicines. You must also present your Medicare card to the chemist.

You can also seek care at a Community Health Centre, which provides care for people of all ages at low cost. Women's care centres provide more specialised services for the community and you can find these in your local *Yellow Pages*. Additionally, your state will have public programs for mental health, disability services and public dental clinics (usually with long wait times). Because of the structure of the healthcare system, patients in Australia may experience a waiting period for elective surgery (surgery that does not need to be done within 24 hours). You can view the data on elective surgery waiting times here: http://www.aihw.gov.au/hospitals/waitingtime_interactdata.cfm

The Australian Government has signed Reciprocal Health Care Agreements with New Zealand, the UK, the Republic of Ireland, Sweden, the Netherlands, Belgium, Finland, Italy, Malta and Norway. You won't be able to use your Medicare card overseas, however the reciprocal agreement covers any medically necessary treatment you may require if you visit one of these countries. You are covered for in-patient treatment and accommodation at a public hospital only, and you would have to pay the full cost of any other medical treatment, public hospital outpatient treatment and prescription medication. You would need to provide local authorities with your Australian passport or a passport showing that you are a permanent resident of Australia and a valid Medicare card.

Resources for medical care

Amcal http://www.onlinepharmacy.com.au
Online chemist shop

Chemist Warehouse http://www.chemistwarehouse.com.au
Online health products and medicines for delivery or purchase in-store

How to choose a GP
http://www.abc.net.au/health/consumerguides/stories/2006/06/19/1837215.htm
Quality article from the Australian Broadcasting Corporation (ABC) website

MyDr   http://www.mydr.com.au/search/gp
Search for a GP by suburb or postcode.

Priceline   http://www.priceline.com.au
Nation-wide discount chemist shop

Royal Australian College of General Practitioners (RACGP)
http://www.racgp.org.au/findapractice

Private health insurance

Private health insurance covers all or some of the cost of treatment as a private patient in private or public hospitals and can also include cover for some services that Medicare doesn't cover such as dental care, optical care and ambulatory services. There are many different health insurance providers and it is important to compare different funds before making a decision and to check all the details carefully before you buy a policy.

The government offers financial incentives for taking out private health insurance such as the 30 per cent Rebate. You're eligible to claim 30 per cent off the cost of care, usually processed by the insurance company so you don't have to actually claim the money back yourself. This will apply as long as you are eligible for Medicare and have a complying health insurance policy that provides hospital treatment, general treatment ('ancillary' or 'extras') cover or both. If you're aged 65-69, the Rebate is 35 per cent and if you're over 70 the Rebate is 40 per cent.

Likewise, you will be penalised if you are what the government considers a high-income earner and you don't take out private cover. If your income is over a certain threshold and you do not take out private insurance, you will have to pay the Medicare levy surcharge (MLS). This is an additional one per cent of your taxable income for people who earn over AUD 73,000 per year for singles and AUD 146,000 for couples and families. The MLS is in addition to the Medicare levy. If this is you, be sure to take out private health insurance cover because you will be paying for it anyway. You might as well spend that money on yourself and your family.

You are also encouraged to take out hospital cover at an early age. If a person takes out private health insurance after 1 July following his 31st birthday, he will pay more for the same level of cover over his lifetime than a person who took out cover before 1 July following her 31st birthday. This cost increases by two per cent each year that a person delays taking out cover. As a migrant, if you are over 30 years of age, you have some time. Migrants do not pay the increased cost as long as they purchase private cover within 12 months from the day they are registered as eligible for Medicare.

Resources for private health insurance

ABC Consumer Guide to Private Health Insurance
http://www.abc.net.au/health/consumerguides/stories/2006/04/17/1837457.htm
This is an excellent article outlining private health insurance in Australia from the ABC website.

Australian Health Plans   http://www.austhealth.com/index.php
Insurance for temporary residents working in Australia on 457 and other visas

Database of private health policies
http://www.privatehealth.gov.au
This is an Australian Government website showing every Health Insurance Policy available from every Health Fund.

iSelect   http://www.iselect.com.au
Compare health insurance plans (as well as life and car insurance and home loans)

Private Health Insurance Ombudsman   http://www.phiac.gov.au

7.

Chapter Seven: Food, products and services - What to expect

Now that you're all settled in and have taken care of the basics, you'll begin your normal day-to-day life in Australia. Part of that life will undoubtedly involve being a consumer. As I've already mentioned, the costs of goods and services in Australia can be pretty high. You may also notice that you can't find some of the products that you're used to here in Australia. In this chapter, I'll discuss all the things there are to spend your money on and hopefully answer some questions about what you'll be able to buy in Australia. I've simply created an A-Z list of general categories of items and services and explained anything that may be unfamiliar in each section.

Alcohol

Beer

Australian domestic beer is excellent, which will be a relief for Americans used to the domestic brands in their home country. And contrary to popular belief, most Aussies do not drink *Fosters*. The most common beer style is lager, though you can find local ales, dark beers and stout as well. Every state has their own unique brands and outstanding microbreweries abound. Due to consolidation in the market, two multinational corporations own almost all the major breweries in Australia. Imported beers are also widely available.

The primary brands in each region are as follows:

NSW: *Hahn*, *James Squire*, *KB Lager*, *Reschs* and *Tooheys*

QLD: *Powers* and *XXXX* (known as 'four x')

SA: *Coopers* (the only independently owned major regional brand), *Southwark*, *West End*

TAS: *Boags* and *Cascade*

VIC: *Carlton Draught*, *Melbourne Bitter* and *Victoria Bitter* (VB)

WA: *Emu* and *Swan*

If you purchase beer in a pub, you can ask for a bottle or for a draught (draft) beer from one of the selections on tap. The better pubs will have a large selection of local and imported beers available. But you'll need to know what you're ordering when it comes to sizes for draught beer. Glassware has different names in different cities, so you should familiarise yourself with these before heading out to the pub.

285 mL (10 fl oz)
Brisbane and Melbourne: pot
Sydney, Perth and Canberra: middy *or* half pint
Adelaide: schooner
Hobart: ten
Darwin: handle
Townsville: ten

425 mL (15 fl oz)
Sydney, Canberra, Brisbane, Melbourne, Perth, Hobart, Darwin: schooner
Adelaide: pint

570 mL (20 fl oz)
Outside Adelaide: pint
Adelaide: imperial pint (not called this everywhere)

1140 mL (40 fl oz)
Jug

Bottled beer in Australia comes in either the Stubby (375 mL) or Long Neck (750 mL) sizes. Recently many beer brands have switched to 330 mL bottles.

Cocktails and spirits

You can find all the major international spirits brands in Australia, though you will probably find them to be much more expensive than you're used to. This is not the case for all brands, but some are particularly dear. Good tequila, for example, is hard to come by at a good price. We're always sure to pick up duty free alcohol when we take an international trip. If you are taking more than one flight in your journey to Australia, you should purchase your duty free alcohol once you're past the security checkpoint to your last connecting flight. This is because you may not be allowed to bring liquids with you through security checkpoints. At the Auckland airport, for example, we found that we needed to purchase our alcohol in the shopping area near our departure gate for the final flight to Melbourne because the airport does a security screening for transit passengers, and they did not allow liquids through that screening point. You can always ask if you are unsure.

Another item to consider when shopping at duty free is the limit. The duty-free allowance per adult entering Australia is 2.25 litres. Any additional litres that you bring into Australia over that amount will cause you to pay duty on the entire amount of alcohol you bring in plus GST. Most of the bottles you will find at duty free shops are 1.25 litres. Generally, you will be okay to bring in two of these (for a total of 2.5 litres) if you go through the 'items to declare' line at customs. This is completely at the discretion of the customs officer, however, I have heard that it can be done with no hassle. You just need to declare it. As with anything else in customs, if you have doubts, just declare it.

The cocktail trend is alive and kicking in Australia and the more upscale bars, restaurants and nightclubs in the cities will have cocktail menus. You can order pretty much anything you want here. Drinking is a major social activity in this country and the market provides for that. I have noticed some differences in cocktails between here and the US, however. Expect a funny look if you ask for a martini with blue-cheese stuffed olives, for example. I've never had a good vodka or gin martini in the smaller towns and cities (they may exist, I've just never found one). On a positive note, I find cocktails here to be less syrupy than in the US, with fresh fruit and ingredients, giving a nice crisp taste to even the sweetest drinks. And there isn't much of a demand for daiquiris here. You'll see frozen mixers behind some bars, but in general these are not like those found in the big daiquiri bars you see in the US.

You will notice a large selection of premixed beverages in Australia as well. Whiskey and coke, gin and tonic, and vodka drinks can all be found in cans and bottles at bars and the bottle shops. Often called 'alcopops' or less formally, 'lolly-water drinks,' these sugary beverages come in many different flavours and are often consumed by younger drinkers and women. I'm not a big fan, but they are available if you're used to drinking wine coolers and those sorts of beverages.

Wine

Aussies are also enthusiastic wine drinkers. And why wouldn't they be when the local product is so good? There are around 60 wine regions across the country. I've described some of the most popular below, but you'll find wine producers in every state.

Hunter Valley (NSW) Semillon is the great wine here, however Chardonnay is also dominant. You'll also find Shiraz, Cabernet and Verdelho among other varietals.

Barossa Valley (SA) This is probably Australia's most popular wine region. Shiraz is the star here, however you can find Cabernet Sauvignon, Chardonnay, Riesling, Semillon and Grenache Mourvedre blends here as well.

Clare Valley (SA) A beautiful area, Clare Valley is a leading producer of dry Rieslings along with Shiraz, Semillon and a distinctive Cabernet Sauvignon.

McLaren Vale (SA) Located on the coast, this green wine region produces award-winning Cabernet Sauvignon, Shiraz, Sauvignon Blanc as well as more unique varieties like Barbera, Fiano, Tempranillo, Mourvedre, Viognier, Sangiovese, Zinfandel and Verdelho.

Mornington Peninsula (VIC) The most significant wine produced here is a distinctive Chardonnay and you'll also find outstanding Pinot Gris and Pinot Noir.

Margaret River (WA) A popular tourist destination, Margaret River produces consistently high quality Cabernet Sauvignon as well as Chardonnay, Sauvignon Blanc and Semillon varieties.

Tasmania Tassie's cool climate is ideal for growing Chardonnay and Pinot Noir as well as remarkable sparkling wines. The producers here also make outstanding Riesling and Sauvignon Blanc styles that are not to be missed.

In addition to the wines mentioned above, you'll find a vast diversity of wine styles in Australia's different wine regions. The country's producers excel at creating sparkling, fortified and dessert wines. Australia is the fourth largest wine-exporting nation after France, Italy and Spain, with Aussie wines found in over 100 countries.

You'll also find great prices on New Zealand wines, which are outstanding in both quality and variety. Most restaurants will offer both Australian and New Zealand wines as well as other internationals. You'll find extensive wine lists in the better restaurants so if you're an oenophile, don't despair. You'll be well looked after in Australia.

Bottle Shops

Oh, the BottleO. Whether you want to drive-up, walk-in or order online, you can find all of your beer, liquor, pre-mixes and wines at your local bottle shop. There are a variety of independently owned shops as well as large nation-wide chains and retailers. Alcohol is not available for purchase in supermarkets, however you will usually find the supermarket's national bottle shop connected to or right next door to supermarket. Just pay for your non-alcoholic purchases in the main store first and proceed to the bottle shop.

You can also find specialty stores for wine and those usually sell beer and spirits as well. If you're looking to save money, here are some stores and websites that you should check out:

Boozle http://www.boozle.com.au
Searches liquor stores in Australia to find the lowest prices on beer, spirits and premixed drinks near your suburb

Dan Murphy's   http://www.danmurphys.com.au
Found in ACT, NSW, QLD, SA, VIC and WA, this store offers a low price guarantee.

1st Choice Liquor Superstores   http://1stchoice.com.au
Offers a price guarantee as well as party and regular delivery.

Legalities

The drinking age in Australia is 18 and you won't even be able to enter bottle shops, bars and nightclubs if you are under age.

Drunk driving is a serious issue in Australia. How much you've had to drink is measured by your blood alcohol concentration (BAC), which is the amount of alcohol in your bloodstream. The police measure this with a breathalyser or blood sample analysis. The Australian Federal Police (AFP) define one standard drink as a 285 mL glass of beer, a 30 mL nip of spirits, a 100 mL glass of wine and a 60 mL serving of fortified wine (such as sherry). You should be aware that bars and restaurants don't necessarily serve standard drinks. They may be larger and your glass could hold two standard drinks or more. Bottles will usually be labelled with the number of standard drinks they contain.

So you'll need to be careful (as you would anywhere else in the world) with how much alcohol you consume if you plan to drive. The legal limit to the BAC level for drivers is 0.05 (you must be *under* 0.05 in VIC), and if you are on a probationary license (P plates) or learner license (L plates) or hold a license in a special category (such as taxi, bus, Commonwealth, heavy or dangerous goods vehicles) no alcohol is allowed. You'll often see 'booze buses' in Australia, where police stop drivers randomly for breath tests. These are usually also 'drug buses' testing for both drugs and alcohol. So don't try to drive under the influence. You will face severe penalties if you are convicted including heavy fines, loss of your license and possibly imprisonment. Even worse than these consequences is the likelihood that you will seriously injure yourself and/or others.

The more you drink, the higher your BAC. Body size, how much food you've eaten, body fat and your gender are all factors that can affect your BAC level and different people can have different amounts of alcohol before they are over the legal limit. The recommendation by the AFP is to have no more than two standard drinks in the first hour and no more than one standard drink every hour after that for men. For women, the amount is no more than one standard drink in the first hour, and no more than one drink every hour after that. But some people need to drink even less to maintain a BAC level below the legal limit.

Bakeries

If you're looking for a good breakfast or light lunch, look no further than the Australian bakery, where you'll find a wide range of bread and pastry products. Most bakeries serve hot savoury pies and sausage rolls all day (see section on 'Pies') as well as cookies, muffins, breads and other sweet and savoury bites.

You'll find some products that are unique to Australia on bakery shelves. Some of these are English products so they will be familiar to expats from the UK. Others are purely Australian. Here are some food items that were new to me when I came to Australia:

Lamingtons: Named for the wife of a Queensland Governor, these are chocolate-coated cubes of sponge cake covered in desiccated coconut.

Pavlova: This is an egg white meringue and sugar confection covered with fruit and whipped cream. Pavlova is a popular dessert found anywhere from summer BBQs to weddings.

Anzac biscuits: These are crisp biscuits of rolled oats, coconut and melted golden syrup. They get their name from being baked, packed and sent to Australian soldiers during World War I by wives and mothers (ANZAC stands for Australia New Zealand Army Corps).

Soldier's cake: This is a tinned fruitcake that was also traditionally sent to soldiers.

There are several national bakeries such as *Brumby's* and *Baker's Delight*. You'll usually find the outlet of a national bakery chain near the entrance to *Coles* or *Woolworths*. But I prefer the independent local bakeries and cake shops. These may be Aussie or run by someone from another culture such as French, Italian, Czechoslovakian or even Asian. You'll find cheesecakes, bubka cakes, slices, shortbread, macaroons, challah, fruit bread, croissants, muffins, scones, Danishes, tarts, éclairs and sponges among many other types of delicacies. You can usually also get a great cup of coffee.

Holiday and festive periods are special times for the bakeries. At Christmas, their windows fill with mince pies, fresh panettone, traditional puddings and even gingerbread houses. Easter is important as well, with swells of hot cross buns, handmade chocolates, breads and cakes. In Australia, wedding cakes are a bit different than in the US. The traditional wedding cakes here are fruit cakes covered in rolled fondant (usually marzipan flavoured) icing. You can get mud cakes and a variety of other cake types at most bakeries, and you can usually also find ganache or buttercream icing for wedding cakes. Just be prepared for the traditional wedding cake if you have or attend a wedding here.

Cupcakes are also a big trend in Australia as in other parts of the world. We have a few different cupcake-specific shops in Melbourne and many people are now opting for tiered cupcake stands in lieu of cakes at weddings. Whatever your craving for a particular baked good, you're sure to find it in Australia. If you long for something from your homeland, ethnic and foreign-owned bakeshops abound, you just need to search your local area.

Books

As I mentioned in the section on saving money, you will want to consider *Amazon* for major purchases of books. Despite the shipping costs, ordering online from overseas can still work out to be less expensive than purchasing them here. You'll find many independent and used bookstores in Australia as well as national chains such as *Angus & Robertson* and *Dymocks*. *Borders* is also here and it sells music and movies along with books. You will probably be shocked at the prices for books in Australia. I use the library when I want to read something, primarily because I don't want to accumulate books (they go out of date so quickly). But as this may not be your preference, you'll want to shop around.

Cars

Buying a car

I've also mentioned that cars are very expensive to purchase in Australia compared to the rest of the world. Many expats purchase used cars once they arrive because buying a new car is so prohibitive. Still, Aussies love their cars and I've found that, in Melbourne anyway, most people prefer driving to catching public transport no matter how short the distance. In sprawling cities like Sydney and Perth, you will probably need to own a car to get around efficiently.

You will want to begin your search in the local newspaper and perhaps the online classifieds websites. Figure out what you want to buy first and be sure to budget for the annual cost of owning a car as well. You'll need to consider things like loan repayments, registration, annual taxes, insurance (Third Party Insurance is compulsory), fuel and maintenance. The market for cars is similar to everywhere else in the world and you can negotiate prices with both new and used car dealers. If you are purchasing a used car, you will need to confirm that there is no money owing on it through the Register of Encumbered Vehicles. Ensure that any used car you purchase has been serviced regularly (ask to see the log book). You can get an outside organization such as the Australian RAC to inspect a vehicle you are interested in.

You will usually have to pay tax on the purchase price of the car so be sure to ask what those taxes will be when negotiating the base price. You'll also pay a registration transfer fee and stamp duty. Warranty laws vary from state to state. If you purchase a car over a certain amount, Luxury Car Tax will apply unless you buy the car from a private individual.

If you aren't staying in Australia for a long time, you may want to look into a buy-back arrangement with a car dealer. You should get an agreement guaranteed in writing that specifies the percentage of the purchase price you will get back on return of the car after a specified amount of time. You will probably find that it is too expensive to hire a car for an extended period of time, and therefore you can save money while getting a vehicle to use during your time in Australia.

Car buying and selling resources

Autoline   http://www.autoline.com.au
Free online vehicle classifieds

Auto Market   http://www.automarket.com.au
Search for vehicles and buy new or used cars.

Carsales   http://www.carsales.com.au
New and used cars and dealer specials

Cars Guide   http://www.carsguide.com.au
News Limited's auto website for new and used cars

Drive.com.au   http://www.drive.com.au
Fairfax Digital's new and used car site

Trading Post   http://www.tradingpost.com.au/automotive/browse
Classifieds where you can find cars for sale

Travellers Auto Barn http://www.travellers-autobarn.com.au
Buy-back arrangements with a guarantee

Some notes on driving in Australia

Australians drive on the left-hand side of the road and most of the cars here are right-hand drive. Therefore, if you are from a country where people drive on the right-hand side of the road, you will need to become accustomed to new road rules such as giving way to the right, especially if an intersection is not clearly marked. The speed limits and your speedometer will be marked in kilometres per hour (km/h) and speeds will be reduced on residential streets and near schools.

Be aware of animals such as kangaroos, which won't hesitate to leap out in front of your vehicle (usually at dusk or dawn). If you see one kangaroo, there may be others with it, as they tend to travel in groups. Livestock also present a problem when travelling in rural areas as not all farmers fence them in. If you see an animal in the road, apply the brakes, dip your lights and don't swerve if it isn't safe to do so.

Speed cameras (multanovas) are increasingly assisting the police to prevent speeding. If someone in the oncoming lane flashes their lights at you, they could be warning you about one of these (or just that you don't have your headlights on). This is illegal, however people still do it. Seat belts are mandatory in Australia. Children must also be in an approved safety car seat and belted in. Parking can be expensive and difficult to find. Ensure that you are allowed to park in a space before you leave your car there by looking for the signs.

Car maintenance resources

Once you own a car, you may want to join your state's association to assist you with emergency breakdowns and you'll also reap the benefits they provide such as touring maps and guides to accommodation and campgrounds. The umbrella organization is the national Australian Automobile Association (www.aaa.asn.au). The state organizations have reciprocal arrangements with each other so you can use the state facilities when travelling interstate if you're a member in your state of residence. The state organization websites are as follows:

NSW, ACT	National Roads and Motorists Association http://www.nrma.com.au
NT	Automobile Association of the Northern Territory http://www.aant.com.au
QLD	Royal Automobile Club of Queensland http://www.racq.com.au

SA	Royal Automobile Association of South Australia	
	http://www.raa.net	
TAS	Royal Automobile Club of Tasmania	
	http://www.ract.com.au	
VIC	Royal Automobile Club of Victoria	
	http://www.racv.com.au	
WA	Royal Automobile Club of Western Australia	
	http://www.rac.com.au	

Here are some additional resources and retail stores for keeping your car in good condition once you've purchased it:

Autobarn   http://www.autobarn.com.au
Quality automotive aftermarket accessories, spare parts, etc.

Mechanics   http://www.mechanics.com.au
Leading directory of auto mechanics across Australia.

Motorpoint Automotive Articles
http://www.motorpoint.com.au/resources.asp

NRMA motoring services maintaining your car tips
http://www.mynrma.com.au/cps/rde/xchg/mynrma/hs.xsl/maintenance.htm

Supercheap Auto   http://www.supercheapauto.com.au
Leading retailer of auto spare parts, car accessories, navigation systems, etc.

Clothing

Aussies are a fashionable bunch, particularly in the cities. I find the clothing here to be unique and fun, though, like everything else, much more expensive than most other places in the world. On the whole, Australia is a pretty casual place. You can wear jeans in most of the restaurants and I find that I only really dress up when going out to a nightclub, expensive restaurant, party or high-end cultural event. But you will need professional clothes for the office if you work a white-collar job and you'll probably find that the dress is smart casual for your other engagements.

My advice is to bring your clothes with you. Don't dump things thinking you can just buy them on the road as you do when you're travelling. Casual items such as jeans, fitness outfits, shorts and other types of relaxed attire are the most expensive comparatively. We don't have retail stores like *Gap*, *Zara* or *Old Navy* here. You can shop at *Target, Kmart* or *Big W*, but you won't find top-quality items there and even the prices at these "discount" suppliers will surprise you. Likewise, the variety of clothes you'll find in Australia is significantly reduced compared to North America and Europe. I find clothes to be very similar across the major retail chains from season to season, and if I want something unique or different I have to go to an exclusive boutique and pay a lot of money for it.

You might choose to order your clothes online from international retailers and have them shipped. This is a great way to mix local basics with unique items at a lower price than you'll find here. We do have outlets and designer discount stores, but the prices still seem high to me compared to what I used to pay for the same items in the US. That said, you can find some really great stuff in Australia. I really enjoy the fashion sense of Australians young and old. It just may take some time for you to adjust to the selections and prices here.

When it comes to shoes and handbags, you'll find the former to be somewhat more conservative than what you're used to if you come from the US or London, and the latter to be very expensive as well. Leather goods in particular are priced high and if you aren't brand conscious you can find the best deals at markets. Shoe varieties can be downright disappointing if you're looking for something very unique or a huge selection (unless you're prepared to pay top dollar).

When it comes to international brands, you'll find quite a few here, from *Guess* to *Gucci* and all the major sporting and athletic companies sell their wares here (*Nike*, *Adidas*, *Puma*, etc.) If you're looking for a good deal on tailored suits, I suggest that you seek the services of one of the many Hong Kong-based bespoke tailors that come through major Australian cities every month or so. They will measure you for a suit and you can choose your fabrics and styles during the fitting. A few weeks later your suits will be delivered to your door and you'll have the option of ordering by phone or email in the future. Our tailor offers to send out fabric sample books and keeps the patterns on file so re-ordering is easy. If you shop this way, you can have luxurious made-to-measure suits at reduced prices to what you will find locally.

Fashion resources

Australian Fashion Review   http://www.fashionreview.com.au
A blog outlining all of the major Australian brands with news and reviews

Vogue Australia   http://vogue.com.au
The website of the Australian version of the magazine with an excellent forum for discussing clothing, beauty and other items of interest with thousands of in-the-know Australians

Coffee

One of the first things I noticed about Australia was the absence of *Starbucks*. I began my life here in Perth where there was not one to be found, though I did notice that Aussies had their own beloved fancy coffee chains like *Gloria Jeans* and *Dome* (local to Perth).

When I moved to Melbourne, I discovered coffee heaven and I can still say that it is one thing that Australian cities have over big American cities. I recently even read about a couple of Aussies setting up Australian-style coffee bars in New York City.

The national coffee chains in Australia are:

Hudsons   http://www.hudsonscofee.com.au

Gloria Jeans   http://www.gloriajeancoffees.com

The Coffee Club   http://www.wherewillimeetyou.com

You'll find some *Starbucks* and *Coffee Bean and Tea Leaf* chains around, but not as often as you see these Australian chains. *Starbucks* recently culled quite a few of their stores. And once you taste the coffee here you'll understand why.

I actually don't recommend the above three chains for coffee. You'll find an exceptional brew in your local café, and you'll probably sit down to drink it out of a cup or glass rather than carrying out a giant paper cup. Aussies definitely do takeaway coffee and you'll see them with cups in hands all over the sidewalks. But having a meeting over a coffee or tea is quite common and there is an appreciation here for good coffee that I think we lost somewhere with the venti-sized cups and flavoured syrups in the US.

If you order a coffee in Australia, you won't usually get a pour from a carafe of pre-brewed coffee sitting on a burner somewhere. So you'll need to know what to ask for. Here is a quick guide:

Short Black   Shot of espresso

Long Black (Americano)   Shot of espresso and half a cup of water

Flat White	Shot or two of espresso with steamed milk (no froth)
Café Latte	Shot or two of espresso with steamed milk and a touch of foam
Mocha	Latte mixed with cocoa powder
Cappuccino	Shot or two of espresso with steamed milk and froth
Macchiato	Shot of espresso with a drop of froth
Iced Coffee	Shot or two of espresso with cold milk, ice cream and whipped cream

You'll also find that tea is very popular in Australia. You can usually find several varieties at your local café or coffee shop. Aussies drink tea with or without milk and/or sugar. If you're ordering a tea for takeaway, be sure to specify your preference if they don't ask. Sometimes 'with milk' is the default option (often called 'white tea').

Dairy

Cows and other milk-producing animals are the same in Australia as anywhere else. But what you'll find on store shelves may be quite different from what you're used to, even if it's just the labelling that isn't the same.

Milk: Fresh milk is widely available in supermarkets, petrol stations, convenience stores and organic/specialty grocery stores. The three main varieties are full-fat (between 3.2 and four per cent fat or 10 grams of fat per glass), reduced- or low- fat (less than 1.5 per cent fat or four grams of fat per glass) and skim (less than 0.15 per cent fat or less than one gram of fat per glass). Check the calcium levels on your chosen milk brand before you make assumptions about which variety or brand has more calcium. Though not a dairy product, you can also easily find soy milk in Australia. Goats milk, buttermilk and lactose- free or reduced milk varieties are also available. If you are looking for long-life milk or canned milk products, these can be found in the non-refrigerated section of your supermarket.

Cream: Double cream (at least 48 per cent fat) may be known as 'rich cream' in Australia ('extra-heavy' or 'manufacturer's' cream in the US). Regular or Pure cream in Australia doesn't have any thickening agents and has a fat content of around 40 per cent. The big difference with creams in Australia (compared to the US) is what is known as Thickened cream. These are whipping creams with a fat content of at least 35 per cent (known as 'heavy whipping' creams in the US) or light whipping creams (known as 'single cream' in the US), which have 18 per cent milk fat.

In Australia you'll also find Clotted or Scalded cream, which is served with Devonshire teas and used in or as an accompaniment to desserts. The fat content can be anywhere from 48 to 55 per cent. You'll also find sour cream in Australia, though it may be thicker than what you're used to, and Crème Fraiche, which contains lactic acid. Long-life and canned creams are also available.

Cheese: Australians love cheese and you'll find many outstanding local producers of all your favourites from brie to cheddar to blue. Australia also imports cheeses, though you won't find any of the delicious, soft French cheeses if they aren't pasteurised.

Butter: In Australia, you'll find salted, cultured, unsalted and clarified butter as well as dairy blends and reduced fat dairy spreads containing other ingredients such as vegetable oil.

Sweet dairy products such as custard, yoghurt (can also be unsweetened) and ice cream are also found throughout Australia.

Resources

Dairy Australia   http://www.dairyaustralia.com.au
This is a great place to start. Not only will you find extensive information on the dairy industry in Australia, the website has helpful tools such as 'Who Makes What' and an explanation of all the Aussie products from milk to custard.

Electrical items

Technology in Australia may be slightly behind, but sooner or later everything that is available everywhere else in the world makes its way over here. These days you don't have to wait too long for new product releases, but you won't get the latest gadgets before they come out in the US or Japan (unless they are made here). For example, the *iPhone* was available in the US before it reached Australian shores.

This can be good because you are only bombarded with the really great electronic products that everyone has to have. Failed products don't usually make it over here. The downside is that, once again, products are usually more expensive to purchase in Australia. The major retailers are *Dick Smith*, *JB Hi-Fi*, *Harvey Norman*, *Good Guys* and *RetraVision*. Appliances such as refrigerators and washing machines are commonly known as 'white goods.' You'll find all the big-name computer brands here, such as *Acer*, *Apple*, *HP* and *LG* as well as all the international electronics brands like *Canon*, *Sony*, *Samsung*, *Sunbeam* and *Toshiba*.

If you're wondering whether you should bring appliances that you already own from your current country of residence, you'll need to consider a few things. First, your appliance's power supply may not be compatible with the 240v 50hz currency found here in Australia. You can check the power supply of each appliance to see which voltages it is compatible with. If the label says '110v – 240v 50-60hz', for example, that will work here. You'll generally see this listed on camera battery chargers and laptop computer power adapters. If this is the case, feel free to bring those. You will just need a plug adaptor. Running 60hz appliances on 50hz cycles will shorten their life spans due to overheating so you should leave those behind. UK appliances should be ok. For US, Europe or Canada, you will need to check with the manufacturer or an electrician if you are unsure. You can buy a 240v-110v step down voltage converter (transformer) if your appliance isn't compatible. But for small inexpensive items, you may just be better off buying a new appliance once you're in Australia.

Your radios will work fine, however televisions and VCRs may have conversion issues. For example, they may receive the picture okay, but not sound. If you are coming from the US, you should probably just sell your TV and DVD player because of format incompatibility. TVs and DVDs manufactured for the US are created for NTSC, while Australia is on the PAL system. A TV or DVD player you buy in Australia will play both, but you'll have problems getting Australian media to play on your US equipment. Additionally, DVD players are region-specific and Australia is in Region 4. Some of the older, cheaper DVD players will play any region. Otherwise you will need a multi-region player or you'll have to have your player converted. The same region issues may also apply to video game consoles such as *Playstation*, *Nintendo* and *X-Box*. I've provided some additional resources on electronics conversions in chapter four as well as below.

Yet another expensive item category in Australia is power and woodworking tools such as drills, lathes, bandsaws, etc., which will cost a lot to replace in Australia. You might run into the same voltage issues as with your other appliances, but the cost and hassle of buying transformers might be worth it. There are some issues you will need to figure out, however, with regards to surge when you are converting power for certain appliances. I highly suggest that you speak to someone, such as an electrician or the manufacturers of your items, if you are considering bringing your appliances. It is easy to burn out the motor of delicate appliances if you don't know what you're doing.

Resources

Aus Prices http://www.ausprices.com
Find the best prices on computers, electronics, jewellery, photography and household items

CNET http://www.cnet.com.au
All the news and reviews for anything digital including car tech

DVD Demystified http://www.dvddemystified.com/dvdfaq.html
All your DVD questions answered, including information about region codes

Shopbot http://www.shopbot.com.au
Compare prices on not only computers, accessories, video games, appliances, cameras, TVs and other electronics, but also wine, fashion, toys and sports equipment.

TechWatch http://prices.techwatch.com.au
Technology news, reviews and pricing

Voltage Converters http://www.voltageconverters.com
Information about power transformers

Fast Food

Aussies are big consumers of fast food and takeaways, with all the major international fast food chains represented. These include *McDonald's*, *Kentucky Fried Chicken* (just *KFC* here), *Krispy Kreme*, *Pizza Hut*, *Subway*, *Dominos* and *Hungry Jack's* (known outside Australia as *Burger King*). Please note that French fries are called 'chips' over here. For something different, try one of the Australian national chains:

Eagle Boys Pizza http://www.eagleboys.com.au
Australian franchise pizza chain

Grill'd http://www.grilld.com.au
Healthy burger joint with an extensive menu and licensed to sell alcohol

Nando's http://www.nandos.com.au
Portugese-style flame grilled chicken

Noodle Box http://www.noodlebox.com.au
Eastern stir fry, soup, rice and noodle dishes

Red Rooster http://www.redrooster.com.au
Roasted chicken and other chicken treats

Salsa's http://www.salsas.com.au
Fresh Mexican grill found in food court and fast casual locations

Sumo Salad http://www.sumosalad.com
Healthy salad bar chain

Trios http://www.trios.com.au
Healthy wraps, salads and sandwiches

Wendy's http://www.wendys.com.au
Scoop ice cream, smoothies and hot dogs.

These are just a few of the nationwide chains (usually franchises) that exist in Australia. You're sure to discover your own favourites. Food courts are found everywhere in Australia and can be an inexpensive option for lunch or dinner.

Grocery

One of the first things I noticed when I returned to the US after being in Australia for a few years was the difference in grocery shopping. Sure I'd missed some favourite items, but I had forgotten how big our supermarkets are in the US and the variety of stores and alternative providers like discount warehouse chains and gourmet groceries such as *Trader Joe's*. You're lucky to fit two shopping trolleys (carts) side-by-side down the aisles of most Aussie supermarkets and the stores are smaller with fewer brands to choose from. In this section (and other food category sections in this chapter), I'll discuss your grocery shopping options in Australia and provide substitution options for some items you might be missing from back home.

Supermarkets

While you may find a few non-chain grocery stores in your state, most of the supermarkets are chains. A typical Australian supermarket has a produce section, deli, butcher, fish shop (usually thawed frozen fish), dairy and dry goods sections, a frozen section and a health products section. You can find basic kitchenware and house and garden products as well. Alcohol is not sold immediately in the supermarket (you will usually find a bottle shop nearby). Australian grocery stores do not have pharmacies.

Supermarkets are often found inside shopping centres and are almost always located in the main shopping area of a suburb. You will generally need a gold coin (one or two dollar) to use a shopping trolley – this is just a deposit and you'll get it back when you return the trolley (it remains in a little unit on the handle). You can also use a hand-carry basket and go through the express checkout lane at the end of your shopping trip if you don't fill it with too many items.

If you're American, ground beef is called beef 'mince' here, 'tomato sauce' is the same thing as ketchup and 'jelly' can be either gelatine or jam. Cookies are called 'biscuits' (as are crackers), sodas are called 'soft drinks' or 'cool drinks' and diapers are called 'nappies.' Eggs may not be in the refrigerated section but they are still safe to eat. If you're cooking or baking and you can't find a required ingredient, try using The Cook's Thesaurus to find a substitute (http://www.foodsubs.com). I've discussed some other important distinctions between what you're used to and what you may find here under specific headers in this section of the book (see dairy, meat, etc.) There is also a list of hard to find items and substitutions where available at the end of this chapter.

While you can find weekly specials and sale items at the supermarket, you won't find programs like double coupon days. Australians don't really use grocery store coupons at all, in fact. And the supermarket is not always the place to get the best prices on food. Most of the major ones have generic products for sale under their own store brand and buying generic can be one way to save money. The variety of major supermarkets used to be greater but, as in most parts of the world, consolidation has reduced the number of brands in operation. I've listed the major supermarket chains below and the states in which they operate.

Coles   http://www.coles.com.au
              http://www.colesonline.com.au

The second-largest chain in terms of market share, *Coles* stores are found everywhere in Australia. The *ColesMyer* group operates several nationwide retailers throughout the country including *Target*, *Vintage Cellars*, *Liquorland* (often found next to *Coles* supermarkets), *Kmart* and *Officeworks*. *Coles* sells a range of generic store brands called *Coles $martBuy*, *Coles*, *Coles Finest*, *Coles Green Choice* and *Coles Organic*. You can purchase *Coles* gift cards as well as *ColesMyer* group gift cards that work across all of the stores operated by the company. *Coles* supermarkets provide a fuel offer for purchases over a certain dollar amount in one transaction for use at *Coles Express* service stations. You can also earn *FlyBuys* rewards points by shopping at *Coles*. Use *Coles Online* for home delivery in some areas.

Foodworks   http://www.foodworks.com.au
The brand name of the second largest independent retail supermarket group, *Australian United Retailers Limited*, *Foodworks* is located in seven states and territories. Its main competitor is *IGA*. *Foodworks* sells *Black and Gold* brand generic products.

Independent Grocers of Australia (IGA)   http://www.iga.net.au
The local variation of the international group, *Independent Grocers Association*, *IGA* stores have different incarnations depending on what state or territory you're in. In ACT, NSW, QLD, VIC and WA you'll find *Supa IGA* stores, which stock a full range of products. *IGA* are the medium-sized shops while *Friendly Grocer IGA* (not found in WA), *IGA X-press* and *IGA Everyday* (not found in WA) are basically convenience stores. In SA, *IGA* stores are branded as *Foodland*. In TAS, you'll find *Friendly Grocer*, which is a convenience-sized store, *Value Plus* in regional areas, and *Supa IGA*, which are full-sized stores. *IGA*'s generic brands are *Black and Gold* and *IGA Signature*.

Woolworths   http://www.woolworths.com.au
Known as "Woolies," this is the largest supermarket chain in Australia. *Woolworths* has its own liquor stores and offers petrol discounts at *Caltex Woolworths*. *HomeBrand* is the store's line of generic products.

If you're in Melbourne, there is a **Costco** membership warehouse club at the Docklands (http://www.costco.com.au). The chain plans to open a Sydney store. You'll find a range of American foods there as well as bulk-sized products.

Specialty food stores

You can find most things at the supermarket, but if you make exotic dishes or are a foodie or health-conscious person, you'll want to branch out. You can find all sorts of shops selling gourmet or specialty products and sometimes you can find better deals on products at the specialty shops.

If you're preparing any kind of Thai, Japanese, Korean, Indonesian, Vietnamese, Chinese or other type of Asian food, I highly recommend checking out some of the Asian supermarkets or food stores for things like noodles, bean curd, pastes, herbs, sauces, oils, rice and beans as well as fruit, vegetables, meat and seafood. Asian cultures have a rich history in Australia and shopping in these stores can provide a wonderful, authentic experience (at a fraction of the cost for some items).

Butchers are the place to get your meats. I rarely purchase meat from the supermarket. You can find butchers from Germany, Italy the Middle East and Asia among many others as well as specialty butchers who take a biodynamic, free-range, Kosher, Organic, Halal or other special approach to stocking their shops. There is always at least one butcher in most suburbs and this is the place to get your pork, sausages, bacon, lamb, chicken, turkey, beef, rabbit and game along with some interesting Aussie selections like kangaroo, emu and wallaby.

Australian delicatessens are outstanding, partly because of the European heritage of its residents. If you want imported cheeses, cold-pressed honey, French butter, Ligurian olives, specialty olive oil, crusty breads, antipasto, pizza bases, pâtés, terrines, figs, jams, chutneys, vinegars, smoked fish and much more, you'll find what you seek at one of the many specialty delis around. They will also stock deli meats, of course.

Other specialty food shops abound, from ready-to-cook meal stores to Italian or Kosher specialty shops to olive oil shops and gourmet variety stores that will enable you to stock your chef's pantry. Greengrocers offer dry goods, nuts, juice bars and dairy alongside more traditional offerings. Indian shops sell authentic spices, curry pastes, rice and sweets. Middle Eastern shops offer fresh Turkish delight, nuts, dried fruits, pastries, Pomegranate juice, chickpeas and couscous. Kitchenware stores carry all the supplies you'll need to cook at home and restaurant-calibre equipment from knives to pans to plates.

I will warn you that it can be just as expensive to gather your ingredients and cook at home as it is to go out to eat the same meal in a restaurant in the larger cities like Sydney and Melbourne. Shopping around will help you to find the best bargains in your local area, but as someone who loves to cook, I rarely do it to save money. The advantages of cooking at home include enjoyment of the activity and control over what is going into your food. But you can find inexpensive meals at your local café or casual restaurant for around the same price.

National speciality shops

Thomas Dux   http://www.thomasdux.com.au
Operated by *Woolworths*, this is a boutique grocery store chain found in NSW and VIC. These stores claim market-fresh fruit and vegetables, artisan-style breads and a range of specialty cheeses, condiments and sauces along with fresh meat, poultry and flowers. This is a gourmet-style grocery that also sells organic, gluten-free and preservative-free foods.

David Jones Food Hall
Found in *David Jones* stores, this department has a huge selection of quality products from Australia and around the world. You can sometimes find your favourite brands from home on the shelves as well as sections for produce, seafood, cheese, dairy, prepared

foods, baked goods, confectionary and a café. You won't find bargains here but it's worth checking out if you're looking for something special.

USA Foods http://www.usafoods.com.au
While the actual shopfront is located in the suburbs of Melbourne, you can order American food, candy and groceries online and have them shipped anywhere in Australia.

British Sweets and Treats http://www.britishsweets.com.au
Located in Bondi (Sydney) if you wish to visit the physical store or you can order British and Irish foods and candies online.

Markets

This is where the farmers come to town to provide fresh seasonal produce and farm-made products. Australian farmers markets can be found in every major city, even if some of them are only open once or twice a month. Established markets have their own fixed locations and are open a few days a week. In addition to the fruit and vegetable stands, most markets also have bakeries, fishmongers, delis, wine shops, butchers, coffee stalls, chocolatiers, organic producers, ice cream shops and small cafes.

Halal

You should have no trouble finding Halal food products in Australia.

Resources

Australia Halal Food Directory http://www.halalaustralia.com.au
Contains a comprehensive list of Australian food businesses that supply halal food products

Australian Halal Food Services http://www.ahfservices.com.au
Recognised Islamic body under the Australian Government Supervisor Muslim Slaughter (AGSMS) system
Halal.com.au http://www.halal.com.au

The comprehensive halal dining guide featuring restaurants, cafes and other eateries

Health

Health-care products and toiletries will probably be similar to what you're used to, but with less of a selection if you are coming from the US. Some items seem more expensive, while others are comparable. If you want to buy things in bulk, you'll need to visit a store like *Costco* (currently only in Melbourne with one coming soon to Sydney). If there is a product you rely on, I suggest that you stock up on it as long as it is something that you are allowed to bring into the country. For example, a friend of mine is lactose intolerant and the tablets she purchases in the US over the counter to help with the problem are not available in Australia. She stocks up when she visits the States. Vitamin supplements are comparatively expensive in Australia, though you will find plenty of variety. Health food stores are easily found in the cities.

The primary two over the counter pain medication brands in Australia are *Nurofen* (analgesic ibuprofen) and *Panadol* (paracetamol). Bulk sizes of these medications are not readily available, so you may want to pack a bulk package of your favourite pain reliever (be sure to declare it). Antibiotic ointments such as *Neosporin* are not available over the counter so you may want to bring these with you also. If you don't, you'll have to settle for antiseptic ointment and there is not a very wide variety.

Hair care and cosmetics products are readily available but again, you may not find your favourite brand. If you're looking for something special, try *Myer* or *David Jones*. Both stores stock a range of international products that you would find in your local drug store back home. Here, you won't find these products at your local chemist, but *Myer* and DJs often stock them (with the department store prices to match). I've listed brands and products that are hard to find here at the end of this chapter. While it isn't an extensive list, you may find something you can't live without on it.

You can check prices and shop online on discount sites such as *ePharmacy*: http://www.epharmacy.com.au/home.asp

Ice Cream and Gelato

In a country with so much hot weather, you can rest assured that you'll find plenty of frozen treats around. Both scoop and soft serve ice cream are popular in Australia and so are pre-packaged ice cream bars from brands like *Peters* and *Pauls*. You can get your ice cream at the supermarket, specialty food shops, markets and scoop shops as well as from ice cream trucks and stands.

As a tasty and lighter alternative, gelato is very popular in Australia. Heaped in giant trays behind refrigerated glass, this colourful treat can be found all over the place. The difference between gelato and ice cream is that gelato has a greater proportion of whole milk to cream so it's lower in fat. It is also churned at a slower speed than ice cream so it has less air whipped into the mixture. And gelato is usually stored and served at a higher temperature than ice cream.

Jewellery

You can find many unique pieces in Australia and the various jewellers create wares to suit all price ranges. Most of the international retail chains are here (*Tiffany & Co.*, *Cartier*, etc.) but you'll also find talented local craftsmen who can make anything you want. Opal is the national gemstone so you'll find plenty of dealers in major cities. Shop around because there are variations in prices and quality.

South Sea pearls from Cape York and the Torres Strait Islands as well as cultured pearls from WA are another type of native gem. You can also find local semiprecious stones such as topaz, garnets, sapphires, rubies and zircon.

If you're looking to buy something special, check out the local *Yellow Pages* in the jewellery section and then just go shopping. Manufacturing jewellers are a great option for those seeking good prices on wholesale diamonds and other precious stones and you can usually design whatever you want. Just be sure you're dealing with a reputable vendor as you would anywhere else in the world.

Kosher

There are over 100,000 Jewish people in Australia[33] and you can find a variety of butchers and other merchants catering for those who keep kosher.

Resources

Jewish Australia http://www.jewishaustralia.com/food.htm
An online portal for Jewish life in Australia

Kashrut Australia http://www.ka.org.au

---

[33] Office of Multicultural Interests, Government of Western Australia http://www.omi.wa.gov.au/omi_guidelines.asp?choice=5

Everything you need to know to keep kosher in Australia including a products guide

Kosher Australia   http://www.kosher.org.au
The foremost Kosher Certification body in Australasia

Legal

The courts in Australia are responsible for interpreting and applying the laws of the country. It is beyond the scope of this book to fully explain the government and how laws are made or changed in Parliament. I've listed some websites that can explain the process to you in the resources section below.

Every person has the right to be represented by a lawyer in court. If you run into problems with the law or have a dispute with another party, or if you just need some legal advice for any aspect of your life in Australia, you will want to contact a professional.

Barristers and solicitors

In Australia, the word 'lawyer' is a general term referring to a person who has been trained in law and has the qualifications to provide legal advice. Solicitors work directly with clients and provide advice. They also prepare contracts, Wills, letters and probate documents. If a matter goes to court, your solicitor will recommend an appropriate barrister to appear as your advocate in Court. Barristers are more specialised and have a deeper knowledge of case law and precedent than solicitors. Your lawyer may be both a solicitor and a barrister.

Wills

You can seek out a solicitor to prepare your will. If your wishes for the distribution of your estate and your funeral arrangements are very simple, there are plenty of online toolkits that are legal and easy to use, saving you a lot of money in the process. We created simple wills with *Australian Executor Trustees* and they provide support once the will is witnessed and submitted (http://www.aetlimited.com.au). You can do an internet search for 'online wills australia' to find more options.

Resources

Australian Government Law topics
http://australia.gov.au/topics/law-and-justice

The Australian Legal System, NSW Government: Lawlink
http://www.lawlink.nsw.gov.au/lawlink/lawlink_libraries/ll_libraries.nsf/pages/LL_Students_centre_legal_system

Community Legal Centres (CLCs)   http://www.naclc.org.au
Provide legal assistance in a wide range of matters

Department of Foreign Affairs and Trade, About Australia: Legal System
http://www.dfat.gov.au/facts/legal_system.html

Find a lawyer in ACT   http://www.actlawsociety.asn.au

Find a lawyer in NSW
http://www.lawsociety.com.au/community/findingalawyer/findalawyersearch/index.htm

Find a lawyer in QLD   http://www.legalaid.qld.gov.au

Find a lawyer in TAS
http://www.taslawsociety.asn.au/web/en/lawsociety/news/pfirms.html

Find a lawyer in VIC   http://www.liv.asn.au

Find a lawyer in WA   http://www.lawsocietywa.asn.au

FindLaw Australia   http://www.findlaw.com.au
Free legal information

Manchester

In Australia, 'manchester' refers to linens: blankets, duvets, pillowcases, sheets, towels, etc. You'll find these items in a wide variety and different levels of cost and quality. However, I've found it difficult to find certain things, such as very high thread-count Egyptian cotton sheets (1000 is the most I've seen and that was at *Target* of all places) and bed skirts/dust ruffles. If you have these items already, I recommend you bring them with you because, guess what: sheets and towels are expensive in Australia.

Bed and sheet sizes in Australia

Therapeutic Pillow International has a helpful chart of Australian and international bed sizes here:

http://www.the-pillow.com.au/resources/bed_sizes

I still use sheet sets from the US, so you don't necessarily have to toss your sheets out if you notice a difference. They will probably still fit, just not perfectly.

Meat

As I mentioned in the section on grocery items, you can find a wide range of meats in Australia, from the butcher to the deli. I highly recommend you check out your local butcher and delicatessen (or you may find your favourite one a few suburbs over) before settling for the pre-packaged meats at the supermarket. I'm not saying that there is anything wrong with those meats, but I prefer to keep it local.

Here is a list of most of the types of meat you'll find in Australia for consumption:

Bacon (for American-style, look for streaky bacon, 'speck' or 'Keiserfleisch' at your deli and ask for it to be sliced into strips)
Beef
Bologna (called 'Devon', 'Polony' or 'Fritz')
Buffalo
Chicken
Crocodile
Duck
Emu
Goose
Guinea Fowl
Ham
Hares
Kangaroo
Lamb
Liverwurst
Offal
Ostrich
Pastrami
Pheasant
Pork
Poussin
Prosciutto
Puddings
Quail
Rabbit
Ribs
Salami
Sausages (often called 'snags' – many varieties)
Squab
Terrine
Turkey (popular for Christmas)
Veal

Venison
Wallaby
Wild boar

Aussies love burgers and you should know that 'burger' does not necessarily refer to a ground beef patty. Australian burgers might have chicken or another type of meet. If you want beef, you should specify that you want a beef burger when ordering. Burgers with "the lot" usually include mayonnaise, lettuce, beetroot, a fried egg, tomato, onion, bacon and BBQ or tomato sauce.

This is a good reference for cuts of meat in Australia:

http://www.themeatboutique.com.au/epages/tmb.sf/en_AU/?ObjectPath=/Shops/meatboutique/Categories/Info/Cuts_of_Meat

Fish and Seafood

Being an island nation, you'll naturally expect plenty of fresh fish in Australia. While I still see more frozen fish than I'd expect in a land surrounded by oceans, there is still plenty of delicious fresh fish and seafood available. I've found Western Australia to have the nicest fish. Your local fishmonger is the person to visit for the best selection of fresh seafood available in your area.

In Australia, you'll find (amongst others):

Abalone (Greenlip, Blacklip, Brownlip, cocktail, Tiger, Paua, etc.)
Barramundi
Bream
Bugs (slipper lobsters; very delicious and several varieties exist in Oz)
Clams, Cockles & Pipis (including Vongole and Surf Clams)
Crabs (blue swimmer, mud, spanner and more)
Dory
Freshwater crayfish (also known as Yabby, Marron and Redclaw)

Mackerel
Mussels
Oysters
Prawns (known as 'shrimp' if you're American; many varieties)
Rays (Stingrays, Eagle Rays, Butterfly Rays, Skate, etc.)
Red Emperor
Rock Ling
Rock lobster (sometimes called crayfish or crawfish; slightly different from lobsters found in the northern hemisphere)
Salmon
Scallops
Snapper
Squid & Calamari
Trevalla
Tuna (including Bigeye, Albacore, Bonito, Yellowfin and Bluefin)
Whiting (13 species: King George, Sand Whiting, Yellowfin, School and more)

Nursery

If you're American, you'll notice some different terminology for baby products in Australia. Diapers are called 'nappies,' strollers are called 'prams,' cribs are called 'cots' and pacifiers are called 'dummies.' In the appendix of this book, I've listed popular parenting websites where you can meet other parents and discuss the best places to find items you'll need for your baby. There are all kinds of retailers for baby items including natural and organic products.

Office

The biggest difference you might notice if you're from North America is the paper sizes at the office. Australians use ISO paper sizes. Instead of 'Letter' sized paper, the most common paper size for general use is A4 (210mm x 297mm or 8.3" x 11.7"). Instead of 'Legal' sized paper, Aussies use A3 (297mm x 420mm or 11.7" x 16.5").

If you need to make photocopies or have business cards, brochures or posters printed, a variety of copy centre businesses exist around Australia. *Kwik Kopy* is a popular chain. You can also have copies made at national office supply stores (listed below):

OfficeMax   http://www.officemax.com.au
Office products and stationery supplies

Officeworks   http://www.officeworks.com.au
Largest supplier of office and stationery products

Pies, Pizza and Pub Grub

Pies

The Australian meat pie is indeed a staple. A buttery thick pastry filled with ground beef and gravy is the traditional version of this popular food item. But you can find all kinds of wonderful and unusual fillings in pies from chicken and leek to liver to lamb and rosemary. You'll find these in every bakery, convenience store, concession stand and airport; in reality, you can get a pie most everywhere casual food is served in Australia. A common way to eat a pie is to smear some tomato sauce (ketchup if you're American) on top and eat it with your hands right out of the package it came in. Sausage rolls are another popular item, consisting of puff pastry wrapped around sausage meat. These are also served with tomato sauce.

You can find pies and sausage rolls in your supermarket's frozen section to bake at home. Popular brands are *Sargent's*,

Four'N'Twenty and *Mrs. Macs*. 'Party pies' are the miniature version of these and they're often on the finger-food menu at informal gatherings.

Pizza

If you're coming from the US, just forget about finding pizza like you're used to. There are some great pizza places in Australia, but they are very different from American pizza, especially if you're used to New York or Chicago-style pies. Australian pizza tends to be more like California-style pizza, with unique toppings and a thin crust.

You'll notice right away that the pizza chains *Pizza Hut* and *Dominos* have made their way to Australia. But the pizzas from these chains are surprisingly expensive compared to the US. All of the pizza places compete and you'll be able to find a better pizza than one of these two for the same price or cheaper.

Pub Grub

I've made it sound gross, haven't I? Actually, you can get an excellent meal in Australian pubs. Some of them are more upscale than others, but you'll be surprised by how amazing pub food can be in Australia. As a matter of fact, it can be a bit of a letdown when you want a classic, unpretentious pub meal and you've unwittingly ended up in a fancy place.

A typical pub menu in Australia will offer:

Potato wedges (these will be seasoned and served with sour cream and sweet chilli sauce in ramekins on the side)
Soup of the day

Steaks
Bangers and mash (sausages served with mashed potatoes)
Burgers
Schnitzels (Chicken Parma is an Aussie favourite)
Meat pies (freshly made)
Fish and chips
Pastas
Salads

These are just some of the items you'll find. Be sure to wash it down with a pint of your favourite local beer and you're all set (see 'Alcohol' topic in this chapter).

Restaurants

If you don't go to a pub when you eat out, you'll find yourself in one of Australia's many wonderful restaurants and cafés. You can get all kinds of food in Australia and every ethnic group is represented. Some of the international cuisine is better than others, of course. Good Mexican food can be hard to find outside of the big cities. But if you're after Chinese, French, Greek, Indian, Indonesian, Italian, Japanese, Korean, Malaysian, Middle Eastern, Thai, Turkish or Vietnamese, you'll have no trouble finding excellent authentic meals.

'Modern Australian' or 'Contemporary' cuisine usually means that the menu will feature fresh locally sourced meat and produce prepared by a chef and attractively presented. Often you'll notice an Asian influence in this style of food and it can be quite light. Calamari, lamb rump, salmon, scallops, pork belly, duck curry and beef fillets are common menu items. Portions in any restaurant are more European than American. And don't even bother asking for a 'doggie bag;' Aussies don't take home their leftovers and you probably won't have much left over anyway. I accidentally ordered too many ribs in a steak restaurant once and when I asked if I could take the remaining half a kilogram with me, the manager came out and told me it was against the law for them to let me take food from the premises.

When you're looking at a menu, the categories of items will usually be separated into 'starters,' which are appetizers. These may be bites in a separate section or the same thing as 'entrees,' which are the first course items. 'Mains' in Australia refer to the main dish. There will also be a section for desserts. If you do not see this on the main menu, just ask, as many restaurants have separate dessert menus that they bring out after the main meal. Some restaurants may offer 'set-price' menus, which provide a certain number of courses for a price if you order off the specified menu. A longer set-price menu will usually be called 'degustation.' Degustation menus can feature many courses, but the more items on the menu the smaller the portions will be to enable someone to eat all of that food in one sitting. These may be paired with wine for an additional cost.

Another sign you will see in restaurant menus or listed in the food guides is 'BYO' (bring your own). This means that the establishment allows you to bring your own alcohol. What you can bring depends on whether the restaurant is also licensed to sell alcohol itself. If alcohol is sold there, BYO probably only refers to bottled wine and you will pay a corkage fee for the privilege.

Meal times are usually from midday (12 pm) for lunch and around 6 pm for dinner. When you sit down in a nice place, the waiter will usually 'lap' you by unfolding your napkin and placing it on your lap. You may be offered 'still' or 'sparkling' water. If all you want is tap water, be sure to specify that. Otherwise you may see a bottle of expensive water appear on your table. Smoking is banned in all restaurants across Australia and in most areas where food is being served. Unfortunately, some of the outdoor seating areas are not smoke-free. If you see ashtrays, that's a sign to sit inside if you don't want to be bothered by smokers, which are still plentiful in number in Australia.

Restaurant guides and resources

Australian Good Food Guide   http://www.agfg.com.au
Food and travel guide, which awards 'Chef's Hats' to the top eateries; restaurants, accommodation, wineries, bars and attractions are featured

deGroots Best Restaurants of Australia http://www.bestrestaurants.com.au
Find restaurants by suburb, type of cuisine and price. deGroots also has listings of gift certificates, venues, clubs and hotels, which you can access from this web page in the upper-right hand corner.

Eat and Drink   http://www.eatanddrink.com.au
Comprehensive fine food and wine guide with critiques of restaurants, bars, cafes, food stores, wine outlets and wedding/party venues along with food, wine and regional guides and an events calendar

EatingWA http://www.eatingwa.com.au
Perth's interactive restaurant guide with reviews, articles and events

Menulog   http://www.menulog.com.au
Find menus for restaurants and get food delivered Australia-wide.

Your Restaurants   http://www.yourrestaurants.com.au
NineMSN's site for restaurants in Sydney and Melbourne; their 'yourTime' guides also cover movies, television, pubs, bars and gigs and you can access these through this web page

Service

The service industry in Australia can be frustrating at times. Aussies are not sticklers about customer service and they tolerate a lot. I regularly walk into the major department stores and stand at the counter, waiting for the salespeople to finish their chat about what they did over the weekend before someone notices me and reluctantly comes over to assist. You won't get very far if you give any kind of a surly attitude to a clerk at the service window of a bank or government office. If there is a line out the door of the post office and it's also time for someone's lunch break, she will take it and there isn't a thing you can do about it. Get used to these annoyances. I don't agree with the egalitarian relationship of customer to service person, but I no longer add aggravation to my day by wishing things were different and complaining about it.

Similarly in restaurants and bars, don't expect every establishment to have perfect service. Australian waiters and bartenders don't work for tips (tipping is not customary here) and therefore they are making the same amount of money whether they knock themselves out for you or not. The no-tipping custom applies also to taxi drivers, hotel employees, hairdressers and everyone else working in the service industry. I've had some amazing service in restaurants. Usually this is at the more expensive places, but sometimes I find myself pleasantly surprised by friendly, conscientious employees who genuinely want to do a great job. I worked as a waitress and a sales clerk for years when I was studying so I always have empathy for hard-working people in the service sector. It also makes me more aware and critical of the truly awful examples. So you won't find bad service everywhere in Australia, but if you don't get what you consider to be good service, don't take it too personally.

Just because Australians don't work for tips doesn't mean that you can't tip. If we go out to dinner and our waiter makes sure we have a great night, we often tip. Not 15-20 per cent of the cheque or (service is built into the price on the menu), but enough to show our gratitude. Servers in Australia are always grateful if you just round up or leave your change. If you go out to a really expensive restaurant, you probably should tip unless your service has been terrible. And don't ever tip if you receive bad service no matter where you are.

Snacks

There's no shortage of sweet and savoury treats in Australia. In this section I'll focus mainly on packaged items and what brands are available from your local supermarket. I haven't mentioned international brands, only the primary Australian ones. There is plenty more available beyond what I describe here and please note that these are just my personal reviews. You may not be able to find your favourite brand of snack food on Australian shelves. Hopefully you'll be adventurous and try a new substitution. Buying imported treats will get expensive after awhile.

Biscuits

These can be either sweet cookies or savoury crackers. *Arnott's* is my favourite brand for chocolate biscuits. They are the makers of the ubiquitous and internationally famous *Tim Tam* range of biscuits. *Tim Tams* are a bit too sweet for me, but *Arnott's* makes a variety of other products that I'm in love with. The key ingredient is the chocolate, which is made especially for the company's products. Try *Butternut Snap*, *Royals*, *Monte* or *Caramel Crowns*. *Nabisco's Oreos* can be found on Australian shelves but only the original variety, sadly. There is also a range of products for children. *Weight*

Watchers products are also sold in Australia if you're looking for a healthy alternative.

Arnott's also makes a range of non-chocolate sweet biscuits and one I'll mention is *Granita*. I love to bake cheesecakes and was sad about the absence of graham crackers in Australia. My mother-in-law uses *Granita* biscuits instead for her cheesecake base and these are certainly a suitable, if much lighter, alternative. I've also heard Americans mention using digestive biscuits as a substitute for graham crackers but I haven't tried using them myself.

When it comes to crackers, *Arnott's* has a great selection again with both regular and healthy alternatives such as the *Vita-wheat* range. *Nabisco Captains Table* and *Ritz* brand crackers are available as are *Carr's*. You can also find *Saltine* style crackers, called *Salada* here (*Arnott's* again). Rice cakes and snacks are popular light alternatives to crackers as well. You might notice 'chicken' flavoured biscuits and potato chips around. While they don't taste like chicken, they have seasoning on them that might be used on a roasted chicken. Give them a try. If you like them, you'll be pleased to know that some restaurants like *Red Rooster* put chicken salt on their chips (fries). Just another Aussie specialty and you can find a package of the stuff at the grocery store for home use.

Chocolate and confectionary

Cadbury is probably the most widely available type of chocolate in Australia. You can get blocks in an assortment of styles from solid to chocolate-covered wafer bars. *Cadbury* also makes the chocolate bars *Boost*, *Dairy Milk*, *Twirl*, *Cherry Ripe*, *Crunchie* (chocolate-covered honey comb), *Flake*, *Picnic* (*Cadbury's* answer to *Snickers*), *Fruit & Nut*, *Time Out* and *Turkish Delight*. The other main inexpensive chocolate brands are *Mars*, *Kinder* and *Snickers*. If you're American, what we call *3 Musketeers* is called *Milky Way* here and standard *Mars* bars are like *Milky Way* in the US. The specialty chocolate brands are *Ferrero*, *Lindt*, *Nestle* and *Whittakers*. If you're happy to spend a couple of dollars per chocolate, head to one of the specialty chocolatiers such as *Koko Black*, *Max Brenner* or *Haigh's*.

The candy brands easily found in Australia are *Allens*, *Chupa Chups*, *Mentos*, *Tic Tac*, *Wrigley*, *Skittles*, *Starburst*, *Werther's* and *Wonka*. Collectively called 'lollies', you can find all types of candies including gourmet treats like *Jelly Belly* and rock candy. Nougat is also popular and eaten just on its own, as are toffees, caramels and other boiled lollies.

Potato and corn chips and popcorn

Twisties, *Cheezels* and *Burger Rings* are the eponymous brands in Australia. These are puffed snacks covered with a salty cheese, chicken or onion powder. The only *Cheetos* brand snacks you'll find are generally Cheese & Bacon Balls. The popular potato chip brands are *Smith's*, *Red Rock Deli*, *Samboy* and *Arnott's Kettle Chips*. Corn tortilla chips are also popular and served with salsa. If you want a lighter treat, microwave popcorn is available from *Uncle Toby's* and *Poppin* brands among others. If you're from the UK, I'm sorry to say that you won't find the wide variety of interesting flavoured crisps that you can get back home.

Other snacks

If you head to the grocer's freezer section, you'll find plenty to pop into your oven. The unique selections are *Chiko* rolls, which are like a large Chinese spring or egg roll. There is no chicken in these rolls but rather mutton, rice and vegetables. You can also find these at events such as football games. Another snack food is the Dim Sim, a Chinese-style meat dumpling that you can buy frozen or at stalls in markets or shopping centres. These should not be confused with Yum Cha. You can also find mini quiches and party pies throughout Australia (see the section on pies in this chapter).

Stamps and shipping

Mail is delivered from Monday through Friday in Australia. You may find a couple of post shops that are open on Saturday mornings, but this is by no means a guarantee that one is operating near you. Most post offices are open during the week from 9 am until 5 pm and these are all *Australian Post Shops*, which also offer a range of services and retail goods for purchase.

The cost of sending a regular-sized letter within Australia is 55 cents. You can buy booklets of stamps from your local post outlet. If you need to send a regular letter overseas, the cost is usually AUD 2.10. Greeting cards are less expensive to send than letters if you are not including any additional paper or items in the envelope. You can also ship parcels within Australia or overseas at *Australia Post* and they have a variety of options for express deliveries, tracking, registered mail and insurance. You can find everything you need to know about Australia's postal service on their website: http://auspost.com.au

Other parcel handling services in Australia

DHL   http://www.dhl.com.au

FedEx   http://fedex.com/au

You can also use courier services. These are listed online or in the *Yellow Pages* for your local area.

Transport

Taxis

Taxis operate throughout Australia and they are similar to taxis you'll find anywhere else in the world. You can hail them on the street, wait for them in a taxi queue (these aren't everywhere as in some countries) or call for one to pick you up. The cabs may not always be yellow in colour, depending on where you are in the country and what company you use. You can generally pay with cash, credit or debit cards. *Cabcharges* are also used by businesses as a way of providing company-paid transportation to their employees or clients. If you have a *Cabcharge* to use, simply present it to your driver at the end of the ride and the fare amount will be charged to the person or business who issued you with the charge.

You may notice that some Australians get into the front passenger seat of taxis instead of riding in the back seat when travelling by themselves. This is part of an egalitarian tradition and perfectly acceptable for you to practice as well. You will not offend the driver if you sit in the back seat, however. Just do whatever you are most comfortable with.

Most taxis have a flag fall, which is a minimum rate applied at the start of your journey.

Cabcharge http://www.cabcharge.com.au
Learn more about this charge account system or implement it in your business.

13CABS Australia http://www.taxisaustralia.com.au
Australia-wide taxi cab booking

Taxi 131008 http://www.131008.com
Australia-wide taxi bookings

Yellow Cabs   http://www.yellowcab.com.au
Map showing phone numbers for Australian taxi companies

Trains

I've covered interstate travel completely in the travel chapter at the end of this book. But if you're travelling locally, Australian cities operate their own suburban or city trains and you should check with your local service provider for specific information, route planners and timetables. In Melbourne, there is also a tram service and in Sydney, a ferry service.

Sydney, city and suburban   http://www.cityrail.info

Melbourne, city and suburbs   http://www.metrotrains.com.au
Melbourne public transport (all)   http://www.metlink.com.au

Victoria, regional   http://www.vline.com.au

Brisbane, Sunshine Coast, Gold Coast
http://www.citytrain.com.au

Brisbane-Townsville-Cairns   http://www.traveltrain.com.au

Perth   http://www.transperth.wa.gov.au

Western Australia   http://www.transwa.wa.gov.au

Adelaide   http://www.adelaidemetro.com.au

Buses

Sydney   http://www.sydneybuses.info

Melbourne public transport (all)   http://www.metlink.com.au

ACT   http://www.action.act.gov.au

Brisbane http://www.translink.com.au

Adelaide http://www.adelaidemetro.com.au

Perth http://www.transperth.wa.gov.au

Tasmania http://www.metrotas.com.au

Airport trains and shuttles

Airport Link (Sydney) http://www.airportlink.com.au
Fast, frequent travel between Sydney Airport and the city centre by train

Skybus (Melbourne) http://www.skybus.com.au

Airtrain (Brisbane, Gold Coast) http://www.airtrain.com.au

There are a number of independent operators wherever there is an airport so consult your local Yellow Pages or online if your city isn't listed or for alternatives to the above airport transfer solutions.

Used goods

If you really need to save money on items for your home or office, consider buying second-hand goods from thrift stores (called 'OpShops' in Australia), consignment shops or private sellers. Aussies frequently recycle goods by selling them or sometimes even offering things for free. You can save a lot of money on quality and sometimes barely used items this way. These shops are also a great source of unique or vintage items. You may consider selling your unwanted items as well.

Websites for buying second-hand

Cracker Classifieds http://cracker.com.au

Ebay http://www.ebay.com.au

Gumtree http://gumtree.com.au
Free classifieds

Tip: Check out the online communities I listed in the resources section of chapter one. People often sell their used goods on these sites in a special section that you can access if you are a member. Expats move around a lot so that's a great place to look.

OpShops and Consignment stores

Opshop.org http://opshop.org/opshop_index.php
Listings by state and territory

HFOC http://hfoc.com.au
Home furnishings on consignment (Sydney)

Vegetables and Fruits

Australian farmers grow some pretty amazing crops and imported fruits and vegetables subsidise what isn't available seasonally. I prefer to buy in season but you can almost always find a produce item that you require at any time of year. You just might pay more for imported items. What may be different for you are the names of items in Australia. Below, I've provided a list of some items that might be called something else here in Australia.

Listed by Australian name (other names)

Amaranth (Chinese spinach)
Beetroot (beet)

Bitter melon (bitter gourd, balsam pear)
Black Sapote (Black persimmon)
Bok Choi (bok choy)
Breadfruit (Sukun)
Broccoflower (hybrid mix of broccoli and cauliflower)
Capsicum (bell peppers: red, green, yellow)
Carambola (Star fruit)
Celeriac (celery root)
Chives (green onions)
Coriander (cilantro)
Currant (red currant)
Curry Leaf (Indian curry leaves)
Dragon fruit (Pitahaya, strawberry pear)
Drumstick (horseradish tree, ben oil tree)
Durian (Civet fruit)
Eggplant (aubergine)
Feijoa (Guavasteen, Pineapple guava)
Galangal (Siamese ginger, galingale)
Garland Chrysanthemum (chrysanthemum greens)
Hairy Melon (hairy gourd, fuzzy gourd)
Horned Melon (African cucumber, horned cucumber, kiwano, prickly cucumber)
Kale (borecole, collard, german cabbage, scotch cabbage)
La Lot (wild betel)
Long Melon (Fuzzy Melon, White Gourd, Winter Melon)
Mabolo (Butterfruit, Velvet apple)
Mache (Corn salad, Lamb's lettuce)
Marjoram (Oregano, Sweet Marjoram)
Nashi (Apple-Pear, Asian Pear, Crystal Pear, Oriental Pear, Sand Pear)
Okra (lady's fingers)
Paw Paw (papaya)
Snow or sugarsnap peas (sweet pea, Chinese pea)
Pepino (Melon pear)
Perilla (beefsteak plant, shiso)

Persimmon (Kaki)
Prickly Pear (Indian Fig)
Pummelo (Pamplemouse, Shaddock)
Rockmelon (canteloupe)
Sapodilla (Chico)
Shallot (Eschallot)
Silverbeet (Swiss Chard)
Soursop (Guanabana)
Spring Onion (green onions, eschalots)
Sprouts (Alfalfa, Bean Sprouts, Mung Bean Sprouts, Snow pea shoots)
Squash (Button squash, scallopini)
Sugar Apple (Custard Apple)
Sweet corn (corn)
Tamarillo (Tree tomato)
Tatsoi (rosette bok choi or Chines flat cabbage)
Vegetable spaghetti (spaghetti marrow, spaghetti squash)
Winged Bean (asparagus bean, goa bean)
Witlof (Belgian endive, chicory)
Zucchini (courgette)

A handy guide to potatoes

http://www.westernpotatoes.com.au/go/consumers/varieties/which-potato-to-use

Water

Most of Australia is drought-prone and wherever you live, you will probably hear about water shortages and conservation, including limitations on the days you can water your lawn, water-saving showerheads and other measures. I've seen houses with outdoor showers rigged so that the water goes into the ground and people also collect water from their laundry (called 'grey water') to give to their plants.

When it comes to drinking water, we've had different experiences. The tap water in Tasmania tastes amazing, while our tap water in Melbourne tastes awful (in three different suburbs). We use *Brita* jugs to filter our water and many people who own houses have water filtration systems installed in their kitchens at the sink. I've heard good things about Sydney's tap water, but I can't confirm anything about the taste of it.

If you don't mind spending the money, you can buy bottled water to drink. Large jug and dispenser-style water coolers are readily available in Australia and you'll see them in most offices. This will depend on your personal preference. Some of my friends in Melbourne swear that their water tastes fine.

Resources

Australian Government web page on water http://www.environment.gov.au/water
A good resource to explain the water situation in Australia

Greywater Information Central http://www.greywater.net
Portal for information about recycled water from the home

Save Water http://www.savewater.com.au
Resource on how to conserve water

Water quality research Australia http://www.wqra.com.au
Research body dedicated to water quality in Australia

Prices for 100 commonly used items in Australian Dollars

Listed below are the prices for commonly sought-after goods located in the CBD or inner suburbs of Melbourne at the time of writing. All prices are listed in Australian dollars (AUD). This list is intended to give you an idea of what things cost here compared to where you currently live. Prices on some items can change quickly so please use this as a general guide only to determine the relative cost of living in Australia. You may find items to be significantly more expensive in regional and rural areas or in cities outside of Melbourne. The prices listed here do not reflect sale or special discount prices.

Air conditioner, 5.2KW Cooling, 6.2KW Heating – *Fujitsu* $1699.

Aluminium foil, 20 metre (m) x 30 cm roll – generic brand $3.66

Anti-perspirant (men's), 78 grams (g) – *Gillette Clear Gel* $6.18

Apples, 1.5 kilograms (kg) - 'Red Delicious' from supermarket $4.95

Bananas, 1 kg – from market $1.99

BBQ grill – *Jackeroo Burwood Roaster* 4 Burner $169.

Beef mince, lean, 500 g – from supermarket $6.00

Beer, 375 mL bottle 24 pack – *Crown Lager* (local premium) $49.99

Big Mac (*McDonald's*) $4.35

Blu-ray disc player - *Toshiba* $279.

Board game – *Monopoly* $39.95

Book, bestselling paperback $22.99

Boxer shorts (men's), 3 pack $15.00

Bread, sliced loaf – *Tip Top Sunblest* Wholemeal, 650 g $3.79

Butter, slightly salted, 250 g - *Lurpak* $4.73

Camera, digital – *Sony Cybershot* 12.1 Megapixel, 3x Optical Zoom $149.

Candy bar – *Mars*, 53 g $1.91

Car, new, base price - *Nissan Maxima 2.5 250 ST-L xtronic CVT* $33,990

Cereal, 775 g box – *Kellogg's Corn Flakes* $6.19

Cheese, 750 g block – *Bega* Tasty $10.89

Clock radio/alarm – *Sony* with *iPod* dock $176.

Coca-cola, 375 mL   24 pack cans $24.84

Coffee, instant, 150 g – *Nescafe Mild Roast* $8.71

Coffee, small latte takeaway $3.25

Computer - *Dell Intel i3* w/ 18.5" Monitor 4GB RAM 500GB Hard Drive $999.

Concert ticket – int'l tour, popular act, best available seat $125

Condoms, 12 pack - *Durex Natural Feel* $7.12

Dishwashing liquid, 600 mL bottle – *Palmolive Lemon* $4.57

Doritos, bag, 200g $3.26

DVD rental, new release, overnight $6.00

Eggs, one dozen x-large cage – supermarket brand $2.50

Fertiliser, All Purpose garden – *Brunnings NPK*, 500g $2.61

Flour, plain, 1 kg – supermarket brand $2.61

Football game ticket, reserved seat $45

Formula, infant, *Nestle Nan Pro Gold from 6mos Follow On*, 900 g $25.69

Foxtel (cable TV), all channels *Platinum iQ* - monthly $120

Glass cleaner, *Windex*, 500 mL $4.24

Greeting card, regular size - *Hallmark* $4.99

GPS system – *Navman MY50T* $236.

Honey, *Beechworth Honey Squeeze*, 375g $5.22

Ice cream, *Bulla Creamy Classics* Vanilla, 2 L $7.50

iPhone 3G handset, 8 GB (does not include usage) $719.

iPod Classic, 160 GB $329.

Jam, strawberry conserve 500 g jar - *Cottee's* $3.77

Kettle – *Sunbeam* 2400 W cordless, 1.7L $44.95

Laundry soap, powder – *Omo Small & Mighty*, 1 kg $11.98

Light globe, mini spiral 18 watt edison screw – supermarket brand $10.88

Magazine, annual subscription – *Good Health* $54.95

Mascara, tube – *L'Oreal Telescopic Explosion* $26.95

Mattress, queen-sized – *Sealy Spinecare Deluxe Ensemble* $999.

Meat, deli roasted ham, 1 kg $15.50

Microwave oven, 1100W – *Sharp Touch control* $199.

Milk, reduced-fat, 2 L – supermarket brand $2.99

Motor oil, 1 L – *Shell Helix Plus 15W-50* $14.70

Movie, *Blu-ray* new release $35

Movie, theatre ticket, one adult $17.50

Mustard, 215 g – *Maille Dijon* $3.90

Nappies – *Huggies Crawler Ultra Dry* 6-11 kg 30 pack $14.98

Nintendo Wii game console $379.

Olive oil, 1 L - *Bertolli Extra Virgin* $13.61

Oregano, dried, 18 g - *Masterfoods* $4.76

Oreo cookies, 300 g $3.48

Paint – *Dulux Designer Silk*, 10 L $169.

Pain reliever, 24 pack *Panadol Gel Capsules* $4.02

Paper towels, 2 pack rolls – *Kleenex Viva* $4.89

Pasta, spaghetti – *Barilla* 500 g $2.73

Perfume – *Calvin Klein Eternity for Women Eau de Parfum* spray 100 mL $120.

Petrol (fuel), premium unleaded, 1 L $1.22

Photo, 4" x 6" print $0.29

Pillow - *HealthGuard* $20

Pizza, large - *Pizza Hut Super Supreme*, ordered online $7.95

Popcorn, microwave – *Uncle Toby's Butter*, 3 family bag pack $4.96

Printer – *HP Laserjet*, 14 ppm black, 1200 dpi $137.

Razors – *Gillette Sensor 3* Disposable 4 pack $7.19

Refrigerator, 410 L Frost Free - *Whirlpool* $899.

Rice – *Uncle Ben's* Long Grain White, 500 g $2.83

Rubbish bin bags – *Glad Wave Top Tie Citrus* 27 L, 72 pack $7.07

Sausages, pork, 1 kg – supermarket brand $7.86

Sheets, queen set (flat, fitted and two pillowcases), 225 thread count $59

Sneakers, men's – *Nike Air Max Tailwind + 2010* $199.99

Soap, bar – *Nivea Bath Care Creme* 2 pack $4.24

Sponges – *Stay Fresh Thick* 3 pack $3.80

Stereo system, compact with 3 disc changer - *Jensen* $179.

***Subway* foot-long *Club* sandwich** $8.75

Sugar, white granulated, 1 kg – supermarket brand $1.62

Tampons, *Carefree* Regular 20 pack $5.19

Tea, English Breakfast, *Twinings Classics* 100 bag pack $9.69

Television, HD, LCD, 32" - LG $799.

Tissues, box – *Kleenex*, 250 pack $3.15

Toilet paper – *Kleenex Cottonelle* 8 roll pack $7.18

Tomato sauce (ketchup), 920 mL – *Masterfoods* $4.57

Toothpaste, 175 g tube – *Colgate Regular flavour* $3.59

Towel, bath, 69 x 140 cm, good quality $17.00

Undershirts, men's, cotton, good quality, 2 pack $19.99

Vacuum cleaner – *Dyson* upright $599.

Vitamins, multi – *Centrum*, 100 tablets $22.99

Vodka, bottle – *Absolut*, 700 mL $41.99

Washing machine, front load, 1000 rpm spin – *Whirlpool* 7.5 kg $699.

Water, bottled – *Frantelle Natural Spring* 600 mL bottle 12 pack $8.27

Wine, 750 mL bottle, good quality Australian red $30.00

Items that are hard to find Down Under (with some potential substitutions)

Anti-perspirant/deodorant in stick form

A1 steak sauce

Big Red gum

Bisquick

Breakfast cereal variety (particularly the wide range of children's ones)

Brown soda bread

Cheese - very sharp (no matter what the label says)

Cheezits

Cherry Coke, Cherry 7-up

Chex Mix

Cool-whip

Crest *toothpaste*

Crisco (try *Copha* or lard)

Crystal Light

Dr Pepper

Fabric softener dryer sheets

Flavoured morsels (for cookies): only milk, dark and white chocolate available

French dressing (American-style)

French-fried onions (the ones that come in a can)

Gerber baby food

Graham crackers (try *Arnott's Granita* or digestive biscuits)

Grape jam

Grits

Haribo candies

Hershey's chocolate products

Jolly Rancher candies

Kool-Aid (try cordial)

Lincoln Logs

Maraschino cherries

Marshmallows (American-style)

Neosporin

Old Bay seasoning

Pampers

Pillsbury

Pop Tarts

Pork pie

Pumpkin (canned)

Pumpkin pie

Ranch dressing

Reese's products

Root Beer

Rubbing alcohol (try *Isocal*)

Scotch eggs

Really sour sourdough bread
Stain remover wipes
Sushi rolls (exotic types)
Tampons with an applicator
Tupperware
24-hour stores
Twinkies
Twizzlers
Tylenol
Unpasteurised cheese
Velveeta

8.

Chapter Eight: Getting along - culture differences and how to meet people

Being an expat makes you a foreigner, which is a condition all its own. The globalised world has made it common for people to live in unfamiliar places: for some people, like me, it is a lifestyle. I've always moved around. It's a symptom of my background as a person whose parents relocated to what might as well have been a different country at the time. As US northerners, or "Yankees" as they are known in the US (the term 'Yank' is used as an annoying term for someone from the US in general), my parents moved to Alabama before I was born for my father's job. I never felt at home there. When I left Birmingham to go off to university in another state, my parents divorced and moved on to new places as well. So I never returned to the city where I grew up, having no family members left there and no real desire to go back. To this day, I have not returned.

That has left me with a freedom that would make most people uncomfortable. For me, the major downside is that I never have a succinct answer when the question, "Where are you from?" comes up. It is probably the most uncomfortable question people can ask me because there is no easy way to answer and I'm sure people are sorry they asked when I give them the back story. But it is a common question to ask people. Most of us have a simple answer.

So if you haven't ever left your home city or country, you're in for a major change. I would call it a treat, but as I've said, I'm a bit on the strange side. Despite the fact that expats are widespread, the situation of being an expat is no less difficult for the individual. Yes, we often notice plenty of foreigners in our hometowns and homelands. Countries like Australia and the US are so made up of immigrants that it is often said that everybody is foreign in these countries. These days, the same can be said for big cities like London and Paris, where cultural clashes have even led to violence. At first, you might feel a gigantic sense of freedom, even recklessness. You will likely be challenged, engaged, stimulated and, no doubt, anxious. If you're a refugee, your feelings will be completely different.

For me, the hardest thing about being foreign in Australia is that I don't think I'll ever completely fit in here. My accent is different and, despite Melbourne's claims to be cosmopolitan, hip and international, heads still spin around when I open my mouth. Unless I've had a few too many drinks, I'm not your stereotypical loud-mouthed American either. My accent, though peppered with Aussie expressions and a slight Australian accent, is still very American. Most people are nice when I chat to them, but there is still a division. In job interviews, customer service and social interactions, 75 per cent of the time I feel a palpable barrier between myself and the Australians I meet. Most of my close friends are foreigners and the majority of them have had very similar experiences.

This is not to say that it's necessarily because of my being American. The times I don't feel this way are the situations in which I'm speaking to a non-Melburnian or someone who has travelled a great deal and lived abroad themselves. You see, Australians are not like Americans in a very fundamental way: most of them stay put in their home states. They may fly off to Europe to go on a

Contiki tour, live in London on a working holiday visa for a couple of years or use their British passports to work and live somewhere else for awhile, but inevitably they all come back to Australia and the vast majority return to (or never leave) the city where they grew up. University students do not typically go to interstate schools, living instead at home with their parents while they study locally. If you're from a country like France, this will seem normal to you. But to transient Americans, this will be a complete and utter culture shock.

So I don't take it personally. My husband, being from Perth, is as much of an alien as I am in Melbourne. Perhaps things would be different if we lived in Sydney, but from my experiences living in Perth and Melbourne, and from speaking to so many people over the last few years about this subject, I can emphatically tell you: don't expect to come here and just fit right in. I'll include a disclaimer here: if you're from the UK, you'll probably have a smoother transition. I am not English so I don't know for certain how it feels to migrate to Australia. However, people from the UK, from what I can see, tend to fare just fine in Australia. The English have been here since Australia's inception and Aussies are comfortable with that. There are plenty of "Pom" jokes and jibes to be sure, but for the most part, the English are accepted.

So how can you increase your chances of a pleasant transition to living Down Under?

Be nice about it

I'm just going to put this out there on its own. Invariably, you're going to find fault and frustration with any new place in which you live. But keep your whingeing and gripes to yourself. Be exceedingly nice and polite. Avoid even the slightest criticisms of the country, the people or how things are done. It is not a good idea to enter someone's home and start redecorating. You will also drive yourself crazy with a negative attitude. Try to look at the positives in everything and remember that you made the decision to become an expat.

You will naturally be difficult to satisfy. Things will be very complicated and frustrating for you during your first months in a new place. Even once you settle in, you'll likely feel homesick and even nostalgic for your life in your home country. And this will intensify with everything you decide to dislike about your new habitat. There will be moments of regret, and remorse and doubt can creep in at any moment. There will be stress and metamorphosis. You will learn new things about yourself that you might not like or recognise.

The transition to a new place is a process. You must be a participant in this process, influencing your own mental state throughout this turbulent time. The wonderful thing about attitudes is that they can be adjusted. Unless you have a mental deficiency, you can choose to feel however you like. Look for the positive things about your new home. Try to think about the reasons you originally thought about migrating from the last place you lived. Write them down if you have to and stash them somewhere for particularly dark moments. At the end of the last chapter I will share my experience of returning home to the US after three years of living full-time in Australia. I did not leave the US because I was unhappy there. But it was very different from the place I left five years ago. At least it seemed different to me.

Transitioning from American English to British English

Because it is a Commonwealth country, Australians speak 'standard' (that is, British) English. Australians also have their own expressions and words that are different from even British English. You will want to begin this transition right away if you are American or if your English language instruction was in American English. While the spoken words for most things sound the same phonetically (except for your accent), many words are spelled differently. If you work in a profession where written English is essential for your job (as a journalist, teacher, writer, editor, etc.), you will want to purchase a comprehensive book on the subject and familiarise yourself with Australian style guidelines immediately. For everyone else, here is a brief crash course in the major differences.

Collective nouns

In British English, collective nouns such as 'team' can be used as plural words ("the team are winning"). American English usually calls for collective nouns to be singular ("the team is winning").

Dates and expressions of time

The date in Australia is written with the day first, then the month, then the year. April 1, 2010 (4/1/10) as written by an American, will be written 1 April 2010 (1/4/10) by an Australian. You may also hear expressions such as 'tomorrow week,' which means a week from tomorrow. A fortnight is two weeks. The 24-hour clock is also used in Australia more frequently than in the US (for example, 18:00 instead of 6 pm). You may hear people say 'half seven' instead of 'seven thirty.'

Past-tense

You may see the past tense and past participle of some verbs written and pronounced as burnt, dreamt, learnt, leapt, smelt, spilt, etc. as opposed to burned, dreamed, learned, leaped, smelled, spilled, etc. It is still correct English to spell these words the latter way. Just be aware that the former usage is also in play in Australia.

Spelling

Vowels: 'o' becomes 'ou', for example: *behaviour, colour, honour, glamour, flavour, labour, neighbour, odour, vapour*

Words that end in –g may have a –ue at the end:
'Analog' and 'catalog' become 'analogue' and 'catalogue'

The letter 'z' (pronounced 'zed' in Australia) becomes 's', for example: 'Analyze' becomes 'analyse' (though use of 'z' is increasingly common).

'-er' becomes '-re' (centre, litre, theatre, etc.)

Others

aeroplane = airplane
aluminium = aluminum
arse = ass
cheque = check
disc = disk
enquire = inquire
enrolment = enrolment
grey = gray
traveller, travelling = traveler, traveling

Terminology

British/Australian	American
arvo	afternoon
'B' road	rural road
barrack for, support	root for, go for
bathers	swimsuit
bench	counter
biro	pen
bitumen	asphalt
block of land	lot
bloke	man
bonnet	hood
boot	trunk
bumper	fender
busker	street performer
car park	parking lot
caretaker	janitor
castor sugar	confectionary sugar, powdered sugar
chips	French fries
chook	chicken
cot	crib
crisps	potato chips
dole	welfare
dummy	pacifier
entrée	first course
elastic, lacky band	rubber band
estate agent	realtor
fairy floss	cotton candy
flaky	unreliable
flat	apartment
flogging	beating
footpath	sidewalk
ground floor	first floor (in Australia, entrance level is the 'ground' floor)

gearbox	transmission
half milk, half cream	half and half
hundreds & thousands	sprinkles
jocks	men's underwear
jumper	sweater
lavatory, toilet	restroom, washroom, bathroom
lift	ride, elevator
lolly	candy
lorry	truck
main course	entrée
mobile phone	cell phone
nappy	diaper
notice board	bulletin board
noughts and crosses	tic tac toe
overtake	pass
paper knife	letter opener
petrol	gasoline, gas
piss; piss off; pissing	beer; go away; raining hard or laughing
polo neck jumper	turtle neck sweater
post	mail
pram	[baby] stroller
punnet	pint
quay (pronounced 'key')	wharf
queue	line
rates	taxes
rego	car registration
rubber	eraser
rubbish	garbage
scone	biscuit
sealed road	paved road
serviette	napkin
singlet	tank top
spanner	wrench
sticky tape	scotch tape
tap	faucet, spigot

ta	thanks
tea	supper (though 'tea' can sometimes just mean 'tea')
thesis	dissertation
tick	check
thongs	flip-flops
3 or 5 door	hatchback
tin	can
torch	flashlight
track suit	sweat suit, sweats
uni	university
ute, utility	pickup truck
wardrobe	closet
whinge	complain
white tea or coffee	tea with milk, coffee with milk
whole meal	whole wheat
windscreen	windshield

An introductory guide to Aussie slang

What they say	**What they mean**
"Battler"	*someone who struggles or tries hard*
"Bogan"	*unsophisticated person*
"Brekky"	*breakfast*
"Bring the esky for beers."	*Bring the ice cooler to keep the beers cold.*
"Buckley's"	*no chance*
"Bunch of pikers"	*Bunch of people who don't pull their weight; chickens*
"Bushbash"	*forcing your way through pathless bush*
"Cark it"	*die*
"Daks"	*pants, trousers*
"Don't get caught in a rip."	*Don't get caught in a strong undertow. (swimming)*

254

"Don't get stroppy with me."	*Don't be ill-tempered towards me.*
"Dunny"	*toilet*
"He dobbed me in."	*He snitched on me.*
"He's a real ocker Aussie."	*He's a boorish or unrefined Australian.*
"Fair dinkum."	*That's honest, genuine.*
"Fair go!"	*Give us a chance; be fair!*
"I'll get a slab."	*I'll pick up thirty cans of beer.*
"I'll put it on lay-by."	*I'll put down a deposit so the store will hold it for me.*
"I'm flat out."	*I'm really busy.*
"I'm knackered" or "rooted"	*I'm exhausted, tired.*
"I'm taking the piss."	*I'm making fun of you.*
"Good on ya!"	*Good for you!* or *Well Done!*
"He cracked the shits."	*He lost his temper.*
"He's taking a sickie."	*He's taking the day off on sick leave.*
"Howya goin'?"	*How are you?*
"I can't be arsed."	*I can't be bothered.*
"I lost money at the pokies."	*I lost money playing the poker machines.*
"I reckon."	*Absolutely!*
"I'm rapt."	*I'm delighted.* (you'll often see this misspelt)
"It's going to be a piss up."	*It's going to be a boozy party.*
"It was a shellacking."	*It was utter defeat.*
"Let's get a sanger."	*Let's get a sandwich.*
"No worries!"	*Don't worry about it! That's okay.*
"She'll be right."	*Don't worry about it. It will be ok.*
"She's a Pom."	*She's English.*
"She's dinky-di Aussie."	*She's a real Aussie.*
"She's a stickybeak."	*She's a nosy person.*
"Spending time with rellies"	*Spending time with family.*
"Stop whingeing."	*Stop complaining.*
"The hoons are out."	*The hooligans are out (can refer to reckless drivers)*
"The place was chockas"	*The place was packed (full).*

"They live in whoop-whoop."	*They live really far away from anywhere.*
"They're having a root."	*They're having sex.*
"Throw snags on the barbie."	*Barbeque some sausages.*
"Was he pervin' on ya?"	*Was he leering at you?*
"What a bludger"	*What a lazy person*
"What a yobbo!"	*What an uncouth, aggressive person.*
"You little ripper!"	*What a good thing.*
"You beauty!"	*Fantastic!*

A final note on Australian English: Aussies shorten the names for everything and everyone. I can tell it really bugs people that my name isn't easy to shorten (one of John's mates finally came up with "Anj," though no one else has ever called me that). Double r's become double zed's (Barry = Bazza, Garry = Gazza). Anything called Paddington becomes "Paddo," registration becomes "rego," television becomes "telly" and so on. It's fun but takes some figuring out when you first hear a shortened version of a word you haven't encountered before.

Aussie social customs

You're yourself: your own person with your own history and way of doing things. I don't think that expats necessarily have to be chameleons and blend in. So stay true to your own nature (if it's a polite and civil one, of course). But it does help to know some Aussie customs and what is typically considered good manners so you know what's going on.

Australians are traditionally relaxed people. Most of them dream of buying their own houses and once this dream is achieved they put a great deal of time and effort into fixing up these homes and tending to their gardens. There is a great deal of pride in this activity and if you become good mates with an Aussie, you might even be invited over to a barbeque or dinner at his home. If this happens, be sure to find out the nature of the invitation: Is it a dinner party? What should you bring? etc. Even if you are told to bring nothing, you should always bring a gift such as wine, chocolates or flowers. If you are told to 'bring a plate,' you should bring a large plate of food to share with the other guests. Usually for barbeques, guests bring their own alcohol and meat to grill. Be sure to ask the person who invited you if you're unsure. And remember to thank your host(s) a day or so after the party or dinner by note or email.

When you go out to a bar or pub, you may notice groups of people buying rounds or 'shouting' drinks. Each person in the group will take turns buying all the drinks for everyone else. Before drinking, Aussies often clink their glasses together and say "Cheers" on the first round. If you are involved in a 'shouting' situation, be sure not to leave until you have bought a round. Otherwise, don't accept a shout in the first place.

You'll hear the word 'mate' thrown around a lot. It took me a few years to really start using this word — it just didn't feel like me until I'd been here for a few years. 'Mate' is a general term of familiarity and you should be prepared to call everyone 'mate' whether you know and like him or not. You can say it to just about anyone (I wouldn't call a much older person mate, though) and I even hear parents calling their children 'mates' from time to time. The word is usually used in place of the word 'friend.'

Formalities (or lack of)

Australian society is relatively informal. You should practice good manners, such as introducing people at their first meeting and greeting business associates in a more formal setting with a handshake and a smile. Aussies tend to use first names regardless of the situation. If someone presents you with a gift, it is customary to open it right when you receive it and you should send a note to thank her again later.

When sitting down for a meal, use continental table manners. This means that you hold your fork in your left hand with the tines down and use your right hand to hold your knife and cut food. When you are finished eating, you can indicate that you're finished by laying your knife and fork parallel on your plate with the handles to the right. Keep your hands above the table and don't put your elbows on it.

Lateness is not technically fashionable in Australia but my experience here is that, like all islands, Australia runs on "ish" time. You should not be more than 15 minutes late for a meeting with someone, but people rarely arrive early to meet each other. Though if you are going to a business meeting, you should be on time and even arrive a few minutes early. Business dress in the major cities is conservative, though you will see people wearing jeans and more casual dress in some industries. Your meeting may feel casual, yet it is taken very seriously if it is a business meeting. You should stick to the facts and make a clear presentation and arguments.

You'll probably find people to be pretty direct when they communicate and Aussies love wit and humour. They can come across as self-deprecating and may downplay their achievements, but this is just because of their propensity to be humble. Don't mistake this for a lack of ambition. Aussies tend to reject pretentiousness and the flaunting of credentials and they are distrustful of people who show-off too much.

Personality differences

I'm going to get into some stereotypes here and I don't believe that everyone fits into them. But I can make some pretty accurate generalisations that may help you to modify your behaviour to fit in a little better, particularly if you're coming from the US. I say this because the negative worldview towards Americans is present in the hearts and minds of many (not all) Australians. A friend told me about a job interview she had at a restaurant. There was another candidate present at the same time and the manager looked at the woman's resume and said, "If I'd known you were American, I wouldn't have called you in for an interview." As it turned out, the woman was actually Canadian but had worked in the US for the last several years. To the manager, it made no difference.

This is not to say that this sort of thing happens everywhere or often. But discrimination does occur and you should be prepared. You should also be ready to feel as if you are taking full responsibility for the political administration of your home country. You'll be asked questions about how Americans think, feel and vote, as if the American population is a uniform body where everyone thinks alike. Americans are actually a more culturally diverse lot than Aussies because of the size of the population and the age of the country, but don't expect rational arguments to dominate the conversation.

I'll ease up a bit now on Australians and suggest that you just smile and don't take these things too personally. Don't react with anger and feel free to explain how you as an individual feel about things in your home country. Aussies have much more in common with Americans than many of them realise. And you'll meet plenty of Australians who don't harbour negative opinions about Americans at all. As I said, just be prepared.

The typical stereotype of an American is an aggressive, pushy person who demands that everything be done quickly and efficiently. Habits are hard to change and I'm sorry to say that I still get frustrated with inefficiency. It is just who I am. But I have never been an impolite person. I always try to be patient with people and this has taken some work over the years because if you have spent most of your life on the east coast of the US as I have, you get used to a certain pace of life. I've heard similar comments from people who came to Australia from London and other large non-American cities. The pace of life and business can be quite slow in some parts of Australia and this is something you will have to adjust to. Try not to exhibit feelings of superiority when dealing with people. Aussies are smart and just because they don't do things your way doesn't mean that their way won't be effective. This is part of the discovery process of being an expat and hopefully one of the reasons you chose this path for yourself in the first place. It can be enlightening to encounter new perspectives and you should embrace them instead of expecting things to always be done the way you are used to.

If you're looking to make new friends (and you should be), accept every invitation you can and even if there is more alcohol at events than you're used to, just go along anyway. You don't have to drink a lot (or at all). Keep a sense of humour about yourself and spend a lot of time listening until you get a good feeling for the cultural norms. This is not to say that you have to clam up and be someone that you aren't. But when you first move to a country, any country, you should always be more reserved and interested in learning about what is going on around you. Once you feel more comfortable, you can reveal more about yourself. Aussies tend to be reserved about their personal lives anyway and discussions can stay light-hearted for hours while people chat about sport or other topics that the group are likely to be interested in or passionate about.

For the love of sport

Most (but not all) Aussies are natural sports lovers. Gambling, including betting on horse races, premiership winners, election results and just about anything else you can think of is rife. I've never passed an empty TAB. Living in Melbourne, we enjoy an extra public holiday for the Melbourne Cup horse race each year.

If you love sports of all kinds, you'll fit right in here. I was actually never a fan of sport, save the odd basketball or hockey game and the Olympics. As I mentioned before, I grew up in Alabama with parents from Chicago and New Jersey, making me the only child in my school who did not support either the Alabama or Auburn college football teams. I grew to hate the pigskin and anything associated with uniformed men chasing around a ball.

How then, did I end up with Mr. All-Sport, who will watch anything involving sports and follows not just the Australian teams (all of them), but also international sports, including soccer, NFL, basketball, tennis, *Formula One*, etc.? It has actually been good for me because I discovered a love for Aussie Rules Football (AFL) and tennis. I even went to a cricket match last year and enjoyed it. So I can now say I am a balanced person, who not only enjoys arts and literature, but also loves to watch football and no longer has to suffer through the weekends when the television is perpetually set to *Fox Sports*.

The most watched sport in Australia is, in fact, Australian Rules Football.[34] With 16 teams to choose from, and plans to add two

---

[34] Australian Football League (AFL) website: http://www.afl.com.au

more teams in 2011 and 2012, AFL dominates the sports pages from March through September. Compared to other sports, your first experience with AFL will likely leave you shocked (or perhaps exhilarated) by how violent it is. The players have no padded equipment protecting their bodies and spend four quarters trying to score goals by marking, kicking and handballing an oval ball around a field, usually with high impact collisions and sometimes aggravated displays of hostility towards the opposing team. It's brilliant! During footy season, expect a tipping competition (with a cash pool for the winner) in your office, where you will pick the winning team for each round. You can also participate in one of two fantasy competitions (once you get your head around the game, this is highly recommended): most big footy fans participate in either AFL's *Dream Team* or *Herald Sun*'s *SuperCoach* fantasy leagues online.

If you are in NSW or QLD, however, you'll probably be exposed to more rugby than footy. There are two different types of rugby: Rugby League and Rugby Union, with completely different rules. Big powerful men, also chasing a ball, attempt to score tries against the opposing team. I've escaped the rugby on most occasions. Only the Rugby Union World Cup (Australia's national team is the Wallabies) is broadcast at our house. The Wallabies play internationally in other tournaments such as the Tri-Nations, which also includes New Zealand and South Africa. Or you can watch the National Rugby League (NRL).[35] If you do love rugby, you'll now find that both types have expanded outside of just NSW and QLD to other parts of Australia.

---

[35] You can learn more about NRL here: http://www.nrl.com.au

And then we have cricket[36]. Yawn. This is another game dear to the hearts of Australians. There is very little action happening in this sport. I always compare it to baseball (with a stern look from my husband) because each team bats the ball with a wooden bat for a number of overs, trying to accumulate runs, the number of which becomes their score for the opposing team to beat when it's their turn to bat. Australia plays in one-day games against other countries and also in test series cricket, the most famous of which is the Ashes against England, occurring every two to three years. The games are very long and you can expect to be in your seat for around seven hours for a day game and that time multiplied by up to five for test cricket. Recently a new form of the game, Twenty20, has been introduced as a shorter format with music and a reduced number of overs to attract more viewers to the game. Not surprisingly, it was quick to dominate ticket sales over the one-day games. Potential boredom aside, test cricket is a beautiful, prestigious show of sportsmanship and its history is part of the national psyche in Australia. Children grow up playing cricket in amateur leagues and even adults play indoor cricket in organised competitions.

Australia also hosts the *Australian Open*[37], one of the four tennis Grand Slams. Every January, usually in extreme heat, international tennis professionals and fans descend on Melbourne to watch day and night matches at the Rod Laver Arena. Other popular Australian sports include soccer (the Socceroos are the national team), with most major cities also having at least one local team, called the A-League.[38] Women, and increasingly men, play netball[39], probably the

---

[36] You can find more information about Australian cricket at the Australian Cricket website: http://www.cricket.com.au

[37] The Australian Open Website: http://www.auspopen.com.au

[38] A-League website: http://www.aleague.com.au

[39] You can learn more about netball at http://www.netball.asn.au

most popular participation sport in the country. Other sports include golf, hockey, yacht races, car racing, basketball and horse and greyhound racing, all of which have a presence in Australia.

Social Resources

Facebook   http://facebook.com
Australians are some of the most active users of social networking sites in the world. You're probably already on *Facebook* and therefore already know how to use it, so why not do a search and look for some active groups and fan pages devoted to topics of interest to you and in your geographical area?

The Newcomer's Club – Australia
http://www.newcomersclub.com/au.html
Designed to give men and women the opportunity to meet and develop friendships with others who live in their local area, many of these groups have general meetings and interest groups that encourage members to learn about their new city, its culture, activities, lifestyle, and to develop friendships by sharing interests and hobbies with each other. Some of the different groups in the directory include Newcomer's Club, American Women's Club and more.

Meetup   http://www.meetup.com
Search for groups in Australia to meet new people.

9.

Chapter Nine: Studying, buying property and other FAQs

This book would go on forever if I discussed all of the possible scenarios in which you might find yourself once you make the move down under. However there are a few key topics that I do want to discuss because they are significant life events that you may very well need some guidance on as an expat right away. This chapter is dedicated to those.

What if I want to study?

Provided you are residing in Australia on a visa that allows you to do so, you can undertake study in thousands of subjects or train for a vocation. Education after high school is usually completed at an accredited university or training program and you will need to apply directly to the school you are interested in. If you are not a permanent resident, you will have to apply as an overseas student and you'll be required to pay overseas student fees. This is something to consider when you are evaluating your costs.

Choosing a program

Your desire to study may be fuelled by curiosity about a subject, an intended career change or to advance your professional career. If you do not already have a bachelor's degree and you want to work towards that, you will want to look into undergraduate university programs. This is the most common type of degree found in Australia. You will need it to get most of the better paying jobs as the job market here is very competitive. If university is not an option for you, or if your career ambitions are better serviced by a more practical qualification, you should look into one of the public Technical and Further Education (TAFE) Institutes. You can also undertake vocational training at private colleges, schools and universities. TAFE qualifications may also be applied as credit to a degree program should you decide to pursue a bachelor's degree later on.

If you already have a bachelor's degree and are looking to advance in your chosen profession, gain additional training or make a career change, then you'll want to look into postgraduate study. You can work towards a graduate certificate, graduate diploma, master's degree or doctoral degree (PhD). Whatever you choose, you will need to begin to think about what you want to achieve through your study and begin looking into schools and courses that will lead to your desired outcome.

Resources

Australian government website for international students
http://studyinaustralia.gov.au/Sia/Splash.aspx

Going to Uni   http://www.goingtouni.gov.au
The complete guide to studying for permanent residents and citizens of Australia; this is a step-by-step resource for all aspects of studying

The Good Universities Guide   http://www.gooduniguide.com.au
An online resource for education, training and career pathways where you can find information about every degree and university in Australia along with performance ratings

Study Abroad Australia
http://www.studyabroad.com/australia.html
This is a comprehensive directory of study programs aimed towards students coming from overseas.

Worldwide Classroom: Consortium for International Education and Multicultural Studies
http://www.worldwide.edu/index.html
This site features a directory and information on over 10,000 primary, secondary, language schools and universities in 95 countries, including Australia.

Costs and applying to school

Once you have decided on a course, you should request application forms by following the instructions on the university's or school's website. This may be as simple as downloading them. You will be required to submit your previous academic records, which must be official copies from the schools where you have studied in the past. You will also be required to prove your English proficiency if you are applying as an international student. University applications will usually require a personal essay and/or statement of purpose to be included in the application, and there may be additional requirements for your particular course. Postgraduate courses, for example, may require you to submit your work history, letters of recommendation and/or a research proposal. You should consult the school you have chosen to find out exactly what you need in order to apply.

If you are applying for an undergraduate program place, you may want to (or be required to) take an entrance exam. Some programs in Australia are very competitive and taking the ACT or SAT test can give you an edge if you score high enough. There may also be more specific entry requirements for some courses. For example, you may have pre-requisite subjects that you will need to have taken and passed in high school. While there are generally no entrance exams for TAFE, you may also have pre-requisite course requirements for these programs.

If you are applying as an international student, you are only able to study in Australia in an overseas fee paying place and international student fees will apply. There is no Australian government fee assistance for non-citizens unless you are in Australia on a permanent humanitarian visa. You can, however, apply for scholarships in order to reduce some or all of your out-of-pocket costs. You can also apply for private loans. I've listed some scholarship directories and programs in the resources section below.

Australian citizens have access to the government loan scheme called the Higher Education Loan Program (HELP). This is often known as HECS-HELP. If you are enrolled in a Commonwealth supported place at your school, these loans can cover all or part of your student contribution. There is also the FEE-HELP loan scheme for non-Commonwealth supported students.[40]

Resources

Australian-American Fulbright Commission
http://www.fulbright.com.au
Promotes and supports cultural and educational exchange between Australia and America; if you're American, this is a good place to look for scholarships

International Scholarships
http://www.internationalscholarships.com
Financial aid, college scholarship and international scholarship resource for students wishing to study abroad

---

[40] You can read more about HECS-HELP here:
http://www.goingtouni.gov.au/Main/Quickfind/PayingForYourStudiesHELPLoans/Default.htm

International Student Loans
http://www.internationalstudentloans.com
Find a student loan for your international education

Universities Admissions Centre   http://www.uac.edu.au
Processes applications for admission to most undergraduate courses at participating institutions (primarily NSW and ACT)

Grades in Australia

The academic grading system may differ a bit from what you're used to. While primary and secondary schools use the A, B, C, D and E system (the letter 'E' stands for failure instead of 'F'), most tertiary institutions will issue your results based on the following:

High Distinction (HD)
Distinction (D)
Credit (Cr)
Pass (P)
Fail (N)

The numerical equivalent to these marks will differ depending on the institution you attend. My university for postgraduate work, for example, issued an HD if you received between 85 and 100 per cent of the raw marks available. Other universities give HD to marks of 80 per cent and higher. A few universities use either the A, B, C, etc. marking system or their own titles for mark categories.

How do I buy property in Australia?

At the time of writing, the property market in almost all metropolitan areas of Australia was red hot. Some people will even tell you that the market is grossly overvalued. It has been this way since I moved here at the start of 2005 and with the building shortages and constant demand for property from both current Australian residents, students and new arrivals, I can not see the property boom ending any time soon. But it is the Australian dream of most people to purchase a home to live in. Unfortunately for some, the realisation of this dream keeps slipping further from their grasp. Prices and interest rates continue to rise and people are finding it harder and harder to save up the requisite amount of money to even put a deposit on a home. Many others do not even qualify for loans in the first place.

If you are in the market to purchase a house, you might find it more challenging than finding and buying property than in other parts of the world. After the global financial crisis, many people across the globe found themselves in similar situations. Perhaps you will find the circumstances in Australia the same as in your home country. We purchased a house in 2006 and therefore I am able to walk you through the basic steps and tell you what you need to know about buying property in Australia. Please note that this is only a general guide to the process of purchasing property and you should do your own research to find tips on negotiating the price of a house, what to look out for when selecting a property and any legal questions you may have at any stage. I am not a licensed real estate agent or buyer's agent.

If you are not a permanent resident or citizen of Australia, your purchase of a house will be subject to review by the FIRB. Generally, if you are living in Australia on a Temporary Entry Visa (with more than 12 months validity) you can buy a residence for yourself - as long as the property is sold when you no longer live in Australia. Students over 18 who are studying at a recognised tertiary institution for more than one year who need accommodation can purchase a house, but a general limit of AUD 300,000 applies to the value of a property acquired by a student temporarily residing in Australia. Other applicants entitled to purchase property are long stay retirees and people in Australia for work reasons who need accommodation. Again, any property must be sold when these categories of buyers no longer live in Australia. If this is you, you may want to consider whether you will lose money on your investment when you sell in such a short period of time due to the one-time costs of purchasing property in Australia such as Stamp Duty (see next section).

Determine how much you can afford to spend on your home

Your first task is to assess your financial situation and determine how much money you have for a down payment on a property and how much you can afford each month to service your mortgage and other costs if you're not buying the property outright. You will also need to factor in the one-off costs associated with buying a property. Be sure to examine the debts you already have because these will affect how much you will be able to borrow to purchase a home.

In Australia, the up-front expenses of buying property are:
- Home loan fees – these will be determined by your lender
- Mortgage protection insurance – for loans over 80 per cent
- Land transfer registration fees – these vary by state
- Taxes – these vary by state
- Stamp duty on property – this varies by state and can be very expensive
- Stamp duty on your mortgage
- Settlement and legal fees
- Building and pest inspection costs for the property you purchase
- Deposit – usually a specific percentage of the price is required
- Body Corporate search (if you purchase an apartment)

- Strata fees (if you purchase a unit, townhouse or villa)

Other ongoing costs you will want to consider are:
- Council rates (annual)
- Utilities
- Home and contents insurance
- Moving costs
- Strata levies (if you purchase a unit, townhouse or villa)
- Monthly mortgage payments – if you take out a variable loan, your payments will increase as interest rates increase; you should not take on a mortgage that is going to cost you more than 30 per cent of your before-tax (gross) income

You may qualify for the First Home Owner Grant. This is a national scheme that provides first homebuyers who plan to live in their homes with AUD 7,000 to offset the costs of purchasing a home. You can learn more about this by visiting the revenue office website for the state or territory in which you plan to purchase property (see resources section below). Your state may also have additional support for homebuyers. Once you have a good picture of your finances, you are ready to visit a few banks and mortgage brokers.

When choosing a lender, you should make your choice based on the best mortgage arrangement available for your situation. Don't feel that you need to be loyal to your bank or make your decision based on any emotional factors tied up with a financial institution's brand. The competition in the financial sector in Australia is stiff and you should be able to find a lender who can accommodate you with little difficulty. Home loans are available from banks, major insurance companies, credit unions and mortgage brokers.

When choosing a lender, you want to look at the complete basket of fees they will charge you and be sure to compare these as well as the interest rate you are quoted. There may be room to negotiate some fees and you should not be shy about asking. You should also ensure that the bank is willing to disclose its appraisal of the security value of the property (valuation). You want to ensure that the value used by your lender is the same as the purchase price of your home or more. I'm thinking ahead for you here. A great way to make money in Australia is to become a property investor. You may not be thinking about this now, but in a few years you may decide that you want to borrow against the equity in your home in order to purchase a second property as an investment. You'll be able to take advantage of a wide variety of tax deductions allowed by the government as well as negative gearing on your investment. You can do your own research on this because it is too lengthy for me to explain here, but you want to keep your options open and be in a good position to invest in the future. A lender on your list gets bonus points if they're willing to revisit their valuation one year after you purchase your home.

You may want to consider using a mortgage or finance broker to shop around for the best deal for you. When we were looking for a house to purchase, we compared a few banks with a couple of mortgage brokers and ended up going with a broker. The larger brokers are doing millions of dollars worth of financing each month and they have the negotiating power to get you the best deal on your loan. Their fees are usually paid by the banks in the form of commission so it doesn't cost you any more to go with a broker.

You will have to choose a financing option and interest rates will be a big factor. As I write this, interest rates, which plummeted after the global financial crisis, are on the rebound and rising by at least a quarter of a percentage point each month. You may only be able to fix your interest rate for a few years, but it's worth it if you're worried at all about price increases. Most banks will also offer you the option to fix the interest rate for part of your loan. You might be wondering why people would choose a variable interest rate. They do this because variable interest rates are the lowest rates offered by banks and you have no risk of locking yourself into a high rate. Interest rates can change frequently and you can think of it in reference to the stock market. You don't want to fix your loan's interest rate too late in the rate fluctuation cycle and risk the rates dropping while you are stuck with a high rate because of your fixed-rate loan. That said, if you can lock-in low rates for as long as possible ahead of major anticipated rises, you will be better off. The trick is being able to predict such things.

Once you choose a lender, you will apply for a loan and receive a pre-approval letter telling you how much you are able to borrow. You should not make an offer on a property without this pre-approval because most real estate agents will expect to see the letter before they consider your offer as genuine. You don't want to miss out on a property to another buyer because you did not have proof of finance.

Resources

To determine the costs of purchasing a home in your state, you should visit the appropriate website:

ACT http://www.revenue.act.gov.au

NSW http://www.osr.nsw.gov.au

NT http://www.nt.gov.au/ntt/revenue

QLD http://www.osr.qld.gov.au

SA http://www.osr.qld.gov.au

TAS http://www.sro.tas.gov.au

VIC http://www.sro.vic.gov.au/sro/SROnav.nsf/Home+Page/SRO~Home+Page?open

WA http://www.dtf.wa.gov.au/cms/index.aspx

Best Brokers http://www.bestbrokers.com.au
National directory of mortgage lenders and brokers

Borrowing Power Calculator
http://money.ninemsn.com.au/property/tools/borrowing-power-calculator.aspx
From NineMSN's money website

Find a mortgage broker
http://www.yourmortgage.com.au/brokers

First Home Saver Accounts
http://www.homesaver.treasury.gov.au/content/default.asp
Tax effective scheme for Australians to save for their first home through a combination of Government contributions and low taxes

Finding a property

Once you have your letter from your lender telling you how much you're allowed to borrow, you're ready to go shopping. Create a list of suburbs where you would like to live. You'll want to look at the attributes of each suburb and think about things like crime levels, transportation, distances from work, local shopping, recreation and schools. Properties in Australia are usually listed through real estate agents and they will be sold by either a private sale or by auction. I've included a list of online websites where you can find property listings. You can also check Saturday's paper in the classifieds section.

In a private sale, you have the ability to negotiate the price with the seller, usually by making an offer on the property to the seller's real estate agent. You may wish to enlist the services of a buyer's agent if you do not feel confident in negotiating the best deal for yourself. If the property is to be sold at auction, you will gather at the property with other bidders on a specified date and bid on the house. There will usually be a minimum price to start the bidding and the house will go to the highest bidder.

If you find a house you are interested in and decide that you want to purchase it, you will have to make an offer to the seller or seller's agent. This can be verbal, however it is better to put it in writing if you are serious. The agent should have a form for the letter of offer (usually called 'Offer and Acceptance' or 'Offer to Purchase') and will assist you in completing it with the details of your particular offer. You need to be certain that you want the property because as soon as your offer is accepted, it becomes a binding contract. You will be asked to provide a deposit at the time the offer is accepted and the amount of the deposit is determined by you in the letter of offer.

Be sure that your letter of offer is conditional, which means that it is contingent on conditions being satisfied that you specify. These conditions may include an acceptable valuation, finance approval and the results of the building and pest inspection report, which you will want to have done as soon as your offer is accepted. If you are buying a unit, townhouse or villa you will need to also have a strata title inspection. Be sure you read these reports carefully and ensure you understand everything contained in them. If you don't understand something, seek professional advice. It is your job to make sure that the property you are purchasing is in good condition.

If you find a flaw in the property that would render your offer invalid, this may be an opportunity to re-negotiate the price of the property if you still want it. Or you can walk away. Be sure that you are happy with the house and contact a professional for assistance if you are unsure about anything. You can lose a lot of money if you back out on the purchase of the home once you have put it under contract.

If the house you want to purchase is going up for auction, you will need to be well prepared. I recommend that you do some reading on buying at auction and familiarise yourself with how everything works before putting yourself in an auction situation. In some states, you will have to register as a bidder with the agent ahead of the auction. You will need to determine a budget and stick to it. If you are naturally competitive, this may require some serious mental control on the day. Try not to get emotionally involved with the house ahead of the auction because this can cause you to spend more than you intended. It will help to know what the property is really worth ahead of the auction to keep things in perspective.

You cannot withdraw your bid once you have made it. If you are the highest bidder, then you have to sign the contract and pay the deposit immediately – there is no cooling-off period as with a private sale. This will mean that you should have had the building, pest and strata inspections carried out, and your solicitor or conveyancer should have looked over the sale contract. In short, be sure you want the property before you go to the auction and be sure you know what you're doing.

Resources

Allhomes (listings)   http://allhomes.com.au

Domain (listings)   http://www.domain.com.au

Local Voices http://localvoices.realestate.com.au
Check out reviews from locals before you sign that offer.

RealEstate.com.au (listings)   http://www.realestate.com.au

Real Estate View (listings)   http://www.realestateview.com.au

Settlement

Once you've made an offer, had it accepted and all conditions of the offer have been met, a date for settlement will be set. This is usually four to six weeks later. The seller usually has control over the date of settlement but it is negotiable. In the meantime, your work isn't over yet. You will need to choose a settlement agent (conveyancer) or solicitor and this agent should not be the same as the seller's conveyancer. You will sign a copy of the contract, as will the seller and you will exchange copies with each other. Conveyancing simply means the process of transferring the property from one owner to another. You also have a cooling-off period (usually a few days) once you sign the contract in a private sale.

The seller will have to provide a number of certificates, which your conveyancer or solicitor will examine to ensure there is nothing incorrect or misleading that will invalidate your contract. The transfer document will then be prepared and all relevant enquiries relating to your land are made. Your lender will prepare the mortgage document, which sets out the terms and conditions of the loan. Prior to settlement, your conveyancer will provide you with a statement and checklist of items to be completed prior to settlement, what monies are due and a schedule. Finally, a title search will be conducted on the day of settlement to ensure that the property has no interest or restrictions against it.

You should also do a final inspection of your property just before settlement. Be sure that you do this and don't make the same mistake we did. When we conducted the inspection there was some large furniture left in the backyard and rubbish lying around. The sellers assured us that they would clean it up so we signed the final inspection release and took them at their word. Well, when we got our keys and went to the property the first time, they had left the mess for us. It can be inconvenient to have to return to the property again when people don't have it ready as they should before your final inspection, but don't let people get away with leaving the property in an unsuitable condition. And don't trust that they will do what they say because you have no recourse if they don't keep their word and you've already signed off on the final inspection.

You usually don't have to attend the actual settlement meeting on the day. Your conveyancer will call you with the good news that your settlement went through without any problems and you can start moving into your new home.

Resources

Australian Institute of Conveyancers
http://www.aicnational.com.au

Homeiown   http://www.homeiown.com
Blog explaining how buying, building or renting a house works in Australia

How safe is Australia?

Australia could be called a relatively safe country. I have not done a comparative analysis of statistics for crime in Australia vs. other countries, however the Australian Institute of Criminology (AIC) releases data every year and I have relied on this information to write about national crime levels here. I can tell you that personally I tend to feel safer here than I did in the US, however I lived in very large American cities in the seven years prior to moving to Australia. The relative absence of guns is a contributing factor to my feeling of safety, however the average person in Australia can purchase a knife easily so I can't say that no guns means no violence. I also don't go out late at night as much as I used to when I was younger, so this may be another contributing factor.

I'll let the statistics tell you the rest. Assaults represent the majority of recorded violent crimes and are on the rise over the last fifteen years. Homicides have decreased and the vast majority of people who are murdered are murdered within a residential dwelling. The entire country only saw 290 incidences of murder or manslaughter in 2008. Sixty-two of those killed were male. Only six per cent of females were killed by a stranger and knives were the most commonly used weapons in homicides in general, followed by physical force. In general, property theft has declined and you are most likely to be the victim of a violent robbery on the street. Other types of property crimes are most likely to occur in a residential dwelling or retail location. Credit card fraud is steadily on the increase in Australia and this, along with scams and identity theft, are other things to be aware of.

If you listen to the media, assault is the biggest problem in Australia when it comes to crime, and statistics confirm this. In Melbourne, we constantly hear about ugly alcohol-fuelled bar brawls amongst young people and the prevalence of knives being carried on the streets. The statistics seem to confirm this: most assault victims are 15-24 year olds. Sixty-one per cent of the victims knew their attacker. Sadly, family members commit 27 per cent of assaults. And assault is seasonal: the number of assaults peaks in the spring and summer months of October to March.

A family member or 'known other' is responsible for 78 per cent of sexual assaults. This is not to say that you are safe from rape by a stranger, but it is yet another statistic to examine when considering your safety. Males aged 15 to 19 years are more likely to commit a crime than any other members in the population. This is also the age bracket in which most female-committed offences occur. You can check out these statistics in more detail on the AIC website: http://www.aic.gov.au/publications/current%20series/facts.aspx

What is my conclusion from all of this? Based on statistics and personal experience living in Australia, I can say that most of the crime you need to worry about will be perpetrated by older teenagers who have had too much to drink and are looking for a fight. A guy I know was 'glassed' (where someone smashes a glass or bottle into your face or body) last year in a club in Melbourne when he was out with his wife because he accidentally bumped into a young man. He had to have plastic surgery and he was hit just above the eye so the attack could have been potentially more scarring than it already is. My advice to stay safe in Australia is to stay off the streets after 2 am and to try not to provoke angry youth. Ensure that you have deadlocks on your doors and home and don't leave the house unlocked. Get an alarm system that is wired to the police if you can afford it. Don't leave valuables in plain sight in your car. But don't be too paranoid either. You need to exercise common sense and awareness in order to protect yourself and your family no matter what country you live in. Australia is probably safer than most.

Resources

Australasian Consumer Fraud Taskforce http://www.scamwatch.gov.au

Childsafety Australia http://www.childsafetyaustralia.com.au

Neighbourhood Watch http://www.neighbourhoodwatch.com.au

Personal safety tips from ReachOut Australia
http://au.reachout.com/find/articles/personal-safety

Stay Safe Online   http://www.staysmartonline.gov.au

When can I become a citizen?

Becoming an Australian is the final step for any migrant who wants to remain here permanently and participate fully in the country. Australian citizens have responsibilities such as serving on a jury and voting in federal and state or territory elections and referendums (changes to the constitution). They also have the right to work in the Australian Public Service or Defence Force, can seek election to parliament, obtain an Australian passport, receive help from an Australian official while travelling overseas and to register their children that are born overseas as Australian citizens by descent.

You will be eligible to apply for Australian citizenship once you have lived lawfully in Australia for the last four years and you must have lived in Australia as a permanent resident for at least 12 months as a permanent resident. The date of your permanent residence if your visa was granted offshore is the date of your first arrival in Australia as a permanent resident. You do not automatically qualify for citizenship; you must apply for it as you applied for your visa to come here in the first place. This is a much simpler process than applying for a visa, however.

The advantage of becoming a citizen, aside from the privileges listed above is that you do not have to apply for a RRV every five years to re-enter Australia if you leave the country. Instead you pay a one-time fee and become a citizen, and then you can leave and re-enter the country on an Australian passport. You should check that your current country of nationality allows dual citizenship before you apply for Australian citizenship because if it does not, you can lose your citizenship in your country of birth. You may prefer to become an Australian citizen and this loss of nationality may not be an issue for you, but you should be aware that not all countries recognise or allow dual citizenship for their nationals.

If you are eligible and have decided that you want to proceed with obtaining your Australian citizenship, visit the government's citizenship website: http://www.citizenship.gov.au You will have to fill out a printed or online application, pay a fee, sit a citizenship test (and pass) and then make a pledge before your citizenship becomes official. You cannot apply for a passport until you receive your official certificate at the citizenship ceremony. For me, the entire process from the date of my application until the date of my citizenship ceremony took about four months. It could take a bit longer for you depending on where you live and the backlog of applications when you apply, but it should not take more than about nine months from start to finish.

What about all the dangerous creatures in Australia?

I did myself no favours on my first flight to Australia by reading a Bill Bryson book about the country. He wrote at length about all the deadly spiders, poisonous snakes and scary sea creatures that were apparently waiting to bite and kill me down here. I already knew about the sharks and crocodiles, but I had no idea that Australia had, for example, six of the top ten deadliest snakes in the world within its borders or killer jellyfish or so many spiders.

Aussies tend to be very relaxed about living in proximity to all these creatures. I myself have mellowed out considerably since I got here and the only time I've actually seen any of the dreaded critters (outside of zoos) is while hiking in Victoria. And it wasn't even one of the most deadly native animals, but the biggest, scariest ant I've ever seen. Called Jack Jumpers, I only knew what they were because we saw a documentary on television about how one little bite can cause anaphylactic shock *if* you are allergic. After a momentary panic, we moved away from the ant and continued our walk.

As my husband loves to tell me, and I think it is very apt for this question of deadly Australian fauna, *awareness* is very important for your time in Australia. It's important when you spend time anywhere in the world for that matter. You should adequately scare yourself by learning all about the deadly moving creatures that can take your life or limbs (don't forget about cars while you're at it) and then just focus on being aware of your surroundings and know how to handle the situation should you come across one of these creatures during your adventures here.

First, let's be sure we're talking about the same dangerous animals. I'm referring to Box Jellyfish, Irukandji (jellyfish), Salt Water Crocodiles, Blue Ring Octopus, Stone Fish, Red Back Spiders, Brown Snakes, Tiger Snakes, Great White Sharks and Funnel Web Spiders. If you're in the city, it is highly unlikely that you need to worry about these creatures, aside from spiders. Venturing into the water at the beach is another story, however, and in some areas you do need to take precautions, particularly at certain times of the year. The deadly jellyfish and the Blue Ring Octopus, for example, live in Northern and North-Eastern Australia near the coast all along the Great Barrier Reef from November to March. Local councils will fence the beaches with a net during jellyfish season and swimmers often wear stinger suits. Crocodiles also can inhabit the waters in this area and in the northeast and NT. You can find them in any river or beach and salt-water crocs lay on the bottom of the ocean or riverbed, so you may not even know one is there until it is too late.

Other dangers lurk in reefs and on the ocean floor in the form of poisonous fish, which you may brush against or step on accidentally. Be sure to wear reef shoes and don't go diving or snorkelling alone if you are inexperienced. Sharks can strike at any time and have even been found in canals in the Gold Coast. Odds are that you won't encounter one, but surfers and swimmers are attacked every year. Look for signs on beaches and don't swim unless you're certain it is safe. I'm not trying to scare you – I myself do not swim in the ocean in Australia. I do not enjoy it in the first place and the presence of dangerous sea creatures and rip currents is just another motivation to keep me out. But I don't believe that you should live your life in fear in Australia. Just learn all about the dangers that might present themselves and practice awareness and you will be okay. There are risks when you get into a car or walk down the street anywhere in the world. You just have to know what you're doing.

Spiders are a real threat and you're probably most likely to come across these little venomous creatures than anything else if you aren't living in the bush. Funnel Web spiders are found most often in NSW and you'll know their nest by the funnel shaped web. Red Backs have a red stripe along their black backs. These are cousins of the American Black Widow spiders. Its web has a cotton shape covering the entrance of the hole it lives in. Watch out for them in backyards, rest area toilets, and even inside your house in your shoes (check inside before putting them on if you live in an area where you have seen these spiders).

Remember that Australian natives live here too and they have been co-habitating with these creatures for a lot longer than you have. If you have doubts about anything such as where it is safe to swim or hike and what to do if you are attacked by an animal, ask the locals. Don't forget also about protecting your children and pets from these animals and teaching your family about what they should keep an eye out for. Here are some web pages and articles where you can get some helpful tips on how to protect yourself:

Ants in Australia http://ezinearticles.com/?Fire-Ant-Bites---Protect-Yourself-Against-Them&id=1435535

Dangerous Animals http://www.downunder-dago.com/113/Usefull-information/Australias-Dangerous-Animals.html

Funnel-Web Spiders http://www.outback-australia-travel-secrets.com/australian_spiders.html#australian-spiders-funnelweb

Redback Spiders http://www.outback-australia-travel-secrets.com/australian_spiders.html#australian-spiders-redback

Saltwater Crocodiles http://www.outback-australia-travel-secrets.com/saltwater-crocodiles.html

Snakes
http://www.outback-australia-travel-secrets.com/australian_snakes.html

Travel in North QLD
http://www.cairnsunlimited.com/safetravel.htm

Finally, you should be aware of the other dangers in Australia such as skin cancer and workplace or occupational health hazards. It isn't wise to focus on one dangerous part of life in Australia while forgetting about the most common ways that you can harm yourself by lack of prevention.

Resources for general safety in Australia

Safety in Australia   http://www.safetlyinaustralia.com.au

Sun Smart   http://www.sunsmart.com.au

Australian Outback Survival
http://www.outback-australia-travel-secrets.com/australian-outback-survival.html

10.

Chapter Ten: Travel - Here, there and everywhere

Now that you're all settled in Australia, you're ready to explore. There are plenty of wonderful places to visit both in and out of the country. If you've ever wanted to see Asia, you're in a prime location to do so. Dreamt about exotic islands in the south pacific? Australians are privy to some amazing deals on flights and accommodation because those islands are now in your backyard. And you're still not too far from the west coast of the US (unless you've moved to Perth). But if that's the case, be comforted by the fact that you're in the best position in Australia to travel to places like Europe, Southeast Asia and the Middle East.

In this chapter I'll give you the run-down on the travel landscape in Australia. This is primarily a directory of travel providers and some informative media outlets where you can go to read about all the wonderful places to visit. Australians love to travel and you'll probably get bitten by the travel bug too once you're here.

A note on booking: If you're travelling within Australia, you need to get used to booking things well in advance, especially if you're travelling over public holidays or the school holiday period. This is how you get the best deals on flights and ensure that your choice of accommodation is available. We always try to book things about six months in advance. That said, you can almost always find last-minute deals on accommodation. But if you absolutely must be in a domestic destination during a specific period of time, you are advised to book well in advance. There simply isn't the large supply of airlines and accommodation that you may be used to in the US or Europe. This is especially true for travel to more rural or regional areas. You can worry less about hotels filling up in the major cities. You'll get better deals when you book flights in advance as well.

Travel within Australia

Your options for getting to where you want to go are car, bus, train or plane. You should begin by booking your travel and then concentrate on accommodation. Most hotels and tourist attractions have websites or are at least listed in an online directory. If you are visiting a national park, it should have a website, generally run by the state or territory in which the park is located. Each state also has a tourism website, which I've listed in the resources section.

Cars: Hire or drive your own

Freeways connect all the states and territories in Australia and you can easily drive from one to the next as long as you don't mind some of the long distances you're likely to experience. If you're travelling outside the major cities, you will find that you require a car to get around because public transportation can be infrequent and limited at best in the country. So if you aren't travelling very far from home and you'll have to hire a car anyway, you're probably best off just driving yourself there. Your Automobile Association membership, if you have one (see chapter seven in the 'Cars' section) will be valid interstate due to reciprocal arrangements. Your only additional cost will be fuel.

If you decide to hire a car, either at your destination or to drive from your home city to another part of the country, you can rent from one of the large national companies (listed in the resources section) or a local company (look in the *Yellow Pages* or conduct a search online). The local companies, while they have better deals, also may have more restrictions, so you should enquire about kilometre limits (if you're driving far you'll need unlimited), whether you can get a one-way rental (where you pick up your car in one city and return it in another) and what the fee for that will be, and whether you can take the car interstate. You must be 21 years old to hire a car from most companies in Australia and there may be limitations or additional charges if you're under 25 years of age. You can also hire four-wheel drives (4WDs) and campervans. If you're planning to drive into remote areas such as the Outback, or you want to do a lot of travel on C roads, you will need to prepare by having the correct vehicle and equipment such as a winch and spare parts.

If you do drive, watch out for animals such as kangaroos, which won't hesitate to leap out in front of your vehicle (usually at dusk or dawn). If you see one kangaroo, there may be others with it as they tend to travel in groups. Livestock also present a problem when travelling in rural areas as not all farmers fence them in. If you see an animal in the road, apply the brakes, dip your lights and don't swerve if it isn't safe to do so.

Resources

Car rental companies:

Apex	http://www.apexrentacar.com.au
Avis	http://www.avis.com.au
Britz	http://www.britz.com (campervans)
Budget	http://www.budget.com.au
Hertz	http://www.hertz.com.au
Thrifty	http://www/thrifty.com.au

WhereIs http://www.whereis.com.au
Detailed online maps and directions (free)

Flights

The lack of competition in air carriers is a primary reason why flights are so expensive within Australia. You will probably have sticker shock at the price of domestic flights if you are coming from Europe or the US. There are three major domestic carriers and a handful of smaller operators that fly regional routes. You can book your airfares online or visit a travel agent, though agents will generally only be able to offer you the same price on domestic flights as you can find on the carriers' websites yourself.

If you fly *Qantas* and you're American, you will be amazed at how luxurious domestic travel in a Western country can still be. A meal is usually included in longer flights along with free beverages and even a snack. You will also generally pay more for your ticket than if you fly with *Jetstar* or *Virgin Blue*. On these latter two carriers, your base fare will be lower and you will pay for any drinks, food or entertainment you consume. They will offer you a menu of items for purchase and you can pay with cash or a credit card right from your seat. Recently baggage charges have been applied and when you book you will have the option of paying a lower fare that will allow you to only bring carry-on luggage with you (usually a 7 kg limit). Or you can pay an additional fee to check your luggage in (weight restrictions will still apply). Be sure you book this in advance because the fees are significantly higher if you wait to book your luggage in at the airport. The major carriers also allow you to check in online 24 hours before your flight. This will not always save you time if you are checking your luggage in (the queue for bag drop is often longer than the line at regular check-in), however it may be the best chance of getting the seat assignment you prefer.

Unlike in the US, it is not cheaper to purchase a round trip ticket from one airline. When you input your flight request into the airline's online booking engine, you will be shown the one-way fare for each leg of your trip. Therefore in some instances, it is a good idea to examine the price of each portion of your journey and compare these across the three carriers. You may find that it is cheaper to fly to your destination on one airline and return on another carrier.

A word about *Tiger Airways*: this is the Australian airline run by *Singapore Airlines*, which I consider to be one of the best quality airlines in the world. *Tiger*, however, has received mixed reviews since it began operating in Australia a few years ago. The fares are cheap. Some people sing their praises for this and swear they have never had any problems. Other people, my in-laws included, have had terrible experiences with cancellations and delays of six hours or more. There are no safety concerns or anything of that sort and apparently the flight experience itself is good (I have not flown with them personally). However I do want to let you know about some of the problems that have been reported in the media since you won't be aware of them coming from outside Australia, especially because my husband's parents had a bad experience with a significant flight delay themselves.

Resources

Airnorth   http://www.airnorth.com.au
This is the major aviation operator in Northern Australia, servicing 12 destinations including Maningrida, Milingimbi, Elcho Island, Gove [Nhulunbuy], Groote Eylandt and McArthur River in the Northern Territory, Kununurra, Broome and Perth in Western Australia, Mount Isa and the Gold Coast in Queensland and Dili in Timor-Leste. New services to Karratha and Port Hedland in Western Australia are planned to begin at the time of this book's release.

IwantThatFlight!   http://iwantthatflight.com.au
Compare prices across the three majors and Tiger.

Jetstar   http://www.jetstar.com/au/en/index.aspx

Qantas   http://www.qantas.com.au/travel/airlines/home/au/en
The national airline of Australia

Regional Express   http://www.regionalexpress.com.au
Servicing the southeast part of Australia including Sydney, Adelaide, Melbourne and Townsville.

Skywest   http://www.skywest.com.au
Offers flights from Perth to regional areas of WA

Virgin Blue   http://www.virginblue.com.au
Run by Richard Branson's outfit, Virgin

Train travel

Travelling by train in Australia is done more for the experience than anything else. You can take a train between major cities or for an interesting scenic experience. A great place to start is at the Rail Alliance Australia (http://www.railaustralia.com.au), where you can click on the link for 'Where can I go?' and choose your rail journey. If you want to take the slow route from Melbourne (VIC) to Launceston (TAS), you also have the option of taking a ferry.

Rail resources

CountryLink   http://www.countrylink.info
Travels to over 365 destinations in NSW, Queensland, the ACT and Victoria

Great Southern Rail   http://www.gsr.com.au
Website of the Indian Pacific (Sydney to Perth via Adelaide), The Ghan (Adelaide to Darwin), The Overland (Melbourne to Adelaide) and The Southern Spirit (Brisbane to Adelaide via Sydney and Melbourne)

Spirit of Tasmania   http://www.spiritoftasmaia.com.au

Ferry service from Melbourne to Launceston

TransWA http://www.transwa.wa.gov.au
Operates rail services throughout the southern and south-western regions of WA, in an area bounded by Kalbarri, Meekatharra, Kalgoorlie, Esperance, Albany and Augusta

Traveltrain http://www.traveltrain.com.au
Services along the Queensland coastline from Brisbane to Cairns, and west to Charleville, Longreach and Mount Isa

V/line http://www.vline.com.au
Victoria's regional train operator

Buses

Australia has an extensive bus network and travelling by bus can be very inexpensive, however it is certainly not the fastest or most efficient form of transportation, especially if you have long distances to travel. You can also look into organised tour operators, which will get you from one place to another but may include guided commentary along the way. You can save money this way and meet a lot of people, but you may prefer the quiet and anonymity of the larger operators. Over the summer and during school holidays, you should book ahead for all services.

Greyhound Australia is the largest national bus service: http://www.greyhound.com.au

Regional operators

Easyrider Adventure Travel http://www.easyridertours.com.au
This is a jump-on, jump-off bus servicing Western Australia.

Firefly Express http://www.fireflyexpress.com.au
Services between Sydney, Melbourne and Adelaide

Integrity Coach Lines http://www/integritycoachlines.com.au

Coach travel in WA with service along the Great Northern Highway between Perth and Port Hedland, including Mt Magnet, Cue, Meekatharra and Newman

Nullarbor Traveller http://www.the-traveller.com.au
Minibus trips from Adelaide to Perth

Premier Motor Service http://www.premierms.com.au
Bus service along the coast from Cairns to Melbourne

Redline Coaches http://www.tasredline.com.au
Tasmania coach service for the northern and eastern coasts

TassieLink http://www.tassielink.com.au
Extensive point-to-point service throughout Tasmania

Transwa http://www.transwa.wa.gov.au
Operates coach services throughout the southern and southwestern regions of WA, in an area bounded by Kalbarri, Meekatharra, Kalgoorlie, Esperance, Albany and Augusta

V/Line http://www.vline.com.au
Coach service to most of the regional towns and cities in Victoria

Wayward Bus http://www.waywardbus.com.au
Offers several different trans-Australian experiences including service from Adelaide to Alice Springs and Melbourne to Adelaide

Additional domestic travel resources

Australian National Parks
http://www.australiannationalparks.com
A comprehensive guide to the parks of Australia

Tourism websites for the states and territories:

NSW	http://www.visitnsw.com
VIC	http://www.visitvictoria.com
QLD	http://www.tq.com.au

WA	http://www.westernaustralia.com
SA	http://www.southaustralia.com
TAS	http://www.discovertasmania.com
ACT	http://www.visitcanberra.com.au/en
NT	http://www.tourismnt.com.au

Wotif   http://www.wotif.com/?country=AU
This is a popular domestic accommodation service, which now also services the international market. You can find great deals on accommodation, especially at the last minute.

Zuji   http://www.zuji.com.au
Australian travel website from Travelocity

International Travel from Australia

Despite the vast array of airlines flying to and from Australia, you will still want to book in advance for the busy times of year, especially for your return flight to Australia. There are international airports in Adelaide, Brisbane, Cairns, Darwin, Melbourne, Perth and Sydney. It can be worth your while to visit a travel agent. There is one on every corner in the major Australian cities and you should have no trouble finding a great deal. It costs you nothing to use a travel agent and the agent will be able to provide you with support throughout your journey. If your travel is simple, you can also book online yourself.

Resources

Direct Flights   http://www.directflights.com.au
International and domestic flights, hotel accommodation, cruises, car hire, travel insurance and activities

Kayak   http://www.kayak.com
Compare hundreds of travel sites at once

Seat Guru   http://www.seatguru.com
Find information on airplane seating, in-flight amenities, and airline information. This site will give you information to allow you to find the best seat before you fly.

Sidestep   http://www.sidestep.com
This site searches all the travel websites to find you the best deals on hotels, flights, cars and cruises.

Travel.com.au   http://www.travel.com.au
Find international and domestic flights, holiday packages, hotel accommodation, travel insurance and car hire, as well as ski, cruise, corporate, family and adventure travel.

Going "home"

It's a funny thing being a foreigner. You leave and change and grow and you forget that your homeland is going to change and grow in your absence. Politics, culture, the economy, your friends — it will all be different when you return from a prolonged absence. The life you remember will not be there anymore. It may look the same. But it won't be because you won't be the same.

This is not to say that returning to your country of origin or your hometown has to be a bad experience. It will just be different and you should be prepared for that. You may feel a sense of loss for what you remember. And this can lead to feelings of anger and resentment. If you've had a bad experience with your relocation and are testing the waters for a return, finding things to be less pleasing than when you left will be especially painful. Or you may not have this experience. Perhaps things are as good as you remember them. Better even. If so, congratulations: you've achieved the best of both worlds, something all expats desire.

I returned to the US last year with my husband to visit friends and relatives and take a much-needed holiday. Many political and economic changes had occurred: the nation had elected the first president of African-American descent. The global financial crisis had shuttered national businesses that had been around since I was a child. Cities in which I had spent a lot of time felt and operated differently. The only constants were my friends and family, though they now had less time for me than they had when I lived there.

At the time we went back, I had a few particular gripes about Australia. I felt that service here was deplorable, the job market unforgiving and the quality of businesses and work attitudes lacking in diligence, creativity and care. Was I ever surprised to find that things in the States weren't much different. We had bad customer service experiences with almost the same regularity as in Australia. My grandfather was very ill in hospital when we visited him and my grandmother at the beginning of the trip, and I noticed that the experience in the emergency room was quite similar to what we'd experience in Melbourne, with long wait times and pre-occupied staff. New Jersey's hospitals had their own inefficiencies, their own brand of poor care.

When we arrived in New York City, we saw the fallout from the market collapse firsthand. Unemployment was high, businesses were bankrupt and housing prices had risen, the combination of these factors driving people out further and further from middle and lower Manhattan. Friends complained (and still complain) about New York State gouging them on things like fines and taxes. The city seemed quite different to me in many ways than when I'd lived there before. It was difficult to put a finger on exactly what it was. It was just a feeling I had. Being different myself, how can I say the feeling was accurate? But since I'm writing this as an expat, I feel that the sentiment is valid.

Each city we went to, and I'd lived in or had long-term experience with all of them, looked different and felt different. I thought that I would leave missing the US, thinking about persuading John to get a green card so we could move back there someday in the near future. But we were both happy to return home. It was wonderful to see our family and friends and we both still love New York, but suddenly Australia seemed more like home to me than my country of birth. Yes, a lot of that probably has to do with being in a relationship with someone: I always say that wherever John is will be home to me. But, despite feeling like a foreigner there, Australia was my new home and it would feel almost disloyal to think about my old "home" possibly being "better." Sure, lots of Americans will tell you that the US is the greatest country in the world. Lots of English people will say that about their own homeland as well. So will French, Japanese and citizens of many other countries (including Australians). But for me, my home was my home. I want to live somewhere I am happy and proud to be at this moment. And the US no longer had that pull for me. What will the experience be like for you?

Appendix

Australian National Holidays

Fixed
1 January   New Year's Day
26 January   Australia Day
25 April   Anzac (Australia and New Zealand Army Corps) Day
25 December   Christmas Day
26 December   Boxing Day

Variable
Labour Day or Eight Hour Day
Easter
Queen's Birthday

Variable holidays can differ because some are celebrated on different days in different states. Likewise, other public holidays are held in different states, territories and cities.

Australia's National Anthem

Advance Australia Fair
Australians all let us rejoice,
For we are young and free;
We've golden soil and wealth for toil;
Our home is girt by sea;
Our land abounds in nature's gifts
Of beauty rich and rare;
In history's page, let every stage
Advance Australia Fair.
In joyful strains then let us sing,
Advance Australia Fair.

Beneath our radiant Southern Cross
We'll toil with hearts and hands;
To make this Commonwealth of ours
Renowned of all the lands;
For those who've come across the seas
We've boundless plains to share;
With courage let us all combine
To Advance Australia Fair.
In joyful strains then let us sing,
Advance Australia Fair.

Resources for parents

Australian Baby Guide http://www.australianbabyguide.com.au
This is the website of the book of the same name, which is a comprehensive resource guide for parents in Australia with children aged up to three years.

Good Schools Guide International
http://www.gsgi.co.uk/countries/australia
Written by parents, this guide reviews schools for English-speaking expats including transitional advice, exams and educational overviews.

Kidsafe Australia   http://www.kidsafe.com.au
Keep your children safe through accident and injury prevention.

Mychild website   http://www.mychild.gov.au
This site provides information on government policies and programs related to early childhood and child care, including assistance with child care costs.

National Childcare Accreditation Council
http://www.ncac.gov.au
This is the government's accreditation body for child care services across Australia. To become Accredited, family day care schemes, long day care centres and outside school hours care services are required to meet a set of standards that focus on the quality of care provided for children. Their website provides the names, contact details and Accreditation history of registered childcare services and you can search for services by postcode or suburb. The site also provides information about quality child care and FAQs from families.

National Immunisation Program schedule for children
http://www.immunise.health.gov.au/internet/immunise/publishing.nsf/Content/nips2

Online communities

Essential Baby http://www.essentialbaby.com.au
For parents of children of all ages, this is the largest of the online parenting communities in Australian, which may or may not be right for you depending on how much of an intimate experience you want to have. It is run by *Fairfax Digital* and contains helpful parenting articles and content as well as a huge community of other parents (mostly mothers), where you can connect and learn about parenting in Australia. There are also meet-up and play groups and plenty of opportunities to meet other parents online.

Bub Hub   http://www.thebubhub.com.au
Another website featuring a pregnancy and parenting community, this site also features a directory and advice for parents. The forums have over 65,000 members, which makes them not nearly as large as *Essential Baby*'s, but large enough that you're bound to

meet plenty of people if you participate. There is a special forum for expat parents living in Australia here: http://www.bubhub.com.au/community/forums/forumdisplay.php?f=238

Natural Parenting   http://forums.naturalparenting.com.au

School holidays

You can find out the school term dates for your state or travel destination via this online portal:

http://australia.gov.au/topics/australian-facts-and-figures/school-term-dates

Other helpful resources

Bureau of Meteorology   http://www.bom.gov.au/weather

Swimming in Australia   http://www.swimaustralia.org.au

Further reading

Almost French: A New Life in Paris by Sarah Turnbull
I know, I know: Australia isn't Paris. Why am I recommending this book? It's a great read written by an Australian journalist who moves to Paris to pursue a life with a Frenchman she falls in love with. I thought it was a really accurate firsthand account of what it feels like to be a foreigner and experience the culture shock that comes with living in a new country. The story is also very entertaining.

GenExpat: The Young Professional's Guide to Making A Successful Life Abroad   By Margaret Malewski

Targeted towards the 25-39 year-old expatriate group, this is a guide to your successful international career. The guide contains tips on every aspect of your move abroad as well as real-life stories.

The Global Citizen: A guide to creating an international life and career, for students, professionals, retirees and families
By Elizabeth Kruempelmann
Think you have what it takes to make it as an expat? This book is part directory, part personal essay and part evaluation tool. You'll find a range of personal accounts, resources to help you find opportunities and exercises to help you determine if your personality traits are compatible with an overseas lifestyle.

A Moveable Marriage: Relocate Your Relationship without Breaking It
By Robin Pascoe
For couples thinking about a move abroad, this is your complete guide to a successful relocation that won't hurt your relationship.